"Therefore let the entire house of Israel
know with certainty that God has made him
both Lord and Messiah,
this Jesus whom you crucified."
(Acts 2.36 NRSV)

THIS JESUS

Martyr,
Lord,
Messiah

MARKUS BOCKMUEHL

InterVarsity Press
Downers Grove, Illinois

Library of Congress Cataloging-in-Publication Data

Bockmuehl, Markus N. A.
   This Jesus: martyr, Lord, Messiah / Markus Bockmuehl.
     p.   cm.
   Includes bibliographical references and index.
   ISBN 0-8308-1875-8 (paper: alk. paper)
   1. Jesus Christ—Person and offices. 2. Jesus Christ—
Historicity. I. Title.
BT202.B52   1996
232—dc20   *96-11251*
                                           CIP

17	16	15	14	13	12	11	10	9	8	7	6	5	4	3	2	1
10	09	08	07	06	05	04	03	02	01	00	99	98	97	96		

Contents

Preface

Passing through London's Heathrow Airport in September 1992 on my way to a sabbatical term in Jerusalem, I happened to pick up a copy of A. N. Wilson's newly released work *Jesus* from a bookstore's best-seller shelf. By the time I reached my destination, I had decided to abandon my intended research project and to write instead a small book on an issue to which I felt a string of recent publications and my own students' questions had given a pressing urgency. At the end of the 20th century, is it possible to affirm a view of Jesus of Nazareth that relates with integrity both to historical scholarship and to orthodox Christian faith? Unable to say everything about this vast and daunting subject, I sensed the need at least to say *something*.

In writing and revising, then, I have had in mind chiefly my students at Cambridge University, St. George's College in Jerusalem and Regent College in Vancouver. For their benefit I have intentionally avoided foreign language quotations and unfamiliar abbreviations, and tried wherever possible to confine the more technical discussion of biblical scholarship to the notes.

While in broad outline this book took shape in Jerusalem in the autumn months of 1992, it contains material revised from earlier publications and reproduced by permission. Parts of the Introduction appeared in *Epworth Review* 21 (1994), pp. 18–31 as "Jesus of Nazareth in Recent Debate"; the other revisions are Chapters Three (from *Crux* 25.3 (1989) 11–18) and Six (from J. I. Packer & Loren Wilkinson (eds.), *Alive to God: Studies in Spirituality Presented to James Houston* (Downers Grove: InterVarsity, 1992), 56–71).

Finally, there remains only a writer's pleasant task of giving thanks to generous patrons and friends. The staff and students from every continent at St. George's College, Jerusalem extended warm hospitality during my sabbatical stay, and offered many constructive questions and criticisms on my lectures delivered during repeated visits there since 1988. Others who have heard and engaged with the arguments include a Learners' Exchange course at St. John's (Shaughnessy) Anglican Church in Vancouver; a 1992 summer school class at Regent College; the Colchester and District Clerical Society; and various Cambridge seminars and congregations, both at the Faculty of Divinity and at Corpus Christi and Pembroke Colleges.

Special thanks are due to those who unstintingly gave of their time in reading various drafts and offering comments: Steve Andrews, Rob Clifton, Frank Griswold, William Horbury, Michael Lloyd, Tom Shaw, Ian Stewart and Tom Wright.

The immortal Mozart invigorated much of the planning and writing of this book, above all with his concertos for the flute, oboe and clarinet. Readers may find their enjoyment of it enhanced by similar accompaniment.

M. B.
Cambridge, Advent 1993

A Note on Abbreviations

Abbreviations follow standard English convention as documented in dictionaries and reference works. For biblical books I have adopted the widely followed conventions of the *Journal of Biblical Literature*. Citations of the Dead Sea Scrolls are according to the standard manual by Joseph A. Fitzmyer, *The Dead Sea Scrolls: Major Publications and Tools for Study*, SBL Resources for Biblical Study 20, revised edition (Atlanta: Scholars Press, 1990).

Some readers may find it helpful to note the following, less familiar abbreviations.

B.T.	Babylonian Talmud
E.T.	English Translation
KJV	King James (Authorised) Version of the Bible
LXX	Septuagint (Greek Old Testament)
NRSV	New Revised Standard Version of the Bible
par.	and parallel(s) [in the Gospels]
P.T.	Palestinian Talmud

Introduction

Which Jesus?

Hundreds of books have been written about Jesus of Nazareth, and the flood of new publications continues unabated. The author of one of the first works on the subject concluded by musing that the world itself could not contain the books required for a comprehensive treatment (John 21.25); but theologians, journalists and critics ever since have been trying, unsuccessfully, to prove him wrong. The last decade alone has received several dozen books on Jesus with varying degrees of acclaim and aversion.

Another Book on Jesus?

What, then, could possibly justify yet another book on the same subject, let alone one of modest size? The world might be a better place if scholars ceased to regard this kind of question as merely rhetorical.

It is the central contention of this book that the life and work of Jesus of Nazareth can be plausibly and credibly interpreted as standing in a relationship of vital continuity with the emerging orthodox Christianity that finds expression in the New Testament and the creeds. This argument as such is not new. But as I hope to explain in a moment, it is here being advanced afresh in deliberate contrast to a climate of both popular and scholarly contemporary Jesus studies which object to precisely this conclusion.

To do justice to the topic would obviously require a major tome. Nevertheless, in some matters it is better to have said a few words imperfectly than to have said nothing at all. I believe the thesis of this book to be one such concern. It is offered simply as one man's concise attempt to revive a neglected argument and give it a wider hearing. If any of my readers were to pick up the gauntlet and pursue the matter further, I should be delighted.

Which Jesus?

Only a fool would deny that many different views of Jesus of Nazareth are in theory *possible*. But it is also true that not all of those views are equally probable. Some can safely be ruled out by sound historical scholarship: among these are Monty Python's *The Life of Brian* and Nikos Kazantzakis' *The Last Temptation*, to name but two popular examples of a long tradition of Jesus fantasies reaching back at least to the second century.

Unfortunately, the problem of distinguishing between the theoretically possible and the historically probable has plagued even serious Jesus scholarship for several centuries. At the beginning of the 20th century the great Albert Schweitzer, in a massive study of the 19th-century quest for the historical Jesus, concluded that many of the books spoke more eloquently about their authors' world view than about that of Jesus.[1] Here was a timely warning that we all are inclined to read into the text our own favourite ideas, to discover a Jesus who agrees with us.[2] Schweitzer concluded that the quest for the historical Jesus had failed because scholars had ignored his thoroughly Jewish apocalyptic view of history.

Others, especially in Germany, went on to assert that the quest had not only failed, but was in fact impossible and in any case irrelevant to the faith of the Church. Much of the so-called dialectical or neo-orthodox theology beginning in the 1920s affirmed this, including such writers as Karl Barth[3] and Dietrich Bonhoeffer[4]. Rudolf Bultmann and some of his students down to the present day have continued to assert that the quest for the Jesus of History is impossible and unnecessary: all we can know is that he existed. Everything else is hidden in obscurity, and in any case of no consequence to the existential response of faith.[5]

As historians of theology since then have variously pointed out, this note of historical pessimism and unreality had as much or more to do with the gloomy post-World War I collapse of continental liberalism and the corresponding rise of existentialism as with the methodological bottleneck in New Testament studies.

Common sense would dictate that such a position of radical scepticism could not last. A "new" or "second" quest for the historical Jesus was launched by E. Käsemann, G. Bornkamm, and other former students of Bultmann in the 1950s and 1960s. This time, scholars focused on careful analyses of forms and traditions in the Gospels, scrutinizing the authenticity of individual sayings, and reconstructing the evangelists' redactional intentions from their handling of the material. By the 1970s, however, this elaborate but often atomistic second effort seemed to be running into the ground.

At the risk of only slight overstatement, one could say that the failure of both movements may have been virtually inevitable. This is due in part to an underlying docetism[6] in the treatment of Jesus' setting within first-century Jewish life and thought. The first questers, as Schweitzer showed, found in the Gospels primarily the reflection of their own Romantic and ethical-liberal views – rather like Narcissus in the well.[7] By contrast, the history of the second quest probably remains to be written: indeed in some quarters that quest continues to ramble on. My own view is that, although appearing to employ far greater methodological rigour in its analysis of Jesus' sayings, the "second quest" tended to be equally impressionistic in its criteria for authenticity, and at times Gnostic in its lack of familiarity, not to say unconcern, with the Galilee and Judaea of Jesus' day. This resulted partly from the influence of R. Bultmann and existentialist philosophy on several of its proponents, and partly from criteria of authenticity which tended to rule out any Jewish Messianic dimensions in the life of the pre-Easter Jesus. In its place, scholars asserted principles like "dissimilarity",[8] the idea that the most reliable core of Jesus' sayings was to be found in the material which contradicted or had no parallels in known (and frequently caricatured[9]) positions of contemporary Judaism. The result was a phantom Jesus, who left even some of the practitioners of this method disillusioned and looking elsewhere for solutions.

Two related developments began to take hold in the 1980s. First, the seemingly moribund "New Quest" received a shot in the arm from a sustained revival of research into gospel origins, focused especially on the hypothetical "Q" document of synoptic Jesus sayings (from the German word *Quelle*, "source"). Secondly, and at the same time, study of the *Gospel of Thomas* and other apocryphal gospels of proto-Gnostic, non-apocalyptic flavour seemed to suggest to some scholars that the Jewish apocalyptic themes even in "Q" needed to be filtered out as later accretions. The original layers of the synoptic tradition, it was argued, showed teaching about wisdom but none about the future, no eschatology. Many of the more prominent authors in this school of thought are or have been associated with the Claremont Graduate School in California.[10]

A related North American phenomenon has been the Jesus Seminar, several of whose members have also been connected with Claremont. These scholars are engaged in the production of gospel editions which indicate the supposed likelihood of authentic Jesus tradition in the Gospels. For each saying or parable, the participants use marbles in one of four shades of red, pink, black and grey to vote on their impression of the relative authenticity. The aim is to publish the Seminar's findings in the form of Red Letter editions of the Gospels.[11]

After a detailed and tenuous redactional layering of the hypothetical "Q" source, the authors in this school present their resulting picture of the earliest teachings of Jesus ("Q^1"). He turns out to be a non-apocalyptic, non-conflictual figure more akin to a wandering Cynic wisdom teacher than to a Jewish charismatic prophet.[12] Stripped of his actions and many of his words, this sort of Jesus seems disembodied of a plausible religious setting in that world of Palestinian Judaism which both his teachings and his actions unmistakably address. According to this theory, Jesus' views on the future coming of the Kingdom of God, the imminent destruction of the Temple and the coming of the Son of Man, among other things, are either excised or become strangely devoid of recognizable contextual sense, taking on their apocalyptic and eschatological meaning only in the course of later editorial revisions.[13]

This vigorous "Q^1-Thomas" school of thought brilliantly identifies divergent perspectives within the canonical and apocryphal gospel traditions. And in general it is true for a mixed Jewish and Gentile area like Galilee that popular Hellenistic philosophical perspectives on power and wealth would have been "in the air", so to speak – even though significant first-century Galilean evidence of itinerant, observant *Jewish* Cynics has yet to be presented. The leading supporters of this view have clearly offered a wealth of new literary critical and social anthropological research, and their achievement must be the subject of a good deal of further debate. Nevertheless, the underlying argument of these scholars often appears to be inescapably circular.[14] Having decided on the basis of complex assumptions about the hypothetical "Q" document that certain parts of the apocalyptic sayings material must be absent from the earliest sayings tradition, one then proceeds to place non-eschatological *Thomas* unusually early and to demote the eschatological sections of "Q" to later redactional layers. Such neatly rarefied, abstracted results not only take us well outside the apostolic interpretation of Jesus. Even from a purely historical perspective, we are left with a highly improbable scenario: a Jewish apocalyptic prophet (John the Baptist) is succeeded by a wandering Cynic disciple (Jesus), whose message of timeless wisdom is in turn corrupted by followers bent on apocalyptic and eschatology.[15] This kind of approach proves in the end unable to provide us with a picture of either Jesus or the earliest Palestinian Jewish Christianity that is suffi-

ciently attached to its inalienable religious and historical
moorings in Galilee and Judaea.[16]

In addition to the "Q[1]-Thomas" research, however, recent
years have also seen the publication of a growing number of
studies that take a very different approach to Jesus. Here, the
concern is first of all to locate and interpret him plausibly within
first-century Judaism, to construct our knowledge of him not
just from his words but also from his actions, and to illuminate
the inquiry by drawing on the mass of relevant archaeological
and literary discoveries as well as the general blossoming of
Judaic studies since World War II. Several dozen authors have
contributed significant works to what has become an identifiable
trend.

Some are even beginning to speak of a "Third Quest" for
the historical Jesus.[17] This is possibly premature, since at this
point it still competes for attention with the mainly North
American "Q[1]-Thomas" group of scholars which I mentioned a
moment ago.[18] Nevertheless, the emerging change in direction is
significant enough to warrant analysis in its own right.[19]

One particularly encouraging aspect in the new
approach's corrective of earlier work is the increasing participation of Jewish scholars in the discussion.[20] Although not
entirely without predecessors in the history of Jesus research,[21]
these writers have brought a new and valuable contribution to
the study. Uninterested in impressionism of either the romantic,
existentialist or "post-modern" kind, and bypassing atomistic
analyses of sayings and hypothetical sources, both Jewish and
Christian scholars in this group are concerned to situate the
stories of Jesus credibly and firmly in the study of first-century
Palestinian Judaism, as we are now beginning to know it on a
much more secure footing.[22] Significant questions and
interpretative differences remain even among these writers, but
there is increasing agreement on methods and sources.

At the end of the 20th century, then, we are in the fortunate position of having a far better documented and, on the whole, much more plausible range of "possible" and even "probable" pictures of Jesus to choose from. What is more, despite occasional publishers' hubris about "first" or "definitive" books on the subject, one senses that more and more authors may have learned a degree of humility and openness from the chequered history of Jesus research. And, not unlike technology designed to be "upgradable" by the addition or substitution of new hardware or software, an increasing number of responsible scholarly accounts in recent years are no longer of the dead-end, "Jesus was the man in the moon" variety, but are subject to refinement in the light of either new hard evidence or more adequate methods of analysis.

From the perspective of sound historical understanding, all this of course is welcome news. Even so, however, we must accept that the full available evidence, cautiously and even sympathetically evaluated, will in all probability still always lend itself to a *range* of plausible views of Jesus, depending not least on the cultural and religious stance of the interpreter. In any case, some of these pictures of the historical Jesus may be compatible with orthodox Christian faith, while others will not be. That, too, should be seen as a welcome state of affairs, both for the ongoing vitality of historical inquiry and to keep Christians from presuming an epistemological certainty which is not to be had this side of the day when all secrets are revealed (Luke 8.17). Even among avowedly "orthodox" accounts, no one picture is possible or perhaps even desirable, as the inclusion of *four* quite different gospels in the canonical New Testament should amply illustrate.

"*This* Jesus"

Against this backdrop, the purpose of this book can be more readily restated. I proceed on the assumption that responsible theological scholarship must present Jesus in a way that is both historically probable and in plausible continuity with the faith of his first followers. To the question, "Which Jesus?", the earliest Christian preaching gave the answer: *This* Jesus, the one who was crucified under Pontius Pilate, who is also the one whom God raised and thereby powerfully endorsed. "Therefore let the entire house of Israel know with certainty that God has made him both Lord and Messiah, this Jesus whom you crucified" (Acts 2.36; cf. 1.11; 2.32; 4.11; 13.38f.; also Rom. 1.3f.). There were evidently different ways of describing that Jesus, but all the apostolic witnesses agreed on the fundamental *identity* of the one about whom they spoke. In these pages, then, I wish to demonstrate that it can be historically legitimate to see Jesus of Nazareth in organic and causal continuity with the faith of the early Church. Writing about the aims of Jesus, Ben F. Meyer recognizes something of this continuity when he concludes, "It is above all *in the tradition generated by Jesus* that we discover what made him operate in the way he did."[23]   My method, further explained below, will be to present what I believe to be a historically responsible account while showing how Jesus' life and teaching can be seen to have given rise to the Church's reception of him.

This is a conscious and deliberate departure from the forced amputation of the "Jesus of history" from the "Christ of faith", which has continued to be the explicit hallmark of too many recent books. Much like love and war, faith cannot be properly described and understood by those who confine themselves to cataloguing the material phenomena and then declare that their sum does not add up to the whole which the adherents claim to see. This activity seems to me rather as if I had invited a friend to a performance of Mozart's *Exsultate, Jubilate* and found him pedantically concluding that the noisy vibrations of various lengths of cat gut and human vocal chords at some distance from our seats could not possibly have any demonstrable connection with the audience's elated response.

My purpose here is to commend that link between the making of instrumental noise and the hearing of beautiful music, for the better appreciation of the whole.

At the same time, and on another level, I hope that this book may serve as a kind of *Let's Go* guide to the relationship between Jesus and Christianity, offering an initial orientation for those with limited time. It is of course merely admitting the obvious to say that in many places our travels will barely scratch the surface. For some this may suffice; others will feel a need to dig more deeply. Can you "do" Switzerland in a fortnight? Well, yes and no. One can travel the length and breadth of the country and see key places and communities. Enough, perhaps, to get a sense of the lie of the land and the people; but certainly not enough for any intimate acquaintance with either. For some travellers such a visit will be entirely adequate: back home, they can now associate sights and sounds with names on a map, and Switzerland will always remain a real place for them. Others will be hungry for more at the end of such a tour, and will plan to return and explore just one or two locations which they found especially enjoyable or intriguing. It is primarily for the benefit of such "serious" tourists that my notes have been designed – not only to document the argument, but also to open a way into further reading.[24]

That being said, we can be on our way.

Sources for the Historical Jesus

It is as well to clear the ground at the beginning with a few remarks about the identity and nature of our sources on the historical Jesus. We begin with the evidence outside the New Testament, as this can be dealt with relatively quickly, and will then raise a few significant points about the canonical material.

Evidence for Jesus Outside the New Testament

Greek and Roman Authors

Fleeting references to Jesus and Christianity may be found in two great Roman historians writing near the beginning of the second century. Suetonius comments on the Emperor Claudius's expulsion of Jews from the city of Rome in AD 48 after repeated unrest within the community which, he says, occurred "at the instigation of *Chrestus*" (*Claudius* 25.4). Scholars have extensively argued back and forth whether this is a reference to internal Jewish disturbances caused by Jewish believers in "Christus", that is, Jesus. While such developments are certainly conceivable in Rome by the late 40s AD, in the absence of additional information it is virtually impossible to be certain of this, and some considerations call for caution.[25] Even if the reference is to Christ, however, this briefest of references tells us only a little about Christianity and nothing about the historical Jesus, other than that he existed.[26]

Tacitus (c. AD 55–117), like Suetonius elsewhere, describes the famous fire of Rome in AD 64, when the Emperor Nero was suspected of arson but managed instead to blame and punish the Christians (*Annals* 15.44:3–4). We are told that these people, loathed for their despicable crimes, were named after their founder:

> Christus, the founder of the name, had been executed during the reign of Tiberius by the procurator Pontius Pilate. The pernicious superstition was halted for a moment, only to break out once again, not only in Judaea, where this evil originated, but even in Rome itself, where all the world's horrible and shameful things collect and find a keen following.

Once again we do not learn a great deal; but here in any case is the leading Roman historian of his day giving independent confirmation that Jesus lived and was formally executed in Judaea in the reign of Tiberius and during Pontius Pilate's office as procurator (technically still a prefect, AD 26–36). That may not seem like much, but it is actually surprisingly useful in discounting two different theories which are still sometimes advanced: first, that Jesus of Nazareth never existed;[27] and secondly, that he did not die by the duly administered Roman death penalty. The latter is a claim which is found in the Koran (Sura 4.157f.) and continues to be asserted in Islam; in a variety of different forms it is also periodically advanced among contemporary Western critics.[28]   Later in the second century, Lucian of Samosata confirms that the Christians worship as god a man who was crucified in Palestine.[29]

Jewish Authors

Flavius Josephus

Josephus, who was born Joseph bar Mattai and later took on the Roman name Flavius, is the single most important source on Jewish history in the first century. We will have occasion to return to him on many occasions, but it will suffice to say for now that he was born of a well-to-do priestly family in Jerusalem c. AD 37 and grew up well educated. Having studied different religious strands of Judaism, he claims to have conformed his life to the Pharisaic interpretation. During the Jewish revolt against Rome in 66–70 he was appointed general of the rebel forces in Galilee. Defeated at the village of Jotapata, he defected to the Romans and later served as a court historian to Vespasian, the victorious Roman general who in AD 68 went on to become Emperor.

Josephus's four surviving works began with a polished six-volume history of the *Jewish War*, published in the late 70s AD. This was followed some fifteen years later (AD 93/94) by a history of Judaism in twenty volumes, known as the *Jewish Antiquities* and designed in part to explain Judaism to a Gentile audience. His autobiography (the *Life*) appeared as an appendix to the *Antiquities*. *Against Apion*, an apologetic work in two volumes, followed not long afterwards.

Aside from a brief and largely uncontroversial reference to the martyrdom in AD 62 of James, "the brother of Jesus who is called the Messiah" (*Ant.* 20.200), there is a longer and more disputed passage about Jesus in *Antiquities* 18.63–64. Most scholars agree that during the history of manuscript transmission by Christian scribes, several additions were inserted: these suggest that Jesus was a supernatural Messiah and rose from the dead. For this reason, some have dismissed the paragraph altogether. Nevertheless, there seems to be an emerging consensus in favour of a version of Josephus's statement which merely removes the identifiably Christian interpolations and leaves what turns out to be a carefully composed, neutral Jewish view of Jesus of Nazareth:

> At this time there appeared Jesus, a wise man. For he was a doer of startling deeds, a teacher of people who receive the truth with pleasure. [He was called the Messiah.] And he gained a following both among many Jews and among many of Greek origin. And when Pilate, because of an accusation made by the leading men among us, condemned him to the cross, those who had loved him previously did not cease to do so. And up until this very day the tribe of Christians (named after him) has not died out.[30]

One could quibble about whether one or two additional statements should be removed or read differently (the second sentence, for example, unless its intention is critical[31]). In any case, it is probably safe to say that this statement, written several decades after both the death of Jesus and the destruction of Jerusalem, reflects the kind of perspective which an educated Jew might reasonably have held about the Jewish sect of the Christians, named after a religious leader executed under Pontius Pilate. Jesus was wise and performed remarkable deeds which gained him a large following. He was put to death by the Romans following a plot among the aristocracy, the reasons for which are not explained.

Jewish Literature Outside Josephus

There is a wealth of other Jewish literature from the time before, during and after the life of Jesus. Much of this is significant and will be drawn on to illuminate the background of the life of

Jesus in the following chapters. Not many texts, however, offer any explicit reference to Jesus. In fact, careful study suggests that outside Josephus few if any of these passages show *independent* knowledge of Jesus. Despite continuing claims to the contrary, there appear to be no references to Jesus in the Dead Sea Scrolls. The same is true for the philosopher Philo of Alexandria (c. 45 BC–AD 25). In the case of Jewish apocalyptic and other non-canonical literature from the Second Temple period, the great majority of scholars would identify the numerous references to Jesus (in the *Testaments of the Twelve Patriarchs*, the *Sibylline Oracles*, etc.) as later Christian interpolations: while many of these documents had their origin in Jewish circles, they became very popular in the Church, where the manuscripts were widely copied and distributed. To Christian scribes the Messianic expectations in these texts often seemed highly compatible with the New Testament's testimony to Jesus; and as anonymous devotional works outside the Bible they were not obviously subject to the strictures which (with notable exceptions) tended to govern the transmission of Holy Scripture in what came to be mainstream Christianity.

This still leaves the vast corpus of Rabbinic literature. Here, a number of texts do indeed refer either explicitly or implicitly to Jesus. None of these are contained in the earliest collections. Without being able to survey all the evidence in detail, I follow here the position of those scholars who regard the Talmudic traditions about the historical Jesus as not only polemical against Christianity (which they invariably are), but also in all probability dependent on popular corruptions of Christian gospel traditions. Examples of this include the repeated references to Jesus as son of "Pandera" or "Pantera", which are found in texts from the third century onward[32] and have plausibly been thought to originate in a spoof on the word *parthenos*, "virgin" (see Chapter One). Similarly one might consider the spurious list of five disciples (including Luke!) or the parody of Matthew 5.17 in the Babylonian Talmud.[33] The

so-called *Toledot Yeshu*, a medieval presentation of the life of
Jesus compiled from earlier traditions, is again of historical
value mainly for understanding the development of Jewish anti-
Christian polemics.[34] It is true that some of these themes recur
in a wide range of sources from different centuries;[35] but their
invariably polemical context and lack of early attestation, along
with the acceptance in these sources of manifestly fanciful
assertions, makes it difficult to treat them on the same level as,
say, the Gospels or Josephus.

In general, it seems safe to conclude that Jewish literature
outside Josephus contains no demonstrably early information
about Jesus of Nazareth which is independent of Christian
sources.[36] Even supposing that an instance could be found
which ultimately depends on independent tradition (e.g. about
the circumstances of Jesus' death: cf. note 35), the material in
question is in any case of such limited extent and significance
for the historical Jesus that not a great deal of value would
derive for our inquiry.

Christian Sources Outside the New Testament: "Other Gospels" and Sayings

Before we turn to say a few things about the New Testament
itself, it is worth commenting briefly on a number of extra-
canonical Christian texts which are sometimes brought into the
discussion.

First, a number of scholars in recent years have argued
for the equal validity and even priority of several other gospels
known to us from manuscript discoveries and references in the
writings of the Church Fathers. Among these are especially the
Gospel of Thomas and the *Gospel of Peter*. We also possess a
Gospel attributed to Philip, as well as quotations from a text
known in the ancient church as the *Gospel of the Nazarenes* or
the *Gospel According to the Hebrews*. Other fragmentary texts
range from quotations of individual statements of Jesus in the
Church Fathers to anthologies of sayings in the Oxyrhynchus

and Egerton Papyrus collections. Clement of Alexandria (c. 150–c. 215), who is generally fond of apocryphal traditions, cites "secret" additions to the canonical Gospel of Mark, including a version of the story of Lazarus.[37]

Perhaps due in part to the curiosity value of these unfamiliar texts, it has become fashionable in certain circles to postulate that they represent early gospel traditions which emerged in parallel to the canonical gospels and must be given equal weight in understanding the historical Jesus. Authors like John Dominic Crossan and Helmut Koester are particularly prominent in this school of thought.[38]

In theory it is certainly possible, indeed likely, that in the process of the Church's transmission and evaluation of the various Jesus traditions, certain sayings and stories were not taken up, and that even whole perspectives on Jesus were found wanting and hence rejected. This must clearly be the case for the traditions of Jewish Christian sects like the Ebionites, about whose views we hear from Church Fathers like Irenaeus in the second century.[39] Might at least some of their Jesus traditions (about Jesus' human parentage, endowment with the Holy Spirit at baptism, etc.) have been based on authentic, independent gospel materials? We may never know. Similarly, we find that a number of Church Fathers quote isolated sayings of Jesus which are not recorded in any of the extant gospels: evidently a variety of oral gospel traditions were still in vogue for quite some time after the canonical gospels had been committed to writing.

Both independent sayings and apocryphal gospels have for many years been the subject of critical studies. A few scholars periodically capture the limelight with "new" revelations about the "authentic" Jesus. Nevertheless, it must be said, with due respect, that majority opinion over the last several decades has continued to hold that every one of the apocryphal gospels can be shown to be dependent on the canonical gospel traditions and shaped by secondary (frequently Gnostic) religious concerns. This is more obviously true for wildly speculative texts like the *Gospel of Peter*, but Synoptic dependence and a Gnostic bias have also been made probable in the case of the more sober (and Synoptic-like) collection of sayings known as the *Gospel of Thomas*. Indeed the best evidence seems to suggest that the circles of early Christianity represented by this document in fact moved *away* from an originally Jewish apocalyptic and wisdom setting towards an increasingly non-eschatological, Gnostic interpretation.[40] The arguments are obviously complex and tenuous in the case of individual sayings, but here too we find at best a handful of sayings to which a majority of scholars might be willing to give serious consideration. The assessment of a mainstream scholar like John P. Meier is typical: "There is nothing here that can serve as a source in our quest for the historical Jesus."[41] In practice this will mean that we should refer to such material with considerable caution, especially where it contradicts more reliable sources.

Critics of claims for the priority of apocryphal gospel traditions have pointed out that such proposals tend to have a number of flaws in common: (i) thin and doubtful evidence masked by the smoke and mirrors of impressive presentation and media publicity; (ii) disregard for the evidence, in the vast majority of early Christian texts, that a basic "mainstream" agreement about the substance of the gospel existed from the beginning (Gal. 2.1–10; 1 Cor. 15.1–11; etc.); (iii) an assumption that primitive Christianity happily carried on with a mass of disembodied sayings, without any narrative or biographical framework about the life, death and resurrection of their supposed author.[42] Quite apart from these and other methodological weaknesses, the results prove unable to provide us with a picture of Jesus and the earliest Palestinian Jewish Christianity that is sufficiently attached to its first-century religious and historical context.

Conclusion: The New Testament Gospels as Our Major Source

These remarks have admittedly and of necessity been somewhat superficial. Nevertheless, for our present purposes we may conclude that, aside from the skeletal corroboration of the New Testament gospels' narrative framework in Josephus, our search for the historical Jesus leads us naturally to the New Testament as our major source, and there especially to the Gospels.

It is true that several other New Testament authors confirm Jesus' human lineage, birth and life (Rom. 1.3f.; Gal. 4.4; cf. Phil. 2.6; Heb. 2.14; 4.15–5.8; 1 John 1.1–3; 4.2) and especially his death on the cross and resurrection. Individual events from the life of Jesus include the tradition about the Last Supper (1 Cor. 11.23–26) as well as the Transfiguration (2 Pet. 1.17–18). A variety of sayings are either quoted or alluded to.[43]

Even this, however, provides only a small and somewhat uncontrolled sampling of the ways in which traditions about Jesus were used in first-century Christian discourse. For the fullest picture, our discussion in the following chapters will therefore turn to the four canonical Gospels.

The Gospels – What Did Jesus *Really* Say and Do?

In a "big" book on Jesus it would be appropriate at this point to spend perhaps a whole chapter on a detailed analysis of the Gospels: their use of sources, their literary and ideological connections, social settings, the relationship between the Gospel of John and the other three, questions of date and authorship, perhaps even a history of Gospels scholarship, and so on.

This is not such a book. Others have repeatedly applied themselves to that task, but our limited purpose here does not call for a lengthy excursus. I will instead offer a few brief comments regarding my working hypothesis, and beyond that attend to the most crucial questions of literary dependence and authenticity as they arise in the course of later discussion.

Everyone agrees that the New Testament Gospels present Jesus from four different perspectives, each with peculiar theological emphases; that the first three relate in form and content more closely to each other than they do to the fourth; and that all four writers made use of earlier sources and traditions. All of them are theologically inclined, and all write their theology in the form of historical narrative.

At various times during the history of the critical study of the Gospels a particular theory of their origin seemed to command almost universal support among scholars, only to be questioned and subsequently modified or replaced by another. Today, many of the pertinent questions are in a greater state of flux than at any other time this century, with several major models vying for acceptance. In some ways this is a welcome state of affairs, as it allows us to proceed cautiously and without having to force all the issues into a grand unified theory. We may operate with a relatively small number of presuppositions, beyond which we can allow the texts themselves to guide our reading.

The Synoptic Gospels' use of sources must be assumed; but a look at a synopsis suggests that the interrelations between them are both intricate and complex. No simple theory is likely to account for them all. Whatever else may have affected the formation of the Gospels, the evangelists were not the sort of paper wizards and sophisticated redactional jugglers which some source critics have made them out to be. It is far more plausible that we are essentially dealing with the literary deposits of the indigenous catechesis about Jesus in Rome, Antioch, and Pauline churches: the similarities and differences reflect forms of teaching inherited from the traditions of the Apostles and tuned to the needs of different local settings.[44]

As for the more specific identification of sources, one fairly common model has been to say that something like Mark and a source of sayings traditions generally known as "Q" were used by Matthew and Luke along with independent traditions of their own. As long as this two-source hypothesis is not seen as the "solution" to the so-called synoptic "problem" (the question of the relative priority of the first three Gospels), it can offer one way of recognizing some of the key interrelations between these accounts. In this book I will assume no *direct* literary dependence, but accept that the Gospels are closely related through common sources. In this way the peculiar concerns of each gospel writer can be recognized and highlighted.

Where does that leave us on the perennial problem of authentic sayings? Without following dead ends like the New Quest's "dissimilarity" criterion or the impressionist, majority vote procedures of the "Jesus Seminar",[45] the following four principles may serve as a general framework.[46]

1. We ought generally to recognize the great advances made in the study of first century *Palestinian Judaism* in the twentieth century, and to agree to understand the person and work of Jesus first and foremost against this background, unless there are good reasons to the contrary.

2. The Gospels are sufficiently diverse both theologically, sociologically and geographically to give a high degree of credibility to sayings with *multiple attestations*. These are bound to be substantially authentic at least to the extent of going back to the earliest Christian church. Even the wording of such traditions, while not unalterable, has been shown in many cases to be subject to the control of rhythmic and other aids to careful instruction and memorization.[47] Linguistic analysis and re-translation into Aramaic have demonstrated in a large number of such instances that an origin in a Palestinian Jewish setting is the most plausible scenario. Indeed the local social and political flavour of many sayings suggest to some leading scholars the existence of written compilations at least as early as the 40s of the first century.[48] And while these considerations are not in themselves sufficient to guarantee the authenticity of a given word of Jesus, they do suggest remarkable constraints on the transmission of these sayings ever

since their earliest settings.

3. In all cases, even those peculiar to just one evangelist, the assumption of early tradition must be a particularly safe bet when the style or theology of the material appears to run counter to the writer's known redactional tendencies.[49] We should add, however, contrary to the assumption of many modern authors, that even a pericope freely composed in an evangelist's own language and theology does not therefore have to be invented out of thin air. Leon Uris's *Exodus* (or for that matter any one of James Michener's novels), for all its evident bias, selectivity and semi-fictional elements, remains a historical novel based on carefully compiled sources and facts. Even if the precise words were not always uttered by the actual characters, it frequently remains true that *some such words and actions* must have transpired for the story – and the history – to make any sense. The illustration is flawed because the gospel writers are not modern novelists, but in fact my point applies to them *a fortiori*.

4. The Gospels were not written as novels, with the primary purpose of entertainment, but as *evangels*: that is to say, they are didactic and persuasive or apologetic works about events which transpired in their own time. This makes it even more likely that questions about the reliability and truth value of their sources were a prominent concern for the authors. All self-respecting Christian catechesis had to keep an eye on public credibility (cf. also Col. 4.5f.; 1 Pet. 3.15f.). This is not to say that the Gospels do not contain elements which may strike the modern literary critic, and even the historian of ancient Judaism, as literary or theological embellishment. Nor is it to claim that they were intended as dispassionate historiography, even to the limited extent that Josephus's *Jewish War* was. But it is to assert as an appropriate rule of thumb that, unless there is good reason to think otherwise, the gospel accounts interpreted in their first-century contexts may be read as broadly reliable in what they *do* affirm about the life and teaching of Jesus.[50]

This approach may rightly be regarded as conservative, if by that is meant that it places a premium on considerations of historical plausibility, continuity, and common sense, at the expense of readings which tend to atomize texts into a profusion of sources in mutual social and religious contradiction. We must indeed affirm the multiformity of our evidence, and refuse to rule out the possibility of finding such contradictions. Nevertheless, my inclination here will be to look in the first instance not for clinical detail in source criticism but for a *whole picture* of both the teaching and the actions of Jesus which makes plausible sense in a first-century Palestinian narrative framework.

It remains to restate my own working hypothesis and proposed argument. I shall assume that in both his words and his actions, Jesus interacted with his contemporaries in ways which were by and large meaningful and intelligible in their shared Jewish social and religious world. Readers may not always agree with my individual judgements about redaction or historical setting. However, the overall argument depends not so much on these details as on the cumulative case for continuity between Jesus and the early church. Granted that there may be a number of possible and even plausible first-century readings of Jesus, and that his influence undeniably impinged on a spectrum of quite different traditions, this book contends that the early church's canonical, apostolic witness to Jesus is indeed one such reading, and that it is a historically legitimate and defensible one.

[margin note: thesis]

The Jesus of History and the Christ of Faith

Although this is in some ways a modest thesis, its implications are highly significant. Just over a hundred years ago, Martin Kähler published his famous book, *The So-Called Historical Jesus and the Historic Biblical Christ*.[51] While there has been considerable debate about what precisely Kähler did or did not mean to accomplish, he contributed greatly to the dichotomy between the "Jesus of history" and the "Christ of faith" which since then has been a hallmark of so much New Testament study and systematic theology.

Looking back on twentieth century biblical criticism, it is ironic that historical scholarship has meticulously investigated and stripped down the texts only to find that even in the very earliest sources one can never discover a "purely historical" Jesus, a Jesus without christology of *some* kind. In the mouths of even his earliest witnesses, Jesus is already the one who died and was raised. There is no such thing as naked historical information. We have seen above that even outsiders like Josephus and Tacitus who speak about Jesus find themselves compelled to discuss him as one who died but whose significance was believed to carry on beyond his death. Yet more than that: suppose for the moment that we could go all the way back to Jesus himself. All the indications are that we would *still* discover a man with a view of himself, God and the world that was already shaped in self-consciously theological, and quite probably christological, terms.[52] Without questioning for a moment that historical issues are important and eminently worth investigating, this does raise the question of whether there can *ever* be such a thing as a "purely historical" portrait, devoid of interpretation. Even for figures like Napoleon, Lenin or Hitler it must remain highly doubtful whether we can ever give a satisfactory answer about who the "real" person was, independent of any definite interpretative framework.[53]

At the end of the day there are always going to be different pictures of Jesus: the Jewish martyr, the failed revolutionary, the unworldly sage, the Messianic Son of God. Many of these are possible views, and on the historical level there can be legitimate disagreement about how best to interpret the evidence. The one thing which we *cannot* do is to go back far enough to find a Jesus of history who is not already a Jesus of his interpreter's faith or unbelief.

But if that is true, it immediately becomes a legitimate enterprise to explore the pictures of Jesus as seen and experienced by apostolic Christianity. This is no escape from the hard work of historical scrutiny, since the Church's view of Christ is firmly anchored in his historical life and work as the one who was also "crucified under Pontius Pilate". Instead, it merely recognizes the conclusion which scholarship has found at last to be inescapable: history and interpretation are inseparably intertwined.

What, then, of Kähler's distinction? Scientifically speaking, this past century of scholarship has confirmed that the "purely" historical, non-christological Jesus remains hidden from view. He is in any case best seen as a figment of the post-Enlightenment imagination. But what we must equally recognize is that for those who first saw him and were called by him, Jesus of Nazareth and "the historic biblical Christ" of their faith were one and the same person. The remainder of this book will seek to relate that conviction to seven critical questions concerning the continuity between Jesus and the faith of the early church.

Chapter One

Where Did Jesus Come From?

If you went out into the streets of London or New York and interviewed people about their knowledge of the life of Jesus or the Gospels, the results would be fairly disappointing. Most people would have heard of Jesus as the founder of Christianity. Many would know that he was crucified, and perhaps that he supposedly rose from the dead. Over and above that, however, one of the very few additional facts which some folk might produce is that he was born in Bethlehem, and possibly even that he came to be known as Jesus of Nazareth.

Among church people, too, Bethlehem and Nazareth hold a special mystique and fascination. Many have grown up with carols like "Away in a Manger" and "O Little Town of Bethlehem". These conjure up rich images of Christ being born in a barn somewhere in a peaceful farming village in the Lake District or in Iowa, with cows and sheep sheltering from the cold and watching the warm and apple-cheeked glow of a baby asleep on a bed of hay. Romantic notions of Nazareth are a bit harder to come by, but some may remember Sunday school lessons or popular films which showed an adolescent Jesus learning the carpenter's craft from his father Joseph in his well-kept workshop in a prosperous hillside village.

→ What can we actually know about the origins of Jesus? As we will discover, there are some knotty questions to be tackled here, with considerable scope for disagreement. Nevertheless, the study is worthwhile in itself and can lead us to an understanding of whether it is possible with integrity to see Jesus' historical origins in continuity with Christian faith as it emerged in the Gospels and later in the Creeds.

In this opening chapter we will look first at Bethlehem

and the birth narratives of the Gospels, and then move on to Nazareth, examining its role in the life of Jesus. We conclude with a few words on Capernaum, which became the home base for Jesus' public ministry.

Bethlehem in Judaea

There were at least two Bethlehems in the land of Palestine, both fairly small and insignificant villages. One was in Galilee, in the territory of Zebulon, on the other side of the valley of Jezreel across from Megiddo. This is mentioned in the description of the land boundaries in Joshua 19.15, and it was apparently the home of Ibzan, one of Israel's judges (Judges 12.8–10). We hear nothing of it for many centuries, although in the Palestinian Talmud it is known as "Tyrian Bethlehem",[1] and today it is the small Arab village of Beit Lahm, 11 km Northwest of Nazareth.

The other Bethlehem is by far the more important of the two. It is located in the hills 8 km South of Jerusalem, just off the main road to Hebron and Egypt. In the Bible it is first mentioned in Genesis 35.19 in connection with the burial of Rachel on the road to "Ephrath, that is Bethlehem". A town called *Bit-Lahmi* in the land of Jerusalem also occurs in a 14th century BC Akkadian administrative letter from Tell el-Amarna in Egypt.[2] In addition to a couple of obscure and depressing stories in the book of Judges (Judges 17, 19), the Old Testament links several well-known episodes with Bethlehem in Judah. In particular, Ruth's mother-in-law Naomi is from Bethlehem, and the two women move there from Moab after the deaths of the men in their family. Ruth marries a local landowner named Boaz, and their great-grandson was King David, born in Bethlehem and anointed there by Samuel (1 Sam. 16). Bethlehem was the site of a Philistine garrison at the time of David (2 Sam. 23.14). David's grandson, king Rehoboam, later fortified the site to guard the approach to Jerusalem (2 Chr.

11.5f.). After the return from the Exile, Bethlehem had a population of well under 200 (Ezra 2.21; Neh. 7.26) and remained an insignificant village until a sustained Christian influence began in the fourth century AD with increasing pilgrimage (visitors included Queen Helena and the Pilgrim of Bordeaux), a church built by Constantine, and later a monastery founded by St. Jerome.[3] Modern Bethlehem is a busy Arab Christian and Muslim town of trade and tourism, with a population a little over 40,000.

The reason Bethlehem continued to inspire the Jewish imagination is due almost entirely to a prophecy in the book of Micah, probably dating from just after the fall of Jerusalem and the Davidic dynasty in 587 BC:

> Now you are walled around with a wall; siege is laid against us; with a rod they strike the ruler of Israel upon the cheek. But you, O Bethlehem of Ephrathah, who are one of the little clans of Judah, from you shall come forth for me one who is to rule in Israel, whose origin is from of old, from ancient days. Therefore he shall give them up until the time when she who is in labour has brought forth; then the rest of his kindred shall return to the people of Israel. And he shall stand and feed his flock in the strength of the LORD, in the majesty of the name of the LORD his God. And they shall live secure, for now he shall be great to the ends of the earth. (Micah 5.1–4)

Clearly this prophecy harbours the promise of a restoration of the royal line of David, and the future emergence of a deliverer who would save his people. Significantly, it need not mean that this Messianic king would be physically born in Bethlehem, merely that he would be descended from the ancient clan of King David.

So where does Bethlehem fit in with the birth of Jesus?

Aside from a passing reference in the Fourth Gospel (John 7.40f., where his opponents assume he was born in Nazareth and therefore cannot be the Messiah[4]), the New Testament only mentions Bethlehem in the birth narratives of Matthew and Luke. Some have even supposed that he may have been born in the Galilean village of Bethlehem, whose proximity to Nazareth would make it much more convenient, and would render Joseph's journey from Nazareth to Bethlehem for a census more plausible.

Nevertheless, while there is little we can say with confidence, it does seem clear that Bethlehem in Judaea is intended. The accounts in Matthew and Luke are entirely independent from each other and, aside from the basic fact of Jesus' unusual birth to Joseph and Mary, actually agree on remarkably little *else* – except that he was born in David's home town.

And although it might of course be theologically convenient, there was really no need to fabricate such a story. Despite John 7.40f., physical birth in Bethlehem of Judaea was *not* widely thought to be a prerequisite for the Messiah, and no such claim was made for several other aspiring first and second-century Messiahs.[5]

In Luke, Joseph and Mary travel to Bethlehem from Nazareth, apparently in order to register for a census under Quirinius the governor of Syria. This is a problematical assertion both because Quirinius only became governor in AD 6, about ten years *after* Jesus' birth, and because a Roman census involved registration at the place of one's normal residence, not at one's ancient place of descent. Luke does not actually tell us where Mary and Joseph stay, except that the baby is placed in an animal food trough because there is no space in the "inn". We also learn that Mary and Joseph remain there for at least five weeks before returning to Nazareth (compare Luke 2.22, 39 with Lev. 12.1–8).

In Matthew, on the other hand, they appear to live in a

house in Bethlehem already. After the birth they seem to stay
on for perhaps as much as two years (see Matt. 2.7, 16) before
escaping Herod's wrath by fleeing to Egypt (2.13–15).
Eventually, after Herod's death perhaps a few months later, they
move North to Nazareth (2.19–23).

Is it possible to make sense of this seemingly con-
tradictory information? There is obviously considerable debate
among scholars. More than a few regard these accounts as
largely legendary, apologetic attempts to establish the Messianic
status of Jesus: in their view, there is every reason to think that
Jesus was born in Nazareth.[6] Given the extant historical
information, many scholars would agree that the census is a
virtually intractable problem. It may be, however, that Luke did
get his facts approximately right in pointing to a census in the
concluding years of Herod's reign. In that case the census in
connection with Quirinius would need to be taken as a very
general reference to the era of the man who was at that time in
charge of the Roman province of Asia and later became
notorious for his association with "the" census of AD 6 (see
Acts 5.37), a more thorough and notorious effort which
subsumed and replaced the earlier ones.[7] (Another serious
possibility worth mentioning is that in Luke 2.2 one could
translate not "this was the *first* census under Quirinius..." but
"this census happened *before* the one under Quirinius...".[8])

Mary and Joseph's trip from Nazareth to Bethlehem in
Judaea is only plausible if at least Joseph was in some
significant sense already resident there: and indeed it is likely
that Joseph's family were residents and owned property in
Bethlehem.[9] This would best account for the fact that Matthew
has them in a "house" (Matt. 2.11), that there was not enough
space for the newlyweds in the extended family's "living" or
"guest room" (Luke 2.7[10]), and that Mary laid Jesus in a food
trough for animals, which were sometimes kept near the
entrance of first-century houses. Possibly this means they
stayed near the front of the kind of cave house known to have

been in use in Bethlehem at this time. Jesus' birth in a cave is in fact attested from very early on.[11] It also agrees with the local tradition of the cave in which St. Jerome stayed in the fourth century, and which is still visible under the Church of the Nativity in Bethlehem today.

The idea of a previous connection of Joseph and Mary with Bethlehem, or at least Judaea, best explains the outline of the story. Even according to Luke, Mary goes to visit her relative Elizabeth in a village in the Judaean hills (1.39): from Nazareth this would be a long and arduous journey, highly unlikely for a pregnant woman.

External confirmation of a sort can be found in the early second-century *Infancy Gospel of James*, a largely legendary collection of stories about the origin of Jesus. Here, Mary is the virgin daughter of a well-to-do Jerusalem couple called Anna and Joachim. She is said to have grown up in the Temple, a legend which might seem a little less far-fetched if she was of priestly descent (note that her "relative" Elizabeth is a descendant of Aaron and married to Zechariah the priest, Luke 1.5).[12] Joseph is here a considerably older man with children from a previous marriage, and he apparently lives near Bethlehem. The suggestion of his advanced age might serve to explain why nothing more is heard of him in the Gospels after the birth, except in reference to Jesus as "the son of Joseph".[13] No specific traditions survive of Joseph's parents, but the two quite divergent genealogies in Matthew and Luke nevertheless trace his descent back to David (albeit through different sons).[14]

This kind of scenario may go some way towards explaining the biblical accounts. Joseph and Mary were residents of the Judaean village of Bethlehem. If Luke is correct, they may have spent a period of time in Nazareth before returning home possibly in connection with a Roman census.

The Birth of Jesus

A slight detour may be in order at this point to offer one or two rudimentary remarks on the controversial question of the virgin birth – or more accurately, the question of whether Jesus was *conceived* by a young woman who had not had sexual intercourse.[15] Although this question is not directly concerned with Jesus' geographic origins, it obviously belongs here in chronological order and is in any case a subject of continuing interest for many Christians and non-Christians alike.

Without wanting to propose a concrete and comprehensive solution, I will begin by stating some basic factual observations, and then to offer a few thoughts on their interpretation.

The only New Testament source to speak explicitly of the virgin birth is the Gospel of Matthew, although in Luke it is strongly implied in the story of the Annunciation. For Matthew, the chief purpose is to show that Jesus fulfils the prophecy of Isaiah 7.14 about a young woman giving birth to a child who will be a sign of deliverance. The Greek Old Testament affirms that this young woman is to be a "virgin" – though the Hebrew original is less clear. Aside from this, and a message of encouragement to Joseph in a dream, not much more is made of this announcement in Matthew (1.18–25).

Luke, on the other hand, emphasizes Mary's surprise at the idea that she should become pregnant without being in a sexual relationship, and the importance of the Holy Spirit and the "power of the Most High" in bringing this about. Referring to Elizabeth, who conceived a child even though she was old and thought to be infertile, the angel assures Mary that nothing is impossible with God. We do not explicitly hear that no man was involved in Mary's pregnancy, but this does seem to be strongly implied.

Mark and John do not mention the virgin birth at all; nor does it appear in the rest of the New Testament. In particular, it seems to be of no great significance for christology until at least the second century, although from the time of Ignatius of Antioch her virginity begins to be discussed and reflected upon.[16] One might think, therefore, that the New Testament stories are nothing more than legendary embellishments of Jesus' origins.

Nevertheless, a number of additional observations call for comment. It is curious, given the Oriental interest in family pedigree and descent, that any talk of Jesus' human father should vanish so completely from the subsequent narrative in the Gospels, when his mother and brothers are repeatedly mentioned. Mark 6.3 refers to Jesus as "son of Mary" – a most peculiar designation in a strongly patrilinear culture. What is more, even in Matthew and Luke the idea of a virgin birth seems in some ways counterproductive, even embarrassing to the writers' redactional purposes. Matthew and Luke clearly go to great lengths to demonstrate Jesus' paternal descent from David, and it seems hardly credible that someone who thought this lineage so important would wish to invent a virgin birth.[17]

In the Fourth Gospel, people on the one hand know Jesus to be the "son of Joseph" (John 1.45, 6.42); but there also seems to be an ambiguously ironic debate about the identity of both his heavenly and his earthly father. Thus in John 8 his opponents first ask him, "Where is your Father?" (8.19), and when Jesus speaks of the Devil as *their* father they retort, "We are not illegitimate children" (8.41) – perhaps implying the charge that he is. While Joseph himself is entirely absent from this Gospel, Mary plays a small but significant role (John 2.1–12, 19.25–27). Overall, it is plausible to conclude that John knows Jesus to be the son of Mary but not of Joseph.[18]

The letters of St. Paul show little interest in the life of Jesus generally, and even less in his family or the infancy narratives. Although he was the Son of God, Jesus was fully human: "born of a woman" (Gal. 4.4) and (lit.) "of the seed of

David according to the flesh" (Rom. 1.3). Although the former expression has sometimes been thought to indicate Paul's familiarity with the virgin birth tradition, the latter apparently does not. Paul does place repeated emphasis on the lowly circumstances of Christ's incarnation (2 Cor. 8.9; Phil. 2.6ff, etc.), but without revealing anything about the identity of his parents.

One conclusion should present itself quite obviously. Even if we did not have Matthew and Luke, the New Testament's information on the paternity of Jesus would be a considerable mystery.

The virgin birth is a puzzling proposition in several other respects, too. The biblical evidence, although scant, is quite clear in what it seems to affirm: a woman conceives a child without the aid of a man. But what is meant by that? Quite apart from the problems it poses for a modern scientific perspective, it is very difficult to see whether even ancient readers could have made head or tail of this. Despite Matthew's quotation from Isaiah 7.14, the idea of a virgin birth was entirely foreign to a Jewish way of thinking: while the Greek word there means "virgin" (rarely "unmarried woman"), the underlying Hebrew means a young woman of marriageable age.[19] Angelic annunciation stories for important births are well attested in the Old Testament (e.g. Gen. 16.10–12; 18.1–15; Judg. 13.2–14); the mothers of great holy men are often barren or old; and even the presence of the Spirit of God is not a problem. In a context of Palestinian Judaism, Jesus could still be Messiah and Son of God if he had a human father: both were titles which applied to other royal descendants of David in the Old Testament (2 Sam. 7; Psa. 2, 89; etc.). To Jewish ears, the idea of a virgin birth would sound distinctly odd.[20]

Greek mythology, on the other hand, tells numerous stories of people with human mothers and divine fathers, including Hercules and Perseus. The idea of divine sonship was not uncommon in Hellenistic thought; similar stories are found in Egypt. But this, too, does not provide a convincing explanation: sons of the gods were always seen as the offspring of *sexual intercourse* between a human woman and a god, who sometimes appears in form of an animal (like a bull or a swan) and rapes the woman. Clearly this is hardly appropriate to our context. The setting is Jewish, and there is not the slightest suggestion of divine sexual intercourse, much less of rape. In fact, in the Synoptic Gospels there is no obvious link at all between Jesus' title "Son of God" and the identity of his biological father.

What, then, are we to make of the biblical account of the birth of Jesus? We cannot here consider the whole history of doctrine, but historically it seems clear that the paternity of Jesus was enigmatic from the start. Joseph or another man might have been the father: in the second century the Jewish Christian sect known as the Ebionites taught the former,[21] while Jewish sources from the third century onward speculate on Jesus' illegitimate origin from a man called Panthera (possibly a corruption of the word *parthenos*, "virgin", to the common Roman soldier's name Pantera).[22] If Joseph was the father, this would not have created undue scandal and there is certainly no need to invent any stories of virginal conception. Joseph's paternity is an implausible suggestion. On the other hand, if someone else was the father, it is peculiar that this accusation is never raised or denied in the earliest documents, and that instead the opponents of Jesus point to his mother, brothers and sisters to stress his unremarkable origins – as if to say, "We know him: this is just Yeshua from down the street." In referring to his brothers and sisters, clearly there is no implication that *all* of his siblings are illegitimate. No one ever seems to doubt Jesus' Davidic descent. And had there been a widespread tradition of his illegitimacy, one would expect to see a lot more evidence of this debate in the New Testament or in second-century apologetics. If it was so difficult in a Jewish setting to establish the idea of a crucified Messiah, how much more if he was generally known to be a bastard![23]

At the end of the day it seems to reflect the evidence most fairly to say that historically the birth of Jesus is shrouded in mystery. Humanly, his paternity must seem doubtful, and it seems most plausible that he was not born to Joseph and Mary in wedlock. On the other hand, the idea of an illegitimate birth, although impossible to rule out altogether, also does not seem to sit easily with the facts.

Thus, the virginal conception of Jesus can be neither proved nor disproved. For those who do not reject the possibility of miracle, Christian belief in the virgin birth is certainly compatible with what *can* be known from history.[24] What is more, on this level of historical plausibility, harsh human reality and theological reflection can meet in a powerful expression of who the biblical Jesus is. The biblical idea of Jesus' virginal conception affirms the glory and purpose of God's work amidst the mixed emotions and hard, down-to-earth consequences of an unplanned teenage pregnancy and single motherhood. For the New Testament authors, glory concealed in humility and God's wisdom in human folly (e.g. 1 Cor. 1.18– 2.16) attended not only his death but his whole incarnation from beginning to end. Here, then, was seen both the utter humanity and the complete otherness of Jesus. In an ironic turn, the doctrine of the virgin birth curiously meets and embraces the later objection of Jesus' opponents (John 7.27): "We know where this man is from; but when the Messiah comes, no one will know where he is from."

The Flight to Egypt

If Joseph and Mary did have some connection with Bethlehem, how did they end up moving to Nazareth, indeed so permanently that the remainder of the gospel narrative links Jesus exclusively with that city? And would they really have fled to Egypt first?

We are obviously in the realm of speculation here. Like

the account of the virgin birth, the historical setting of the story of the magi and the flight to Egypt in Matthew 2 is not one which scholarship is well placed to adjudicate or verify. There is a lot of theology in Matthew which makes it very significant for him that Jesus should go to Egypt. Jesus is seen as the representative of Israel, the one who fulfils the will of God in all righteousness and restores the people to their originally intended relationship with God. Matthew sees Jesus' return from Egypt as a fulfilment of God's statement in Hosea 11.1, "When Israel was a child, I loved him; and out of Egypt have I called my Son." The identification of Jesus with Israel is obvious, and clearly the implication is that Jesus' life and work constitute a new exodus, a new redemption for the people of God. In this context, the motif of a hostile king killing the male babies after being warned by sages is also reminiscent of the story of Moses, especially as told by Josephus (*Ant.* 2.205ff.). For Matthew at least, the primary significance of the story of the Holy Family's flight to Egypt seems to be literary and theological: Jesus is the one in whom the Old Testament story comes to its appointed fulfilment.

Having said that, the biblical story is not altogether without historical plausibility. Astrology was held in very high regard in the ancient world, and even educated writers confirm the great influence which heavenly portents would have had, not least in Babylonia. A kind of Jewish horoscope is attested even in the Dead Sea Scrolls.[25] As for Herod the Great, he was indeed a cruel and extremely insecure ruler, and Bethlehem a tiny but highly symbolic place on the doorstep of Herodion, one of his key fortresses – not a good place to tolerate even the slightest hint of sedition. True, there is no historical evidence for his execution of all the male babies of Bethlehem. From all we know of him, however, he was easily capable of such an idea, especially since the number of children involved would have been small enough (likely less than a dozen) not to attract a great deal of public attention.

Egypt, on the other hand, was a favourite place for refuge ever since the earliest biblical times, and it had always been relatively accessible from Palestine. (Jeremiah 41.17 even mentions a roadside hostel near Bethlehem on the way to Egypt.) With around a million Jews it had the largest Jewish diaspora community, and the vast city of Alexandria in the Delta of the Nile had a particularly large and vibrant Jewish community enjoying frequent contact with Jerusalem and the Holy Land. If the family of Jesus did feel threatened by a violent ruler and sought shelter in Alexandria for a few months until his death in 4 BC, they were quite possibly not the only ones to do so.

In the end it is impossible to assess the historical value of this story, since we have only Matthew's word for it. It does seem entirely conceivable in its historical setting; at the same time, Matthew's primary point is a theological one.

Nazareth

We are told, then, that Jesus moved to Nazareth with his parents; and his family remained resident in the area. The third-century Palestinian Christian writer Julius Africanus suggests that relatives of Jesus were still living there in his day (Eusebius *Eccl. Hist.* 1.7.14): a man named Conon who was martyred in Asia Minor under the Emperor Decius claimed to be a descendant of Jesus from Nazareth.[26] In any case, that Jesus grew up in this obscure location in Lower Galilee is not in doubt.

The first-century village of Nazareth was nestled on the slopes of a secluded valley in the hill country 25 km West of the Sea of Galilee and 8 km West of Mount Tabor. It was off the beaten track. Outside the New Testament and Christian sources, Nazareth is never mentioned before about AD 300, when it occurs on an inscription from Caesarea listing the priestly courses and their bases in Galilee.[27] It does not appear in the Talmud. Nathanael's first reaction to Jesus in John 1.46 is revealing: "Can anything good come out of Nazareth?" Part of the reason for its relative obscurity may also be the close proximity of more important places: Japha, two miles Southwest of Nazareth, was the largest village of Galilee, Flavius Josephus's base during the Galilean campaign in the war against Rome (AD 66–67) and the site of an important battle (*War* 3.289ff.; *Life* 230, 270). A little more than an hour's walk away was Sepphoris, the largest city in Galilee (*Life* 232) and the home of pro-Roman, Sadducean Jewish landowners.[28] After its destruction in 3 BC by the Roman general Varus, Herod Antipas's splendid reconstruction of the city in Hellenistic style provided the area with an economic boost that may well have played a part in the carpenter Joseph's decision to settle in nearby Nazareth.[29]

Archaeological evidence suggests the area was first settled by the Middle Bronze Age. Houses and tombs from a variety of periods have been discovered, including several interesting specimens from the Herodian era. However, the site may in fact have been uninhabited during the Persian and early Hellenistic periods.[30] Rough calculations of the remains surveyed suggest a maximum population of around 500,[31] although the village's spring, now known as the Fountain of the Virgin, could in theory support several times as many people. Nazareth today is an active, mostly Arab trading city numbering around 50,000, including the industrial Jewish suburb of Natzeret Illit.

The Childhood of Jesus

The New Testament tells us virtually nothing about Jesus' childhood and adolescence. Luke relates one story of Jesus at the age of twelve on his family's annual pilgrimage to Jerusalem for Passover (2.41–51). The boy is so fascinated with the legal and theological discussions going on in the Temple that he

misses his family's caravan departure for Galilee. When his
parents turn back and eventually find him in the Temple, he
displays an acute desire to be "where the action is", as it were,
foreshadowing his keen interest in the Temple later in life.

Aside from this little vignette, we hear nothing of Jesus'
childhood. Luke alone attempts to give us an impression when
he says that after the Temple incident Jesus returned to
Nazareth with his parents, "and was obedient to them. ... And
Jesus increased in wisdom and in years, and in divine and
human favour" (2.52). Attempts to fill the gaps are largely
apocryphal, if not ludicrous: for instance, suggestions that Jesus
went off to India, to Glastonbury, or to the North American
Indians, as has been claimed in various quarters. He must have
had a normal Jewish childhood and adolescence, in which he
would have been taught to read and (probably) write from the
Torah, and would have learned his father's trade.[32] In Mark 6.3
Jesus is called "the carpenter", which suggests that he may well
have worked as a village carpenter in Nazareth for a number of
years. The carpenter's profession would have placed the family
of Jesus in the position of lower middle-class craftsmen, possibly with some religious or community responsibilities even in
the local synagogue. There may have been additional work at
Japha or Sepphoris. On the other hand, it is worth noting that
the Gospels never show Jesus visiting either Sepphoris[33] or
Antipas' controversial new capital of Tiberias,[34] quite possibly
because of a critical attitude towards these cities and their
inhabitants.

Capernaum

This brings us very near the beginning of Jesus' ministry. At
some point in his late twenties Jesus was caught up in the
message and ministry of John the Baptist, which was causing
considerable spiritual revival in Palestine: John offered a sense
of national renewal along with a hope for God's redemption of

Israel.[35] Jesus' own baptism by John was a profound spiritual experience. The Gospels assert that in this context he had a heavenly vision affirming his calling as the Messianic Son of God, and this vision came to be tested and confirmed in the course of his subsequent retreat for prayer and fasting to the Judaean wilderness (Mark 1.9–13 par.). John the Baptist gradually came to be seen as a political threat by Herod Antipas, who had him arrested and put to death (Mark 6.17–29 par.).

At some point in the unfolding of these events Jesus moved to Capernaum (possibly to avoid hostility due to his known sympathies for John: see Matt. 4.12f.). This town, whose Hebrew name *Kfar Nahum* means "village of Nahum", lies in a picturesque location on the Northwestern shore of the sea of Galilee. In the first century its population of perhaps 1,000–1,500 enjoyed the use of a large synagogue built of local basalt, the remains of which have been identified underneath the extant fourth-century limestone edifice.[36] Luke 7.5 suggests it was funded by a local patron in the Roman army. The presence of this man, called a "centurion" in Luke 7.1/Matt. 8.5 and a "royal official" in John 4.46, is made more plausible by the recent discovery of a Roman bath house and other Roman public buildings. Aside from fishing, agriculture, and presumably construction, some employment would have been provided by small-scale glass making and purple-dye industries which the same excavations have brought to light.[37] Matthew 9.9 indicates a nearby highway customs station: this seems plausible as the border with the Tetrarchy of Philip was only 4 kilometres away.

John 2.12 speaks of Jesus going to Capernaum with his mother and brothers. Perhaps there were family connections in the village. In any case Peter and Andrew, his first followers, had a house in Capernaum (Mark 1.29; John 1.44 says they were from the neighbouring village of Bethsaida), and Jesus is found in the house of Peter's mother-in-law early in the gospel narrative. Intriguingly, an Aramaic dedicatory inscription from the fourth-century synagogue mentions people with some of the same names which we encounter in the Gospels: "Alphaeus, son of Zebedee, son of John, made this column; on him be a blessing."

It was here that Jesus made his home: Capernaum is called "his own town" (Matt. 9.1; Mark 2.1). The accounts of his ministry and teaching relate intimately to the life of this rural district in the Galilean countryside. Thus we find stories and parables of fishing on a temperamental lake, small grain fields amidst rocky terrain, widespread indebtedness, absent landlords, and hired workers in large private vineyards. Jesus teaches in small villages, on the hills or even from a little boat just offshore in one of the many small coves around the lake.[38] We hear of only one episode at the very beginning of his ministry when Jesus is found in Nazareth (Luke 4). He was evidently not accepted there as a prophetic leader: familiarity breeds contempt. So it was from his base in this lakeside village of Capernaum that Jesus began to preach the good news of the Kingdom and to gather his first followers. In this sense, Capernaum can be seen as the home of the very first Christians.[39]

Conclusion

In this study of Jesus' personal origins we have discovered a combination of the humble and the sublime, the undistinguished and the truly extraordinary. Jesus was probably born in the small town of Bethlehem in Judaea, whose former importance for the history of Israel had long since faded away. His paternity seems to have been a puzzle at the time, and in the absence of convincing answers it remains concealed and encapsulated in the Christian confession that he was "born of the Virgin Mary". After a possible brief stay in Egypt, perhaps in Alexandria, Jesus spent his entire youth in an insignificant town in Galilee and became known as Jesus of Nazareth. It was not until he moved down to Capernaum that he emerged from the shadows of a hidden and unremarkable Palestinian Jewish life and set out on the mission which God had confirmed to him at his baptism by John and subsequently in the Judaean desert.

It is surprising how few modern books on Jesus have anything whatever to say on the subject of *Christmas*. The Apostolic accounts of the birth and infancy of Jesus offer a rich heritage of reflection about the nature of the incarnation, without which the Christian understanding of Jesus is incomplete. The early church's confession about Jesus' humble origins expresses the sheer wonder and surprise of suddenly finding a light shining in the midst of darkness and death: God's saving presence had come to stay among his people in the very ordinariness and poverty of their lives, "to guide our feet into the way of peace" (Luke 1.79; cf. Matt. 4.16).

Looking back decades later on the hidden origins of Jesus, his followers could not help but interpret his birth in this way. Of course, to do so required a knowledge of his whole story as it later unfolded. But Christmas is precisely where that story took its beginning: "when the fullness of time had come, God sent his Son, born of a woman..." (Gal. 4.4–5).

Chapter Two

Was Jesus the Messiah?

Since the very beginning of the Church, perhaps the most foundational Christian belief about Jesus has been that he was the Messiah promised in the Hebrew Scriptures, the redeemer figure appointed by God to liberate Israel from servitude and sin. In the account of the earliest Christian sermon ever preached, the Apostle Peter says this about an Old Testament prophecy:

> David spoke of the resurrection of the Messiah, saying, "He was not abandoned to Hades, nor did his flesh experience corruption." This Jesus God raised up, and of that all of us are witnesses. ... Therefore let the entire house of Israel know with certainty that God has made him both Lord and Messiah, this Jesus whom you crucified. (Acts 2.31f., 36)

But was Jesus really that promised Messiah? On what basis could we decide? And if he was, what does that mean? Why did some Jews think that he was, and others that he was not? These are some of the questions I would like to discuss in this chapter. I shall begin with a survey of who the Messiah was expected to be in the Old Testament and in first-century Judaism, followed by an evaluation of whether and how Jesus met those expectations.

The Messianic Hope in Ancient Judaism

Hope for the ultimate salvation of Israel was almost universal in ancient Judaism, although it took many different forms. It was not always and everywhere connected with one redeeming figure called the Messiah. Nor was there an identifiable orthodox system of beliefs by which one could measure deviation or conformity. Some scholars, indeed, have taken to speaking of *Judaisms* as a better way to reflect this diversity, although others still prefer to highlight a basic "common" set of practices and beliefs as underlying all or most of the different manifestations of Judaism.[1] But be that as it may: as long as we allow for considerable variation and breadth of definition, the following skeletal outline may serve to capture something of the nature of ancient Jewish Messianic expectations (along with Jewish eschatology in the wider sense).

The Term "Messiah"

The term "Messiah" itself derives from the Hebrew word *mashiah,* which literally means "rubbed with oil". This term, in English usually rendered "anointed", and in Greek *christos* (hence the name "Christ"), denotes a ritual action used to designate and appoint someone for a special task. The two most important applications are the offices of *Priest* (e.g. Aaron, Exod. 28.41, etc.) and *King* (the most famous instances are Samuel's anointing of Saul, 1 Sam. 10, and of David, 1 Sam. 16), but later also that of *Prophet* (Isa. 61.1).

Royal Theology

Numerous biblical traditions are important for the understanding of Messianism in the first century. Some passages first came to be related to the Messiah when Christians began using them as prophecies fulfilled in Christist. Others were already regarded as Messianic in first-century Judaism; but many of these, too, had "become" so only at a relatively advanced stage of Jewish reflection on the subject.

By far the most powerful and formative influence on the early development of a Messianic expectation was the ideology of *kingship* in the united monarchy of Israel and later in the

Southern Kingdom of Judah. Antecedents of this can be seen in the leadership tradition expressed in the stories of Moses and Joshua, and later those of the Judges. The decisive influence, however, must be sought in the court theology of the dynasty of David. (This theology, in fact, may well have flavoured the biblical accounts about the earlier leaders.)

Generally in the Ancient Near East, kings and royalty were considered specially favoured by the gods. Unlike our modern views of government, the authority of oriental kings was given to them not by the people they governed, but by divine appointment. The king was seen as enjoying a particularly close and favoured relationship with the gods, so that he could be portrayed as the divine agent and representative on earth.

Such a perspective on the monarchy is also found in the Old Testament, particularly in the so-called royal Psalms (especially Psa. 2, 18, 45, 89, and 110). Divine power was seen to guarantee the power of the king and to symbolize and apply the reign of Yahweh over Israel and all the earth, resulting in prosperity and success for his people. In this capacity, the king could even be called the "son of God", a term which both distinguished him from the rest of Israel and made him the representative of his people (see especially Psa. 2.7; 2 Sam. 7.14; 1 Chr. 17.13, 22.10). Thus he had many divine privileges, but also a significant number of religious and moral obligations: he was the guarantor and enforcer of God's covenant with Israel. Some kings fulfilled this role well and some badly: the Old Testament assesses them by exclusively moral and spiritual criteria, with little or no regard for their political prowess and achievements.

The House of David

All this might simply have made Israelite royalty a powerful traditional institution with important religious roots, but not necessarily more than that. What planted the seeds of hope for a Messiah firmly in the royal ideology of Israel was the early belief in the permanent rule of the house of David. The key story here is of course Nathan's prophecy to David in 2 Samuel 7.11–16: "Your house and your kingdom shall be made sure forever before me; your throne shall be established forever" (cf. 1 Kgs. 2.3f.; Psa.18.50 (18.51 in Hebrew); 28.9; 89.4, 29–38).

In addition to this growing conviction that the house of David would endure forever, various pre-exilic prophets developed the image of the ideal king, a man who (unlike most of the contemporary rulers) would be of the calibre of David, doing all that God required, and delivering his people from their increasingly threatening enemies. The prophet Isaiah spoke of a powerful prince of peace to be born as king on the throne of David (Isa. 9.6; cf. e.g. 11.1; 16.5); similar ideas occur in Micah (5.2–4), Jeremiah (e.g. 17.25) and Ezekiel (34.22f.; 37.24f.), and then increasingly in post-exilic texts (e.g. Zech. 3.8, 6.12; and probably Amos 9.11).

By the time of the Exile, therefore, the promised glorious Davidic king had become an established part of the Judaean royal ideology. The almost continuous decline since David and Solomon meant that a return to the former glory was a treasured hope. Nevertheless, at the destruction of Jerusalem the royal line of David was suddenly finished – for good. Although the descendants of David were still being traced after the Exile,[2] no Davidic ruler was ever to govern a sovereign Israel again. There was indeed great excitement after the Exile when Joshua was High Priest and Zerubbabel, a Davidic descendant, briefly became governor of Judah under the Persians. Thus Zechariah identifies Joshua as the "Branch", a term used for the Davidic Messiah promised by Isaiah and Jeremiah (cf. Zech. 3.8; 6.12 with Isa. 11.1; Jer. 23.5; 33.15). This hope, however, came to nothing.

Nevertheless, the loss of the Davidic dynasty had caused great soul-searching during and after the Exile. The gradual revival of Israelite religion and culture on the basis of the Torah and a rebuilt Temple brought about an increasing re-affirmation

of hope in the promise of a redeemer king in the line of David.
In the light of this, post-exilic Judaism witnessed a powerful
development of eschatology, specifically of the hope in a future
national and spiritual restoration. Passages like 2 Samuel 7
kept alive the hope for another anointed Son of David
(expressed with great urgency in Psalm 89), and Deuteronomy
18.15 raised the hopes of a great "prophet like Moses". (Since
the time of Malachi, this prophet may also have been understood as someone coming in the spirit of Elijah: see Mal. 4.5
[=3.23 in Hebrew].)

At least in some circles, a glorious high priestly figure
was also expected. There was a prediction in 1 Samuel 2.35 of
a new and faithful priest who will "go in and out before my
anointed one forever". David himself, moreover, had acted as a
priest in offering sacrifices and pronouncing blessings,
2 Samuel 6.17f. Later reflections of such a priestly ideal can be
seen in Phinehas in Sirach 45.34 or in the glorious image of
Simon ben Onias in Sirach 50.

Post-exilic prophecy developed the hope of restoration in
a variety of powerful ways. Redemption was sometimes linked
to a vaguely described Messianic figure, but sometimes simply
seen as the work of God himself (e.g. in Isa. 56–66). As a
result, while the Old Testament provides plenty of fuel for the
continuing development of Jewish Messianic expectations, it
does not clearly describe one particular coming Messiah, but
instead uses different metaphors to speak about human agents
whom God will appoint (and "anoint") to bring about the
coming redemption.

Kingdom and Redemption

Several other features of post-exilic belief are worth pointing
out. First, the hoped-for deliverance had a *universal* dimension,
in that it applied to God's dominion over the whole world and
creation. In this it was indebted to the Hebrew prophetic
tradition. On the other hand, there was also a strongly held

national Jewish *particularism* which focused on God's relationship with the Jewish people often to the virtual exclusion of the Gentiles. In addition to this collective nationalist emphasis, moreover, Judaism also shared in the increasing interest in _individual salvation_ which arose in the Hellenistic world. The belief in providence, resurrection and the coming Messiah was something which was understood to give assurance not just to the nation but to the life of the individual believer as well.

In a situation where the wicked and the oppressors seemed perpetually to flourish at the expense of God's people, a real belief in salvation could only be linked with an affirmation of God's *future Judgement,* in which all wrongs would be punished and all rights affirmed and vindicated.

Even so, first-century Jews still anticipated salvation and the Kingdom of God as a material, political reality *on earth.* There can sometimes appear to be a tension between the evidently political hopes of salvation (expressed, for instance in Daniel, the *Psalms of Solomon* and in revolutionary circles) and the more transcendent, utopian ideas of a world to come and new creation (examples include the New Testament epistles and certain apocalyptic and rabbinic texts). This tension occurs, for instance, on the subject of the resurrection, which some understood as strictly physical, others as more spiritual, and which was discounted altogether by yet others (like the Sadducees[3]). On the whole, however, it is important to note that Jews understood salvation holistically and comprehensively. Precisely because it brings about *God's* Kingdom, the Messianic Age must be eminently transcendent and new in character. But whatever else this may mean, the Messianic salvation of real people also can certainly be nothing *less* than the real, tangible, embodied fulfilment of God's covenant promises to Israel.

Along the same lines, heaven and earth were seen as closely intertwined. The contest of good and evil on earth reflects a larger struggle of God and his angelic hosts against the spiritual forces and powers which oppose his purposes and which he or his Messianic agent must overcome as part of the saving design. What is more, every significant event that happens on earth has its prior counterpart in heaven. For this reason, the Messiah is already present in heaven before he appears on earth.

Although some of these new ideas reflect the influence of the surrounding Persian and later the Graeco-Roman cultures, they were all developed in the context of an intense and increasingly sophisticated study of Scripture. It is probably fair to say that when new ideas take hold in Judaism, they are never a complete innovation: revelation is always based on what has previously been revealed.[4] This same pattern of new ideas developing through an intimate dialogue with Scripture and traditions of interpretation also characterizes Jewish thinking about the Messiah, as well as New Testament reflection about the person of Jesus.

This complex picture of Jewish Messianic belief continued in post-biblical Judaism, with different religious groups and literary sources presenting a variety of views about the future salvation. The believing community of Israel experienced a great deal of religious and social alienation and oppression at the hands of one foreign power after another. Partly because of that, almost all Jewish writers were agreed on the hope of a restoration of Israel. But there were very different pictures of what that might mean and how it might come about. Indeed it is generally true that Judaism permits greater diversity in the area of belief than in that of conduct. Allowing for this complexity, then, I want now briefly to sketch some of the key features of the Messianic hopes in the first century AD.

First-Century Messianism

It is possible to describe in a kind of narrative outline the basic features of first-century Messianism. Not all features are represented in all the sources. Indeed there is probably no one document that contains every feature mentioned. Nevertheless, most or all forms of Jewish Messianic hope fit somewhere within the outline given below, and certain elements are central to all expectations. My aim is not to give a checklist but an impressionist portrait, which can then be discussed in relation to the Gospels' portrait of Jesus.[5]

The Birth Pangs

One or two items usually precede the coming of the Messiah. The most important of these is the period of general tribulation and suffering expected just before his arrival. It will be a time of evil, wars, famine, earthquakes, and godlessness among the people. This is often (even in the New Testament) referred to as the "birth pangs" of the Messiah, sometimes linked with cataclysmic events in nature – the darkening of sun and moon, the stars falling from heaven, and all manner of other omens.[6]

The Coming of Elijah

Malachi 4.5f. (3.23f. in Hebrew), preceded by the promise of the "prophet like Moses" (Deut. 18.15), raised the hope that Elijah, the greatest of the classical prophets, would be sent to help Israel just at the time of her greatest need. Although the New Testament treats the return of Elijah as a precursor of the Messiah, this is not always clear in other texts. At times it even appears that "the prophet" is an important eschatological figure in his own right, without necessarily being linked to the Messiah (compare also John 1.21, 25 with 6.14; 7.40).

The Coming of the Messiah

Sometimes the Messiah is pre-existent in heaven and is then revealed on earth; sometimes he is straightforwardly born as a descendant of David; quite often he is seen as already present in obscurity among Israel but suddenly appears in public (in the New Testament see especially John 1.31). Almost always he is a fully human figure, born of human parents although divinely anointed to be king. Nevertheless, in apocalyptic circles he can be assigned additional exalted features such as his presence before God in heaven prior to appearing on earth (*1 Enoch*, 4 Ezra, *Sibylline Oracles* 5, 11QMelch). Neither a virginal conception nor a birth in Bethlehem are normally anticipated, as we saw in Chapter One.

A multitude of different titles was used for the Messiah, reflecting different emphases in the various traditions: Son of David, Shoot or Branch of David, Son of God, the Righteous One, the Messiah [anointed] King, and very occasionally Son of Man.[7]

Occasionally an ideal High Priestly figure is envisioned, as we saw earlier (cf. Sir. 50; *Testament of Levi*). In some circumstances there are perceived to be two messiahs, one who will be the ideal High Priest and one who will be the ideal King, as in the case of Qumran's Davidic and Aaronic Messiah (e.g. 1 QS 9.11; CD 12.23; 4QPBless 3f.).

In one strand of ancient Jewish thought, the Messiah dies before the end of the old world order arrives.[8] The concept of a suffering Messiah, too, is a rare but not altogether unlikely idea. Although difficult to document explicitly before AD 70, it fits in with a long-standing Jewish and biblical tradition of redemptive suffering of the righteous (Isaiah 53, probably understood as Messianic in some circles; Job, the Lament Psalms; also Wisdom 2; 2 and 4 Maccabees). The Messiah's sufferings are attested in a variety of rabbinic texts, several of which appeal to these and other biblical passages which are also adduced by early Christian writers.[9] A later tradition contrasts the eschatological prince of peace descended from David with another Messiah, a warrior descended from Joseph (or Ephraim), who goes to battle on Israel's behalf.[10]

The Work of the Messiah

The political and spiritual powers of evil are oppressing the people of God and are gathered under the leadership of an evil prince ("Antichrist") in a final attempt to defeat God's purposes. The Messiah will conquer and destroy these godless forces. A new Jerusalem will be rebuilt (or will descend from heaven) and usually there is an expectation of a glorious new Temple. Israel in the diaspora will be gathered in from the four corners of the earth. A kingdom of utopian splendour and peace will be set up in the Holy Land, under the King Messiah. This will be the Kingdom of God, since God will be its supreme ruler. According to many expectations, its boundaries will extend to incorporate all the Gentile kingdoms as well, and they will bring tribute to God in Jerusalem and participate in the worship of God.

All those who have died (or, in some cases, all the *righteous* dead) will be resurrected and will participate in this kingdom of glory. Creation and the cosmos, too, will be renewed. There will be a final judgement, chaired by the Messiah as Judge and based on heavenly books in which people's lives are recorded. The righteous will participate in the eternal kingdom of God, while the wicked are subject either to destruction or eternal damnation.

Sometimes the earthly kingdom of the Messiah is seen as temporary, but in these cases it is expected to be superseded by an even greater renewal of the world which will then endure forever.

Was Jesus the Messiah?

Did Jesus fulfil these expectations? Was he justifiably received as the Messiah anticipated in the Old Testament and subsequent Jewish expectation?

First of all, of course, it is significant that the Jesus at least of the Synoptic Gospels never purely and simply stands up to claim, "I am the Messiah." He comes close on one or two occasions and we will look at these in a moment, but he never actually volunteers this information, or even refers to himself as "the Son of David". In Biblical scholarship, the dramatic narrative effect of a gradual disclosure of his identity in the Gospels has come to be called the "Messianic ooorot". However, the original reasons for Jesus' hesitancy on this subject may well have to do with his reluctance to endorse the strongly political, violent Messianism of a growing Jewish resistance movement, with whom Jesus radically disagreed about the manner in which the Kingdom of God would come about.

Nevertheless, despite Jesus' relative silence it is certainly possible to detect in the Gospels an overall scheme of Messianism which agrees with many of the familiar themes of contemporary Jewish hope. The apocalyptic theme of birth pangs preceding redemption, of cataclysmic events in politics and in creation, is reflected in Jesus' speech about the future (Mark 13.8 par.), although he does not relate it to his own present ministry. The issue of Elijah or "the prophet" also arises repeatedly (Mark 9.11–13 par.); indeed Jesus himself repeatedly appears in the guise of a prophet.[11] The Gospels present Jesus as a true descendant of David, and this does not appear to be disputed by Jewish opponents. The circumstances surrounding his divinely favoured birth are evidently important to Matthew and Luke as Messianic evidence, even though they do not figure in the rest of the New Testament and have few if any parallels in contemporary Jewish sources.

It is important, too, to take into account Jesus' deeds, especially his healing miracles, his demonstration in the Temple and his "triumphal" entry into Jerusalem (more on this below). Jesus normally rebuffs direct questions about his identity. But in Matthew and Luke, when John the Baptist (whom Jesus highly respected) sends word from prison to ask if he is the Messiah, Jesus gives a plausibly indirect answer, by referring to his miracles and message: "The blind receive their sight, the lame walk, the lepers are cleansed, the deaf hear, the dead are raised, and the poor have good news brought to them" (Matt. 11.5 par. Luke 7.22). In light of the prophecy of Isaiah 61, Jesus' healing and preaching have a self-authenticating Messianic significance, especially given the contemporary interpretations of the Isaianic prophecy.[12]

Jesus does not typically speak of his *pre-existence* in heaven. Occasionally, and in veiled terms, the Synoptic Jesus does use the language of being "sent" (e.g. Mark 12.6 par.) or having "come" (e.g. Mark 2.17 par.) for a particular purpose. But on the whole the sending theme and especially the idea of pre-existence are developed only later in the Fourth Gospel, as well as in the letters of Paul.[13]

A priestly role of Jesus, although it is profoundly developed in the letter to the Hebrews, does not appear in the Gospels. Indeed, in spite of Jesus' vehement criticism of the Jerusalem Temple, there is no indication that he understood his own role as priestly.

Jesus' kingly role, on the other hand, occurs in a wide range of contexts. Although his use of the term "Son of Man" is often simply a common Aramaic idiom of referring to oneself (or to humanity in general), Jesus does sometimes speak of a coming heavenly Son of Man, in the tradition of Daniel 7 and apocalyptic literature, who will come as a ruler and Judge. Matthew and other early Christians identified Jesus with this Son of Man – a disputed identification but one which, I would argue, is implicit in Jesus' own words. Examples include Mark 8.31, 38; 14.62.[14]

Even the pre-Easter Jesus speaks of his *kingdom,* and alludes to the authority implied in it. Luke 22.28–30 conveniently sums up a number of themes found scattered throughout the Synoptic Gospels:

> You are those who have stood by me in my trials;
> and I confer on you, just as my Father has con-

> ferred on me, a kingdom, so that you may eat and
> drink at my table in my kingdom, and you will sit
> on thrones judging the twelve tribes of Israel.

In his final triumphal entry into Jerusalem, Jesus deliberately procures a donkey to ride into the city from the Mount of Olives. This is an intentional appeal to the prophecy in Zechariah 9.9, where the king comes to Jerusalem riding on a donkey. Jesus appears to identify himself as the son of the king in the parable of the wicked tenants (Mark 12.1–11par.). Popular expectation of him was very high, and the Fourth Gospel reports of the occasion when people wanted to take him by force to make him king (John 6.15). Before the High Priest he is asked point blank whether he is the Messiah Son of God, and here at last Jesus answers clearly in the affirmative (Mark 14.62 par.). Moreover, his appearance before Pilate involves the related charge that he is king of the Jews, which in the end is posted as the official charge against him on a public notice on the cross (Mark 15.26 par.).

Having said that, however, there are several aspects of the work of Jesus which very clearly fall short of the Messianic expectation. It is true that Jesus picks up and positively affirms many of the key Messianic expectations discussed above: the final battle leading to the destruction of the godless empire (usually identified with Rome) and the restoration of the throne of David, the ingathering of the exiles, the renewal of the Temple, the general resurrection, the final judgement, and the Messianic kingdom. We must note that Jesus evidently *shared* and did not reject these aspects of the Jewish Messianic hope. Indeed he even declared them to be imminent, about to occur in the lifetime of his contemporaries (Matt. 16.28 par.; Mark 13.30; Matt. 10.23).

Nevertheless, by any straightforward estimation Jesus did not accomplish these things in his lifetime, and thus did not meet some of the most widely held expectations about a Messiah or about the Messianic Kingdom. He was arrested on the expedient charge of sedition, put on trial, humiliated and then shamefully executed. Despite occasional Jewish notions of a death of the Messiah preceding the ultimate Kingdom of God, in the public mind this kind of ignominious death would have meant the end of any Messianic claim. A righteous man he might be – after all, even the highly regarded Maccabean martyrs had suffered a violent death. But he could not be the Messiah.

Here, surely, lies one of the reasons why the Passover crowd in Jerusalem, after its enthusiastic welcome for Jesus, could so suddenly turn against him when he was arrested and put on trial. Judaea at this time was frequently buzzing with anticipation of various Messiah figures, and there had already been several candidates who all turned out to be failures. Everyone knew, too, that the hope for a Messiah was politically subversive, and the priestly aristocracy of Jerusalem with their private police gangs worked closely together with the Roman authorities to crack down at any hint of insurrection (see Chapter Three below). Although Jesus would have had a considerable measure of support and high expectations from many people, even the behaviour of the disciples shows that this support was highly volatile. In the present political situation it was too dangerous to back a loser. At the first sign of trouble, most people did the safe thing and turned against him.

Obviously this raises a closely related question to which we shall return in due course (see Chapter Four). Not: was he or was he not the Messiah according to Old Testament and contemporary Jewish expectation, but: did Jesus fail or succeed in relation to his *own* aims and expectations?

For now, I would like to conclude by suggesting why the early Church did come to the conviction that Jesus was the Messiah.

There are a number of reasons which arise from within

Jesus' own ministry and his self-understanding: they include especially his close relationship to God as Father and his interpretation of his own ministry. Scholars are increasingly coming to recognize the historical setting and importance of miracle stories in the ministry of Jesus.[15] It is now commonly accepted that other contemporaries, like Honi or Hanina ben Dosa,[16] had also performed miraculous actions. Unlike them, however, Jesus explicitly understood his healings and exorcisms as inaugurating the Kingdom of God and spelling the defeat of the reign of Satan:

> But if it is by the finger of God that I cast out the demons, then the kingdom of God has come to you. When a strong man, fully armed, guards his castle, his property is safe. But when one stronger than he attacks him and overpowers him, he takes away his armour in which he trusted and divides his plunder. (Luke 11.20–22)

We will have occasion to discuss these areas in detail later, because they relate to the question of Jesus' *own* aims and whether or not he achieved them.

Nevertheless, all these perspectives depend for their validity on the most important source from which all early Christian theology derived: the belief in Jesus' vindication through his resurrection. We must note that the disciples' reported reaction to the death of Jesus did not fundamentally differ from that of other people. If Jesus had ended in this way, he obviously could not have been the Messiah. Cleopas summarizes these feelings in Luke 24.21 (cf. Mark 8.31f. par.): "But we had hoped that he was the one to redeem Israel." This had been the disciples' hope, but Jesus' crucifixion meant that evidently they had been fooled and he could not be the promised redeemer.

However, after Easter Sunday the disciples' Messianic faith in Jesus was unexpectedly restored. Indeed Peter's sermon, quoted at the beginning of this chapter, affirms the resurrection

to be the certain guarantee "that God has made him both Lord
and Messiah, this Jesus whom you crucified" (Acts 2.36).

This is of course a statement of faith, to which we shall
have to return for a closer examination in Chapter Seven. For
the early Christians, however, this was the only conclusion they
could come to: given their knowledge of Jesus and his teaching,
and given their experience of the empty tomb and the
resurrection appearances, their only possible interpretation of
this was that God had raised Jesus from the dead and thereby
vindicated and endorsed him as the Messiah. One even finds the
claim that God's promises to Israel have come to fulfilment
specifically in the resurrection of Jesus (Acts 13.32f.,
attributed to the Apostle Paul).

The logic of this Christian reasoning is suggested in the
resurrection stories themselves. In Luke 24, the risen Jesus
leads the disciples through a tour of Old Testament prophecies
which speak about a suffering Messiah, and he appeals to his
own pre-Easter predictions of suffering and death. The
implication is that all of a sudden many things that he had said
and done before seemed to make sense. Indeed the abundance
of Old Testament motifs in the passion narratives indicates the
early authors' desire to establish that even Jesus' sufferings
show him to be the Messiah promised in the Scriptures.[17]

Moreover, Chapter Four will suggest that the powerful
theme of the suffering righteous in biblical and Jewish thought
had already formed an increasing part of Jesus' *own* reflection.
In the second part of his ministry, as the opposition of the
authorities and the likelihood of his own suffering became
increasingly obvious, he explicitly considered the significance of
his own likely suffering.

Does that settle whether Jesus was the Messiah? Clearly
the early church did regard the resurrection as the divine
vindication of Jesus. But the Messiah's task of defeating the
enemies of God, judging the earth and establishing God's
Kingdom still was not accomplished. It is significant that in

Luke's account in Acts the disciples immediately press the risen Jesus on that issue: "Lord, is this the time when you will restore the kingdom to Israel?" Significant, too, is Jesus' reply:

> It is not for you to know the times or periods that the Father has set by his own authority. But you will receive power when the Holy Spirit has come upon you; and you will be my witnesses in Jerusalem, in all Judaea and Samaria, and to the ends of the earth. (Acts 1.6–8)

Jesus does not rebuke the disciples, as we might expect, but instead he says that the completion of the Kingdom of God is still to come at a time which God alone has appointed. The Kingdom of God has begun to come in Jesus, and it is certain to be fulfilled in the future. And, by implication, it is continuing to come in the life of the Church and the proclamation of the gospel to the ends of the earth (cf. Acts 14.22).

Conclusion

Was Jesus the Messiah? If by that we mean that Jesus of Nazareth entirely fulfilled the promised hope of Israel, the answer can only be "maybe" in some respects and "no" in many others.

But according to the early Christians, that question is too narrow; in some ways it is the wrong question. For them, Jesus *was* the Messiah as the suffering Righteous One, he *is now* present by the Spirit of the Messiah, in the gospel of deliverance proclaimed to Jews and Gentiles, and he *will* come as Judge and King to bring God's new world to completion at his return. This threefold perspective emerges in a remarkably suggestive passage from another early sermon of Peter (Acts 3.17–20). Through the death of Jesus,

> (1) God fulfilled what he had foretold through all the prophets, that his Messiah would suffer [Jesus *was* the Messiah].

(2) Repent therefore, and turn to God so that your sins may be wiped out, so that times of refreshing may come from the presence of the Lord [Jesus *is* the Messiah, cf. 5.42; 9.22; 10.36; 17.3; 18.5, 28; also 3.16, 9.34 Jesus himself continues to heal],

(3) and that he may send the Messiah appointed for you, that is, Jesus [he *will be* the Messiah; cf. Rom. 11.26; 1 Thess. 1.10; Phil. 3.20].

Was Jesus the Messiah? The argument of this chapter has been to suggest that it is possible to answer with a qualified but unambiguous *yes*. This Christian answer takes into account not just Jesus' life and death, but also his resurrection, the affirmation of his presence in the preaching of the gospel, and his future return as Judge and exalted King. In this sense the early church affirmed that Jesus *was, is,* and *will be* the Messiah, the Saviour of the people of God.

Chapter Three

Why Did Jesus Predict the Temple's Destruction?

Having considered the question of Jesus' messiahship, we turn in these next two chapters to a consideration of his basic aims and purposes, beginning with the specific question of his attitude to the Temple. Whether they choose to concentrate their study of Jesus on his actions or, more conventionally, on his words, scholars generally agree that Jesus' perspective on the Temple and the priestly authorities is possibly the single most important issue in understanding his ministry in Jerusalem and the ultimate cause of his arrest.

Jesus' Temple Prophecy

One of the more puzzling questions in this regard arises from the claim that Jesus publicly predicted the Temple's destruction forty years before the actual event. It was apparently an issue which came back to haunt him during his trial (and his followers after his death: Acts 6.13f.). Did Jesus make such a prediction, or is this an apologetic attempt of the Gospel writers to justify Christianity's superiority to Judaism after the fall of Jerusalem in AD 70? If Jesus did predict this, what sense can we possibly make of it in its first-century setting?

The Temple

After the first Temple of Jerusalem had been destroyed by the Babylonians in 586 BC, a second, rather less spectacular Temple was built on this site after 520 BC. The next major architectural change relating to the Temple took place under Herod the Great, who ruled Palestine from 37 to 4 BC. He began in 20/19 BC to construct an entirely new gold-covered sanctuary to a height of 50 metres, as well as vast administrative buildings. He also extended the Temple platform and outer courts to quite enormous dimensions (c. 300m x 470m, more than enough for a dozen football fields[1]). Only in 62–64 AD was the work finally completed.[2]

This grandiose new structure briefly became one of the wonders of the ancient world. Ancient writers, including the Roman historian Tacitus (*Hist.* 5.8), marvelled at its great opulence, and the first-century Jewish historian Josephus describes its lavish construction and the use of gigantic blocks of hewn stone in building the platform (*Ant.* 15.391–402; *War* 5.184–226). Some ashlars of quite staggering size can still be seen in the wall today. The stones uncovered at the Southwest corner of the Temple mount weigh 50 tons, while another one, now accessible in the so-called "Western Wall Tunnel", has been measured at 12m x 3m x 4m, with an estimated weight of 400 tons.[3]

The Temple had a steady supply of fresh water through spacious cisterns, an aqueduct, and a sophisticated drainage system (parts of which have also come to light). Thousands of labourers were employed in the construction. Josephus claims that when it was completed, 18,000 men became at least temporarily unemployed (*Ant.* 20.222). An early passage in the Babylonian Talmud says, "He who has not seen Jerusalem in her splendour, has never seen a desirable city in his life. He who has not seen the [Second] Temple in its full construction has never seen a glorious building in his life."[4]

Nevertheless, although this most spectacular Temple must have seemed indestructible, it was also the most short-lived. In the year 70, the Tenth Legion of the Roman army under their general Titus destroyed it by fire as part of their crushing of the First Jewish Revolt.

Jesus' Prediction of Destruction

In the Gospel of Mark, we read the following episode at the beginning of Chapter 13: "As Jesus came out of the Temple, one of his disciples said to him, 'Look, Teacher, what large stones and what large buildings!' – Then Jesus asked him, 'Do you see these great buildings? Not one stone will be left here upon another; all will be thrown down.'"

Did Jesus really predict the destruction of the Temple? Or did the early church only attribute this saying to him after the year 70? And if he did predict it, what kind of background can we assume for such a statement? The chief purpose of this chapter will be to address this second question, the Why of the prediction.

In the 19th and early 20th centuries, scholars commonly assumed that the various predictions of the Temple's destruction were basically "prophecies after the event" (*vaticinia ex eventu*), history written in the form of prophecy. Many such *vaticinia* exist in the literature of the Hellenistic era, in writers as diverse as the Roman poet Virgil and the Maccabean editor of the Book of Daniel. The existence of similar genres in the New Testament should not, therefore, be excluded in principle.

For a while, the supposed presence of these predictions was taken as evidence that the Gospels were written after the year 70. Especially in German scholarship, for instance, this type of reasoning is still found among commentators on the predictions contained in the Gospel of Luke (Luke 19.43f., etc.). This is in spite of the generic, non-specific character even of Luke's version of the prediction.[5]

However, more recent critical scholarship even in Germany has tended to regard at least the basic core of this prediction as genuine and coming from Jesus himself. It has been recognized that such a prediction would be quite in keeping with Jesus' other criticisms of the Temple, as well as with his apparently strong apocalyptic views. In particular, contemporary writers on this subject see a close connection with the demonstration, or the so-called "cleansing", which according to all four Gospels Jesus staged in the Temple. Other arguments in favour of authenticity include the recurring accusation, both in the Gospels (Mark 14.58 par. Matthew 26.61; cf. John 2.19) and in Acts (6.13), that Jesus had *threatened* to destroy the Temple;[6] and the fact that while Jesus' prediction seems to envision a *razing* of the Temple ("no stone shall remain upon another"), the historical accounts (and all "real" *ex eventu* prophecies) of the event clearly indicate that the Temple superstructure was in fact *burned down*. (Such a feat was in any case rather easier to accomplish than a literal razing, since the water enclosures of Jerusalem limestone cause it to crack when burned.)

In the following discussion, then, I shall assume the authenticity of this basic core prediction, and concentrate instead on why it was given. This problem involves significant economic and political as well as sociological and theological considerations. My primary intention, however, is to advance one relatively modest argument: namely, that Jesus' prophecy must be seen against the background of *an existing Palestinian tradition of interpretation*, according to which the biblical prophecies of the Temple's destruction (and restoration) had not yet been fulfilled. It is this which serves as the key to understanding Jesus' relationship with the Temple.

Other Predictions of the Temple's Destruction

It may come as a surprise to some readers that the historical evidence points to a good number of *other* predictions of the Temple's destruction before the year 70. We will look at just three of these here, to see what light, if any, they may shed on our question. Several others could be adduced, although it is not always straightforward to establish a date before 70.

The Jewish historian Flavius Josephus tells of an eccentric peasant called Jesus the son of Ananias (Ben

Hananiah) who suddenly began uttering a strange oracle of judgement against Jerusalem and the Temple. Beginning at the feast of *Sukkot* (Tabernacles) in the year 62, and continuing for more than seven years, he went about the city madly announcing its destruction. His oracle remains difficult to make sense of:

> A voice from the East,
> A voice from the West,
> A voice from the four winds;
> A voice against Jerusalem and the Sanctuary,
> A voice against the bridegroom and the bride,
> A voice against all the people.[7]

We cannot say a great deal about this with confidence. Josephus describes this Ben Hananiah as a "rude peasant", and the subsequent account suggests a man whose mental health would certainly seem to border on the neurotic. Indeed Josephus tells us that he was arrested, flogged, and released on the grounds of insanity. Just before moving on, however, I would briefly like to point out one feature of this oracle which will be of significance later on. The reference to Jerusalem, the bridegroom and the bride seems to allude to an Old Testament passage of judgement from Jeremiah 7.34 (lit.): "And I will bring to an end the voice of joy and the voice of gladness, the voice of the bridegroom and the voice of the bride." What is more, this same judgement discourse in Jeremiah 7 also contains God's explicit prediction of the destruction of the *first* Sanctuary: "Therefore, I will do to the house that is called by my name, in which you trust, and to the place which I gave to you and to your fathers, just what I did to Shiloh" (v. 14).

More interesting, though admittedly not a great deal less enigmatic, are the next two examples. In AD 66–67 Josephus himself was the general of the Jewish rebel forces in Galilee. At his first defeat at the town of Jotapata, however, he became disillusioned with the rebel cause and staged a dramatic defection to the Romans. In his work *The Jewish War*, he describes how he had experienced a series of dreams and meditations about certain Scriptural prophecies – though unfortunately he does not tell us which ones. On this basis he became convinced that God was now on the side of the Romans, and he correctly predicted that the Roman general Vespasian would become emperor (*War* 3.401). This "prophecy" is independently attested by the Roman historians Suetonius (*Vesp.* 5.6) and Dio Cassius (*Hist.* 65.1, 4), and perhaps implicitly by Tacitus (*Hist.* 1.10; 2.1; 5.13). As the narrative unfolds, Josephus goes on to reiterate on several occasions that the destruction of the Temple was foretold in various Scriptural oracles. Once again, it is unfortunate that (perhaps because of his Gentile readership) he remains unspecific about the identity of these biblical passages; he speaks only in vague terms about "ambiguous divine utterances" (*War* 3.352).[8]

Having said this, however, there are in fact one or two places where Josephus does hint at his scriptural sources for the prophecy of Jerusalem's destruction. In Book 10 of the *Antiquities*, he says that the biblical prophet Jeremiah, in addition to predicting the destruction of Jerusalem by the Babylonians, also "left behind writings concerning the recent capture of our city" (*Ant.* 10.79). We have here, then, another indication of the belief that the prophecies of Jeremiah applied to Josephus's own day. Secondly, and of much greater importance for Josephus, there are the prophecies of the book of Daniel. He describes these at great length, and takes especially the prediction of the Roman conquest of Jerusalem as proof of divine providence (*Ant.* 10.276).[9]

Quite intriguingly, early rabbinic literature contains a similar report about Rabban Yohanan ben Zakkai, traditionally regarded as the founder of rabbinic Judaism. Unlike the early Jewish Christians, who according to Patristic tradition fled Jerusalem for Transjordan when the revolt began,[10] Yohanan stayed in Jerusalem. We are told that he attempted unsuccessfully to persuade his countrymen to accept Vespasian's generous terms of surrender. By this time the rebels allowed no one to leave the city alive, so he had his disciples carry him out of the city in a coffin. The story has it that he went straight to Vespasian and predicted his succession to the throne. When asked for an explanation, he cited Isaiah 10.34 (lit.), "Lebanon shall fall by a mighty one."[11]

This curious identification of Lebanon and the Temple is worth looking at for a moment. "Lebanon" is a common midrashic figure for the Temple[12]: according to one rabbinic interpretation, it is based on a play on words involving the root *lbn* – the Temple "makes white" the sins of Israel.[13] The use of this metaphor is well-attested in the Bible and Jewish literature of the Second Temple period. The cedars of Lebanon adorned the Temple, and so in some sense "Lebanon" could stand for the glory of the Temple (e.g. Isaiah 60.13). This identification is made explicit in Ezekiel's parable of two eagles and a vine (Ezekiel 17.3, 12), and it may also be directly in view in Jeremiah 22.23, a declaration of woe upon King Jehoiakim of Judah as the "inhabitant of Lebanon, nested among the cedars". Psalm 92.12f. provides a more positive parallel: "The righteous flourish like the palm tree, and grow like a cedar *in Lebanon*. They are planted *in the house of the Lord*; they flourish in the courts of our God." In the same sense, Sirach 50.12 compares Simon ben Onias the High Priest to "a young cedar on Lebanon".

Another early example worth noting is Habakkuk 2.17: "The violence done to Lebanon will overwhelm you." In the Targum, the Aramaic paraphrase for use in synagogues, the passage is explicitly taken to refer to the Temple. Qumran's Habakkuk commentary, on the other hand, following the typical Essene and early Christian identification of the Temple with the community, foresees here the destruction of the wicked priest of Jerusalem because of the violence he did to "*Lebanon*, that is the Council of the Community".[14]

(In a curious reference in the first-century work *Lives of the Prophets* 12.11, we are told that Habakkuk predicted the destruction of the Temple "by a Western Nation". Since there are no other, more specific clues here of a post-70 date (and the context seems to betray no knowledge of an actual destruction), we may be dealing with another genuine prediction. It is also worth noting, in addition to the reference to "violence done to Lebanon" in Hab. 2.17, that the "Chaldeans" in 1.14–17 could be seen as coming from the sea, and thus from the West.[15])

Given the early currency of the "Lebanon" metaphor for the Temple in Jewish interpretation, it is not unreasonable to grant that the Old Testament judgement oracles applying to Lebanon might therefore have been transferred to the Temple as well. In Greek-speaking circles, moreover, the connection with the Temple will have been even more obvious in view of the use of *libanos* to mean "incense".

Let me return to Rabban Yohanan ben Zakkai and his interpretation of the prophecy that "Lebanon shall fall by a mighty one" (Isa. 10.34). As the context shows, the Rabban evidently took this passage to mean that the imminent destruction of the Temple could be accomplished not by a common soldier but only by a king, a "mighty one". The Temple would be destroyed; Vespasian was evidently the general who would bring this about; *ergo*, Vespasian must either be or become emperor. In another early rabbinic passage which attributes to Yohanan the prediction of the Temple's destruction, he quotes Zechariah 11.1: "Open your doors, O Lebanon, so that fire may devour your cedars!"[16] Once more, "Lebanon" stands for the Temple according to this interpretation. It may speak for the authenticity of both passages that they go against the trend of later rabbinic interpreters (like the Targum and Rashi), who did *not* apply the prophecies from Isaiah 10 and Zechariah 11 to the Temple.

There are several other predictions of the destruction of the Temple, or at least of the need for the present one to be replaced by a new one. Some of these references are

notoriously difficult to date, but others are generally assigned
with some confidence to the period before AD 70. Several seem
to involve exegetical connections with the Old Testament
prophets.[17]

Reasons for the Vitality of this Interpretative Tradition

We have seen evidence that there were several predictions of a
destruction of the Temple before the year 70, and that they all
seem to relate implicitly or explicitly to previous prophetic
Scriptures as their authority. Why would such an interpretative
tradition flourish in the first century? As I indicated earlier, we
cannot unfortunately deal here with these questions in depth; but
it is worth offering a few brief remarks.

Theological Reasons

Theologically, the first and most important reason was that the
restoration promises of the biblical prophets had not been
fulfilled. Prophecies about the Exile and subsequent return to
the land under ideal conditions and with an ideal Temple were
obviously unfulfilled. Isaiah 40–66 and Ezekiel described
situations which were a far cry from what the present Temple
represented. This awareness is found already in the pre-
Maccabean book of Tobit (13.16–18, 14.5)[18] as well as in the
book of Daniel (9.17, 26f.). In particular, the corruption and
decline of the Hasmonean dynasty and subsequent occupation
by the Romans had dashed the hopes of a fully liberated Jewish
kingdom. What is more, several groups had doubts about the
Maccabees' complete cleansing of the Temple. This is clearly
true for the Essenes and perhaps the author of the Psalms of
Solomon (8; 17), as well as some of those who frequented the
alternative Temple at Leontopolis in Lower Egypt.[19] If, despite
its glory, the Temple of Herod was not the promised Temple,
and if the purity of the Zadokite high priestly line was at all a

matter of concern, then it was only logical to conclude that the present corrupt system would need, sooner or later, to give way to a new one.

Social and Political Reasons

In addition to this, the corruption of the priestly aristocracy in Jerusalem invited comparison with the earlier prophetic oracles of judgement and destruction. Of key significance must have been the offensive fact that of the 28 high priests between 37 BC and AD 70, all but two came from four power-hungry, illegitimate non-Zadokite families.[20] But quite apart from this, recent historical study is making increasingly clear that the operation of the Temple, which most devout Jews regarded as the physical centre of their religious practice, was in the hands of a vast economic and religious power network. The priestly hierarchy which controlled the operation of the Temple also appears at least indirectly to have overseen a virtual monopoly on the sale of sacrificial animals and most other commercial transactions relating to the regular worship. In fact, this is bound to be true particularly for the customary commerce in wood, bird and drink offerings which was conducted in the Temple precinct itself.[21] According to one intriguing line of argument, the offensiveness of this trade to Jesus could also be linked with the possibility that traders had only very recently moved into the Court of the Gentiles at the invitation of Caiaphas, having previously operated their shops mainly on the Mount of Olives.[22] The Mishnah gives evidence of hugely inflated price fixing for sacrificial doves, which were the offering of the poor; and it suggests that this so much concerned the mid-first century Pharisee Rabban Simeon ben Gamaliel that he successfully set out to lower the price by publicly teaching that under certain conditions the customary sacrifice was not required.[23]

The legitimate and necessary operation of the Temple was supported by a maze of intrigue, nepotism, and corruption, which is amply reflected in Josephus and early rabbinic sources. In particular, the hierarchy operated agents and hit squads known as "men of violence" and the "big men of the priest-hood".[24] Included among these was the Levitical Temple guard, whose armed forays on behalf of the Sanhedrin are also encountered on the pages of the New Testament.[25] Josephus records that thugs employed by the High Priests used to rob the tithes intended for the (lesser) priests.[26] And a well-known early passage in the Babylonian Talmud complains about the four illicit high priestly families who so ruthlessly exercised power over the Temple and its treasury:

> Woe to me because of the house of Baithos [Boethus]; woe to me for their lances! Woe to me because of the house of Hanin [=NT Annas, Jos. Ananus], woe to me for their calumnies! Woe to me because of the house of Qatros, woe to me because of their reed pens! Woe to me because of the house of Ishmael ben Phiabi, woe to me because of their fist! For they are high priests and their sons are treasurers and their sons-in-law are Temple overseers, and their servants smite the people with sticks.[27]

It is of some interest in this regard that a stone weight inscribed with the name "Bar Qatros" was found in the so-called "Burnt House" in the Jewish quarter of Jerusalem, and an ostracon with a very similar name has come to light at Masada.[28] What is more, it appears that the Qatros family may have been the same as that of Joseph Caiaphas, the High Priest mentioned in Josephus and the New Testament. This man, in office from AD 18 to 36 (when he was deposed by the Romans, along with Pontius Pilate), was moreover related by marriage to the powerful "house of Hanin". Jewish sources, along with gospel texts like John 11.50 and the passion narratives, suggest that during those two decades Annas and Caiaphas together enjoyed unrivalled power as a result of successful collaboration with the occupation forces of Rome.[29]   (It is of more than incidental interest in this regard that the rock-cut family tomb of Joseph Caiaphas may have been discovered in Jerusalem in 1990.[30])

Josephus and the rabbinic writings also concur in offering some most remarkable descriptions of the utter luxury and extravagance of the priestly aristocracy in Jerusalem before the First Revolt against Rome (AD 66–70).[31]   Archaeological corroboration of this has now come to light in the excavations of some fabulously appointed aristocratic residences of Herodian Jerusalem which were opened to the public in 1987 (Wohl Archaeological Museum).

This evidence does not perhaps make for an incontestable argument.   But my case here is at any rate cumulative rather than strictly deductive, and more material could undoubtedly be adduced.[32]   In any case, if the historical data were to confirm even just sporadic cases of conspicuous corruption in the Temple hierarchy, it is not hard to see how this might have caused a good deal of social and religious tension.   Poorer Jews from the countryside (including Galilee) would find themselves powerless in the face of the inflated prices charged in Jerusalem, and shocked at the Sadducean lifestyle, culture, and religion which they encountered in the city.   Several groups, including the Qumran sectarians, could not resist the comparison and re-application of the earlier prophetic judgement oracles to the present Temple.

Reasons for Jesus' Prediction

It is against this background that we can begin to understand Jesus' prediction of the destruction of the Temple.   The context of John 2.19 sets this prediction in close relation to Jesus' so-called "cleansing" of the Temple, in which he staged a demonstration of overturning the money-changers' tables and driving out the merchants of sacrificial animals.

It is of course true that the presence of money-changers

served to provide worshippers with the needed Tyrian currency for the payment of the Half-Shekel Tax from which public daily whole offerings for atonement were financed (Exod. 30.16); the Mishnah suggests they used to set up their tables in the Temple on the 25th day of Adar, the month before Passover.[33] Sellers of sacrificial animals, too, were clearly required near the Temple for the legitimate operation of the sacrifices.

Some scholars have gone on to conclude from the legitimate function of money-changers and merchants that Jesus' action therefore must have been entirely incomprehensible to any contemporary Jews.[34] However, it really is not inordinately difficult to see how Jesus' action might have appeared in the eyes of pilgrim bystanders. First, his apparently regular presence and participation in festivals at the Temple suggests his *approval* of Temple worship in principle (see note 50 below); indeed according to all four gospels Jesus continues to teach in the Temple after the "cleansing".

Secondly, however, Jesus *was* apparently opposed to the collection of the Temple tax: he saw it as inappropriate to Israel's status as children of the King (Matt. 17.24–27).[35] (At the same time, the story of the widow's mite in Mark 12.41–44 shows that his opposition did not extend to *voluntary* giving.[36]) In any case, that Jesus' concern was fundamentally for the holiness and purity of the Temple may also be indicated by Mark's note in 11.16: Jesus stopped people from carrying things through the Temple, presumably because they were using it as a shortcut. To treat the Holy Place in this fashion is an offence which the Mishnah rates along with spitting in the Temple or entering it with unwashed feet.[37]

If our earlier description of the corruption of the priestly hierarchy is even partly correct, then it is easy to see how Jesus' demonstration in the Temple could have been a reaction against the perceived economic and spiritual injustice of the unscrupulous operators of the Temple system. The commercial transactions in the Temple court were not as such the object of his anger,[38] since these were of course necessary if pilgrims were to bring their sacrifices. In the context of a whole nexus of racketeering and exploitation, however, it makes sense for Jesus to complain that the authorities have turned a house of prayer for all the nations into a cave of robbers. There is here an implied judgement, perhaps not unlike that expressed by the Qumran sectarians, which pertains not to the sacrificial system *as such* but to the injustice and abuse of power which have polluted the Temple and all who actively participate in its corrupt dealings.[39]

In this context it is particularly significant to consider Jesus' citation of the two prophetic passages in Mark 11.17, a saying which, despite repeated assertions to the contrary,[40] is arguably authentic[41]: "Is it not written, 'My house shall be called a house of prayer for all the nations' (Isa. 56.7)? But you have made it a 'den of robbers' (Jer. 7.11)." The passage from Isaiah speaks of the universal access to Temple worship for all the nations. Jesus' point here may be the reference to the eschatological Temple to which all the Gentiles will come to pray. It may be significant in this regard that the merchants' business was conducted in the large outer court, which was the only part of the Temple to which Gentiles had access. The passage from Jeremiah 7 discusses the hypocrisy of the people who sin by callous oppression and then pretend to serve God in the Temple. God responds by asking, "Has this house, which is called by my name, become a den of robbers in your sight?" (Jer. 7.11).

Jesus' citation of this verse is highly significant for several reasons. First, the Jerusalem Temple is also called a seat of robbers in several Qumran texts, an indication that Jesus' thinking could well be *intelligible* to his contemporaries.[42] (This may be further corroborated by the fact that the prophecy of Jesus ben Hananiah also alludes to the same biblical chapter.[43]) Jeremiah 7, moreover, goes on in the immediate context to announce that God will destroy the Temple at

Jerusalem as he destroyed the sanctuary at Shiloh. Jewish bystanders, therefore, would probably have realized the connection and significance of Jesus' Scripture quotation on the one hand and of his symbolic demonstration on the other. Mark 11.18 (cf. Luke 19.48) may in fact offer a hint of a sympathetic reaction by at least some people: the authorities could not arrest Jesus because "the whole crowd was spellbound by his teaching."[44]

In his belief that the Temple would be destroyed, Jesus consciously appealed to the biblical prophets and their condemnation of moral injustice in the cult of Yahweh. Because of his expectation of the imminent eschatological kingdom of God, Jesus belongs to a tradition of interpretation which saw the present corruption of the priestly aristocracy as doomed to destruction. This present system surely could not be the Temple of the new Jerusalem that was promised in the prophets. But if indeed this was *not* the Temple of the restoration, then the prophetic judgement oracles must still apply to it.[45]

There is no doubt that this threat to the Temple made Jesus, perhaps not unlike Jeremiah six centuries before him,[46] religiously offensive and a political liability at least to the priestly hierarchy and to the many ordinary citizens of Jerusalem whose social and material *status quo* depended on the Temple trade.[47] As a result, his popular support at least in the capital was highly volatile and, in the event, easily swayed (Mark 15.11, etc.), no doubt partly on pragmatic grounds of expediency in a politically explosive climate (John 11.50[48]). Jesus was arrested and hurried through an informal trial on a trumped-up charge of sedition. In effect, he was condemned on a mixture of religious and political grounds, chiefly (i) for having threatened to destroy the Temple, and (ii) for being an insurrectionist, "King of the Jews" (the formal charge for Roman legal purposes: John 19.19f. par.[49]).

Conclusion

In this brief discussion we have not been able to address the arguments exhaustively. Two conclusions, however, can be affirmed.

1. We have discovered an established interpretative tradition, supported in a wide range of first-century Palestinian sources, which appeals to prophetic judgement and restoration texts in holding that the present Temple must be destroyed. In addition to oracles involving the "Lebanon–Temple" cipher, Jeremiah 7 and Daniel 9 figured most prominently among these texts. The existence of this tradition further corroborates our working assumption that we are not dealing with a prophecy "after the fact".

2. In Jesus' ministry, the prediction of the destruction of the Temple is closely connected with his demonstration in the Temple. That demonstration symbolically expresses his objection to the corrupt racketeering practised by the Temple authorities, and it is linked at the same time both with prophetic texts expressing God's eschatological judgement on this Temple, and with a saying which points to a fervent hope of restoration.

What significance does Jesus' attitude to the Temple have for Christian faith? As far as we can tell, Jesus himself did *not* describe his own death as the sacrifice to end all sacrifices, even though Christian interpretation, beginning with Hebrews 8–9 and strengthened by the events of AD 70, went on to view it in this fashion. Nor, apparently, did Jesus regard the Temple as obsolete and effectively replaced by his ministry, even though John 2.19–22 may interpret a version of his Temple prophecy in these terms. Had Jesus spoken so explicitly on the subject, it is inconceivable that the New Testament would have gone on to depict not only Jesus himself but even the Apostles, from Peter and James to Paul, as continuing to participate in Temple worship and sacrifices.[50]

What we *can* say is (i) that Jesus unmistakably criticized the existing operation of the Temple as a corrupt system, bound for destruction in connection with the arrival of the Kingdom of God which he heralded and inaugurated in his ministry and person. Given the importance of this theme in his life and destiny, moreover, it is clear that this criticism of corrupt power and privilege was not merely cosmetic but fundamental to his concern. Power corrupts, and absolute power corrupts absolutely – in religion no less than in politics. The historical message of Jesus does not offer comfortable reassurance to those who personally benefit from the *status quo*.

But furthermore, we can assert (ii) that Jesus probably *did* use sacrificial symbolism to interpret his impending death. At least the solidly attested tradition of the last supper (Mark 14.24/Matt. 26.28/Luke 22.20; cf. possibly Mark 10.45par.[51]) attests the fact that Jesus increasingly regarded his impending death as of far-reaching consequences: his blood shed on behalf of the covenant would be profoundly instrumental to God's purpose of redemption. Returning to this issue in the next chapter, we will see that the idea of righteous martyrdom as sacrificial and redemptive for the nation was not without good Jewish precedent. Meanwhile, however, we can begin to get a glimpse of how, for those who came to believe in him, a sacrificial interpretation of his death, if justified, could offer a powerful assurance for the ultimate meaning of their own experience and destiny. At the same time, it is not hard to see how the combination of themes (i) and (ii) might reasonably have led the Fourth Evangelist or the writer to the Hebrews to the conclusions they reached – especially after Jesus' prediction came to be fulfilled in the events of AD 70.

But we are getting ahead of ourselves. Jesus' attitude to the Temple and to his own death can really only be meaningfully understood if we can give a positive answer to this other question: did he succeed or fail in what he was trying to achieve? That is the subject of Chapter Four.

Chapter Four

Did Jesus Fail?

The title of this chapter is not frivolous, as if to introduce some newfangled theory dreamed up at an academic sherry party. Instead, I am concerned to ask a genuine historical and ⟵ theological question about Jesus of Nazareth, namely: <u>what were his aims and expectations, and did he succeed in achieving them?</u> Although the nature of our evidence is such that we can never hope to reconstruct this fully, it is clearly a legitimate question to ask. What is more, quite a lot depends on it for our assessment of Jesus and the faith of the early church.

Jesus died a criminal's death, like so many unsuccessful Jewish rebels against Rome.[1] According to the earliest account his dying words were, "My God, my God, why have you forsaken me?" (Mark 15.34 par.). Pagan and Jewish observers for the next two or more centuries accused the Christians of venerating a wretched criminal, obviously a man whose botched career ended in tragedy.[2] Many writers to this day conclude that Jesus of Nazareth ended in failure.[3]

Did Jesus fail? In Chapter One we encountered Flavius Josephus's short note about Jesus (see p. 12, in which he seems to take a relatively ambivalent position, quite possibly typical of the attitude which many first-century Jews will have held about Jesus. Jesus for them was probably a good man, who seemed to have much to offer. But in the end, like so many, he was a victim of his own illusions, who left behind a strange and motley crew of loyal followers as others had done before him – John the Baptist, Qumran's Teacher of Righteousness, the false prophet from Egypt, and so on. (In this regard the perspective of a moderate like St. Paul's teacher Gamaliel the Elder also seems quite credible as reported in Acts 5.34–39: time will tell whether the Jesus movement is just another passing religious craze.)

On the other hand, for the early *Christians* Jesus clearly was the promised Messiah; we examined the reasons for this belief in Chapter Two. The earliest datable *Christian* testimony to Jesus which survives in writing is Paul's first letter to the Thessalonians, probably written in AD 50, which affirms, "We believe that Jesus died and rose again" (4.14; cf. also 2.15). Paul's other letters contain additional information about Jesus (e.g. 1 Cor. 11.23–26; 15.3–5, dated c. AD 55); and of course the four Gospels, although probably edited later, contain a great many early Palestinian traditions. The earliest Christian historical narrative about Jesus probably sounded something like this account of Peter's speech at the house of Cornelius:

> God anointed Jesus of Nazareth with the Holy Spirit and with power; ... he went about doing good and healing all who were oppressed by the devil, for God was with him. We are witnesses to all that he did both in Judaea and in Jerusalem. They put him to death by hanging him on a tree; but God raised him on the third day and allowed him to appear, not to all the people but to us who were chosen by God as witnesses, and who ate and drank with him after he rose from the dead. He commanded us to preach to the people and to testify that he is the one ordained by God as judge of the living and the dead. All the prophets testify about him that everyone who believes in him receives forgiveness of sins through his name. [Acts 10.38–43.]

Roughly speaking, this is what the earliest outline of the preaching of the "gospel", the Christian message, must have looked like. The emphasis of the story is on the death of Jesus and on what happens afterwards. That perspective takes for granted that Jesus was the Messiah, but it does not accentuate what he *himself* thought he was doing, *before his death*. All we are told is that "he went about doing good and healing all who were oppressed by the devil".

In order to dig a little deeper into Jesus' own purposes and self-understanding, we will examine the gospel accounts in four steps. First, there are Jesus' relevant statements in the early part of his Galilean ministry, up to the turning point in Caesarea Philippi. Following this, we will look at developments in the second half of his ministry, followed by the question of why Jesus had to die and how his death related to his aims. Finally, I hope to suggest whether Jesus failed or succeeded in meeting those aims.

The Aims of Jesus: The Galilean Ministry

The Call Vision and its Significance

Jesus appears on the scene of first-century Palestine within the context of John the Baptist's ministry, which is described both in the New Testament and in Josephus. John was a popular charismatic wilderness preacher who urged people to prepare for the coming Kingdom of God by being baptized as a seal of their repentance and of God's forgiveness of their sins. Jesus was caught up in the popular renewal movement which John's ministry initiated, and his baptism by John in the River Jordan appears to have been a profound and life-changing spiritual experience. In this connection we hear of his powerful call vision, in which he saw the Holy Spirit descending on him from heaven like a hovering dove.[4] At the same time he heard a voice which in the language of Psalm 2 and Isaiah 42 addressed him as "my Son, the Beloved; with you I am well pleased" (Mark 1.11 par.).

Within a first-century Galilean context, this kind of language would have considerable significance. "Son of God" and "Beloved" were ways of referring to the Messiah (cf. Chapter 1); and in the Old Testament, talk of the Holy Spirit "coming upon" people usually means that they are being divinely appointed (and hence "anointed") for a particular task.

In this fashion the 70 elders are designated to help Moses (Num. 11.16–25), Balaam is to prophesy (Num. 24.2), various Judges are to rule, and Saul is to be king (being changed "into a different person", 1 Sam. 10.6). Of particular significance would have been Isaiah's end-time prophecies about the Davidic Prince of Peace on whom the Spirit of God would rest (Isa. 11.2), and about God's Chosen Servant in whom he delights (42.1–4; cf. the heavenly voice, Mark 1.11) and on whom he has put his Spirit.

The First Crisis: Temptation in the Wilderness

Immediately after this, the Gospels describe Jesus undergoing a profound personal crisis in the wilderness. Others before him, like John the Baptist (Mark 1.4) and Bannus (Josephus, *Life* 11), had withdrawn to the desert for individual meditation and reflection. In Jesus' case, this reflection apparently centred on the meaning of his baptismal vision, especially his being called God's "Son". Matthew and Luke present the Tempter as concentrating his challenge on the question of his divine appointment: "If you are the Son of God..." (Matt. 4.3, 6; Luke 4.3, 9).

This crisis having been weathered, Jesus' specific identity seems less explicitly in the foreground in the following chapters. He begins to gather a group of both male and female followers from a variety of social and cultural backgrounds, the core group of which eventually numbers twelve men – a significant symbol of the twelve Old Testament patriarchs (sons of Jacob) and thus of a reconstituted twelve tribes of Israel.[5]

Early Ministry and Message of the Kingdom of God

Unlike John the Baptist, Jesus heals and teaches mostly in *public*, in the towns and villages of Galilee.[6] Like John, however, he calls people to repentance in view of the impending Kingdom of God (note Matt. 3.2; 4.17 par.), although apparently with a reduced emphasis on baptism (contrast the Synoptic Gospels with John 4.1f.) and a markedly less ascetic lifestyle (Matt. 11.18 par.). And like his predecessor he calls disciples, trains and commissions them, initially just to replicate his ministry and message. In the first commission Jesus sends the disciples out primarily to cast out demons, to heal, and to announce the Kingdom; they do not preach *Jesus* (Mark 6.7–13 par.).

The favourite and most important subject of Jesus' teaching is clearly the Kingdom of God. Like many Jews of his day, he saw this as the promised era of God's universal rule and the restoration of the chosen people to wholeness and relationship with God, an era where his will comes to be done on earth just as in heaven. Jesus' teaching about this Kingdom is simple and memorable, and like the rabbis he frequently tells parables, popular stories used to illustrate and drive home a point about the nature of God's purposes. But he also makes use of powerful, direct moral instructions whose forcefulness strikes the audience as being "not like the scribes" with their more academic, deliberative style (Matt. 7.29).

Kingdom Praxis and Initial Controversy

This first part of the gospel narrative describes the time in which Jesus "went about doing good", as Peter's summary has it in Acts 10. In some ways Jesus would have looked much like any of several other first-century Galilean charismatic figures who healed and taught and were known for their close personal relationship with God.[7] Nevertheless, even now there is a peculiar urgency and restlessness about Jesus: in his conviction that the Kingdom "has come near" (Mark 1.15), he seems increasingly to understand his own ministry as instrumental to that Kingdom, as symbolizing it and even inaugurating it. He begins to contrast the newness of his message with the "old" of conventional scribal theology, for instance in parables about new wine and old wineskins (Mark 2.22 par.). In practically applying this conviction, his ministry began to overstep the bounds of propriety and of conventional religion, more controversially and more blatantly than did those of other charismatic leaders of his day.

Not only did Jesus come to see his message and ministry as instrumental for the coming Kingdom, but he began to act in the light of it, regarding the needs and demands of the Kingdom as paramount above all other concerns already in the here and now. He claimed authority as a human being to declare a paralytic's sins forgiven (Mark 2.1–12 par.; cf. Matt. 9.8). In demonstrating God's Kingdom power to drive out evil spirits, he seemed to be employing magical practices of exorcism which the theologians regarded as suspect (Mark 3.22 par.). He healed in public and in synagogues even on the Sabbath, declared life-saving and restoration to wholeness as more important and more in keeping with the purpose of the Sabbath than the customary interpretation of the Sabbath law, claiming even that a human being could be "lord of the Sabbath" (Mark 2.27f). He flouted the established oral tradition of conventional Pharisaic religion where it seemed to constrain the requirements of his Kingdom ministry, breaching the bounds of religious propriety by allowing his disciples to snack in the grain fields on a Sabbath (Mark 2.23 par.), taking a liberal view of Pharisaic food laws (Mark 7.1–23 par.[8]) or telling a potential disciple to leave his father's burial to others and give priority to following him (Matt. 8.22 par.). Similarly, he gave prior loyalty to his disciples over that to his own family (Mark 3.31–35 par.). An unusual feature in first-century Judaism was the relative prominence of women among his followers,[9] and Jesus seems to have baffled even his own disciples by his high regard for children (Mark 10.13–16 par.).[10]

Perhaps most controversial of all, however, Jesus seemed to some people to be blurring the line between piety and immorality in that he freely associated with tax collectors, prostitutes, and others of highly dubious reputations, accepting them into table fellowship without *first* requiring them to repent and mend their ways. Many a Pharisee would have extended this kind of treatment to repentant sinners who had mended their ways, but Jesus made himself odious by extending his fellowship and God's unconditional grace to people as they were.[11] Repentance, which others would have made a precondition, was often left to follow on in due course as the sign that salvation had indeed come.

At the same time, one should resist the cliché that Jesus kept company only with the poor, the outcast and marginalized. His contacts and acquaintances include people like a synagogue president, various rich businessmen and well-to-do ladies, senior aristocrats in Jerusalem, even a Roman centurion. He did want to reach "sinners", "the lost", and the "sick" – but they (*as well as* the "righteous" and "healthy") were to be found in all walks of life.

Theological Disputes and Growing Opposition

At the same time as his following grew, Jesus clearly began to attract the ire of the religious establishment. One should not exaggerate this for the Galilean situation, where synagogal authorities and priestly aristocrats were not nearly as powerful as in Judaea and Jerusalem. But the notion of investigators coming down to Galilee from Jerusalem (Mark 3.22), or of powerful interests identifying Jesus as a political risk to be addressed (Pharisees and Herodians, Mark 3.6; cf. Luke 13.31), is not perhaps as far-fetched as has sometimes been assumed.[12]

In disputes and discussions with the theologians and religious leaders, Jesus repeatedly disagreed over points of Scriptural interpretation and religious practice. This was not in itself a major problem. In fact, several of the issues were still unresolved at the time, so that Jesus' opinion would have had the support of other factions within Judaism.[13] On more than one occasion later rabbinic opinion ended up adopting the view represented by Jesus: examples include the principle of life-saving on the Sabbath[14] or the cancelling of vows in view of the duty to provide for one's parents.[15] Nevertheless, Jesus' persistent clashes with religious leaders over such matters would not have helped their impression of him.

In any case, along with his public Kingdom ministry there are growing signs of Jesus' awareness of opposition: disputes in synagogues; his avoidance of cities; private teaching to his disciples which recognized that, as with the prophets, the majority of Israel was hardened against his message (Mark 4.10–12 par.); and the unbelief of his family and home town (3.21, 31–35; 6.1–3).

At the same time, the theme of growing opposition goes hand in hand with *the increasingly pressing question of Jesus' role and identity.* The issue is raised by the lunatic at the synagogue of Capernaum, by the crowds amazed at his healing and teaching, and by Jesus' various claims to a special Kingdom status and authority (forgiveness of sins, lord of the Sabbath, the bridegroom at the feast). Even more acutely, the question was raised by a number of unusual experiences of which apparently only the disciples were aware, like the stilling of the storm (Mark 4.35–41 par.), the feeding of the five thousand (Mark 6.34–44 par.; cf. 8.1–9 par.), and Jesus walking on the water (Mark 6.47–51).[16] Whatever original incidents may underlie these stories, they certainly serve to illustrate the pressing need for an answer to the disciples' terrified question, "Who is this, that even the wind and the sea obey him?" (Mark 4.41 par.).

It is by no means clear that Jesus' own message and ministry at this stage provided an answer or even an obvious direction in this regard. There was obviously a great deal of puzzlement on the part of both disciples and outsiders alike, and his own attempts to restrain publicity, at least in Galilee, suggest that perhaps he himself may not have wanted to let the issue come to a head (note Mark 1.44, 3.12, 5.43; and contrast 5.19 in the Gentile territory of Decapolis).

The Execution of John the Baptist

At this stage in his Galilean ministry, one event must have done more than any other to force Jesus to come to terms with the likely outcome of his career and therefore with the true nature of his calling. So far, Jesus' ministry appears to have operated to a certain extent in the shadow of John the Baptist, from whose work and teaching he had derived much benefit (compare Matt. 3.2 with 4.17). Herod Antipas was Rome's appointed puppet ruler (tetrarch) in Galilee and Perea beyond the Jordan during the years 4 BC – AD 39. Because of his morbid fear of public unrest, and John the Baptist's public disapproval of his questionable marriage to his half-brother's wife Herodias, Antipas had John arrested as a political liability and imprisoned at his desert stronghold of Machaerus, East of the Dead Sea. There he was eventually executed, apparently at the instigation of Herodias (Mark 6.17–29 par.; cf. Josephus, *Ant.* 18.116–119).

Although he had been arrested before Jesus' public Galilean ministry began (Mark 1.14 par.), John was apparently still more widely known than Jesus (note Mark 6.14–16 par.). Nevertheless, when Jesus heard about John's execution, he withdrew with his disciples to a lonely place (Mark 6.32 par.), probably realizing that this news spelled trouble for his own ministry as well. Indeed, Luke reports of certain Pharisees who advised Jesus to leave immediately because Herod wanted to kill him (Luke 13.31f.). It also appears that, in the wake of growing controversy, a significant number of followers may have deserted Jesus (John 6.60–66).

The Turning Point and the Second Half of Jesus' Ministry

Caesarea Philippi

Not long afterwards, Jesus appears to have taken his disciples on a journey into what is now known as the Golan Heights, outside the jurisdiction of Herod Antipas and in the Tetrarchy of Herod's estranged half-brother Philip. They found themselves at a place called Caesarea Philippi (Paneas, modern Banyas in the Golan), in the extreme North of Philip's territory. This would have been a safe haven, and indeed an ideal place from which even to leave Palestine altogether and abscond to the security of Syria, had Jesus wanted to do so. Other stories say that Jesus did in fact spend time in "the region of Tyre and Sidon" as well (Matt. 15.21; cf. Mark 7.24, 31).

In this situation of relative peace and safety, Jesus appears to go through a time of searching, perhaps a second identity crisis after his earlier temptation in the wilderness. This is when he consults his disciples: "Who do people say that I am?" The reported reactions identify him with a variety of prophetic and Messianic figures: John the Baptist, Elijah, or one of the prophets. When pressed about their own assessment of him, Peter makes the famous statement, "You are the Messiah" (Mark 8.29; all four gospels agree in substance). As on earlier occasions when the subject of his Messianic status had come up, Jesus urges strict silence about this matter. But then there is clear evidence that a turning point has been reached in Jesus' own self-understanding. He appears at least tacitly to acknowledge Peter's confession.

This amply attested event reflects perhaps a realization that even though he might be unwilling to identify himself publicly as the Messiah, some people would inevitably draw that conclusion from his teaching and miracles (Matthew 11.2–6 suggests that he himself encouraged the imprisoned John the Baptist to do so). However, that conclusion in turn meant his life was in danger. And if he was to continue in his God-given ministry, his calling would inevitably involve suffering and quite possibly execution.

Here, then, is a point of decision. In accepting Peter's confession, Jesus not only acknowledges the likelihood of a violent end if he returns to continue his ministry in Palestine.

To do that, however, would require a *positive incorporation* of ⟵
martyrdom in his self-understanding. It is highly significant,
therefore, that all three Synoptic Gospels insert here the first in
a series of reflections on Jesus' imminent suffering and death:

> And he began to teach them that the Son of man
> must undergo great suffering, and be rejected by
> the elders, the chief priests, and the scribes, and be
> killed, and after three days rise again. (Mark 8.31
> par.)

Given Jesus' political and historical context, some such "mid-
career" reflection on the meaning and likely outcome of his
ministry carries a very high degree of historical probability.
The *purpose* of this suffering is here not yet explained, but a
critical point has clearly been reached in that Jesus now affirms
that a violent end may well be an integral part of what he is
called to do. Interestingly, he is said to formulate that decision
in the context of a second crisis experience of being tempted by
"Satan" (Mark 8.33 par.).

It is difficult to say with certainty whether Jesus did in
fact speak about his own resurrection at this point; or if he did,
what he meant by it. But the possible allusion of "after three
days" to Hosea 6.2 and his mysterious talk about a "sign of
Jonah" (cf. Jonah 1.17 with Matt. 12.39f.) means that Jesus'
self-understanding in the biblical tradition of the suffering
righteous may well have included the equally biblical hope of
some kind of subsequent vindication – which, since it follows
death, might indeed be phrased in terms of resurrection.[17]

Transfiguration: Divine Confirmation of Jesus' Call

In all three Synoptic Gospels there follows the narrative of the
transfiguration. How, where and why this took place is
probably impossible to reconstruct. The story describes a kind
of visionary experience involving Jesus and his three closest
disciples. In this mountain-top vision,[18] Jesus is transformed

into a brilliant appearance and seen to be conversing with
Moses and Elijah, the two greatest Old Testament prophets,
both of whom had significant Messianic connotations in Jewish
thought.

That Jesus was a man of visions and mystical experiences
should not come as a surprise. Apocalyptic literature and other
Jewish writings from the centuries before and after his birth
share very similar perspectives on mysticism as a way of
experiencing more deeply and immediately the spiritual realities
of faith, including God's coming kingdom. We have already
found Jesus in the gospel accounts undergoing a powerful vision
of divine appointment at his baptism, followed by his personal
confrontation with Satan in the wilderness. Luke 10.18 records
that Jesus greeted the report about his followers' mission of
healing and exorcism by interpreting it in light of another apocalyptic vision: "I watched Satan fall from heaven like a flash of
lightning" (cf. Rev. 12.9; *2 Enoch* 29.3f., etc.). His heralding
of the Kingdom and defeat of the powers opposed to it was a
subject of ardent spiritual and mystical reflection for him (see
also p. 127 below).

Whatever this experience may have been (appearances of
Moses and Elijah are paralleled in certain rabbinic stories), the
gospel accounts indicate that the disciples were clearly left with
an exalted impression of their Teacher's significance in relation
to the great prophets of Israel. In Luke, moreover, the focus of
Moses and Elijah's meeting with Jesus is precisely on the
coming climax of his kingdom ministry in Jerusalem (9.31).
What this story might mean for Jesus' own self-understanding is
of course hard to assess without undue speculation. But if some
such vision did form part of his pre-Easter ministry, it would
naturally come as a re-confirmation of his divine call at
baptism: we should note particularly the repetition of the
heavenly voice which declares, "This is my Son, the Beloved"
(Mark 9.7 par.).

Departure for Jerusalem

It seems that not long after this, Jesus decided to make his usual pilgrimage to Jerusalem for the Passover season, aware that this was in all likelihood his last time. (It is interesting to note John 11.54–57: Jesus hid with his disciples in Ephraim in the Judaean hills before this Passover.)

In Matthew and Mark, this decision ushers in the last phase of his ministry, although Luke at this point inserts nine full chapters of material which Matthew and Mark placed in the Galilean setting (Luke 9.51–18.30). Even Luke, however, intimates that Jesus deliberately went up to the capital despite the danger to himself "because it is impossible for a prophet to be killed outside of Jerusalem" (Luke 13.33) – a recognition that one way or another his fate must come to a head in that city.

The synoptic accounts consistently give the impression that from now on *Jesus began to act much more deliberately with a view to his approaching suffering and death.* He incorporated it explicitly and implicitly in his teaching, setting his Kingdom message much more clearly in a context of the judgement and Messianic restoration of Israel, the coming glorious day of the Son of Man, for which somehow his own suffering and rejection would be instrumental.

> The days are coming when you will long to see one of the days of the Son of man, and you will not see it. And they will say to you, 'Look there!' or 'Look here!' Do not go, do not set off in pursuit. For as the lightning flashes and lights up the sky from one side to the other, so will the Son of Man be in his day. But first he must endure much suffering and be rejected by this generation. (Luke 17.22–25)

This awareness and affirmation of future suffering is evident also in his well-attested reply to the request of James and John that they might sit to his right and left when he attained to his throne: "You do not know what you are asking. Are you able to drink the cup that I drink, or to be baptized with the baptism with which I am baptized?" (Mark 10.38 par., cf. 10.45).[19]

Jesus also affirmed the idea that his suffering would be somehow redemptive, would contribute to the salvation of Israel. This idea has quite extensive roots in the Jewish tradition. Not only is a positive evaluation of righteous suffering widespread in the Old Testament Psalms of Lament and the book of Job (note also the persecuted son of God in Wisdom 2), but a variety of texts positively interpret such experiences as of saving significance. Of particular influence in Jewish interpretation was the story of Abraham's willingness to sacrifice his son Isaac, which according to Gen. 22.16–18 procures a special blessing on his descendants and all the nations of the earth. Similarly, the death of the second-century BC Maccabean martyrs, who apparently inspired the author of Hebrews as one of the great examples of faith,[20] was at least in some circles interpreted as an atoning sacrifice for the sins of the nation (4 Macc. 6.29; 17.21f.; cf. 2 Macc. 6–7). Aside from its potential roots in the story of Gen. 22, this interpretation of martyrdom goes back in any case at least to Isaiah 53, where the life of God's innocent servant is seen as a sacrifice for the sins of the people (vv. 4–6, 8, 10) – an idea which became the subject of continuing reflection in later Jewish texts.[21] Jesus himself now gives expression to this tradition in passages like Mark 10.45 and parallels, mentioned earlier: "The Son of Man came not to be served but to serve, and to give his life a ransom for many." This notion of redemptive suffering comes perhaps to its clearest statement in the accounts of the Last Supper, as we will see. Given the Old Testament and Jewish background to the statements of Jesus, it is legitimate to suggest that Jesus came to affirm his impending death not merely as the tragically inevitable outcome of his career as a righteous prophet, but in fact as an integral part of God's will for him.[22]

And at this point it also becomes significant that the earliest accounts of the resurrection appearances go out of their way to stress that the Messiah's suffering and resurrection were in fulfilment not only of his own predictions, but of the prophecies of Scripture (cf. John 20.9; Luke 24.27; 1 Cor. 15.3f.; Peter's speeches in Acts 2f.). This emphasis on prophecy and confirmation is of course partly apologetic, intended to buttress faith in the Cross and resurrection against the charge of unscriptural innovation and false prophecy (cf. Deut. 13.1–4). Yet even if the particular constellation of biblical prophecies in this context has a uniquely Christian application, the very existence of motifs like the vicariously suffering righteous indicates that Jesus certainly would not have been without biblical guideposts in reflecting on the imminence of his own undeserved death.

The "Triumphal Entry"

Despite growing reflection on his likely suffering, it appears Jesus also continued to sound a note of Messianic self-consciousness. The most dramatic demonstration of this is his so-called triumphal entry into Jerusalem (Mark 11.1–10 par.), in which he deliberately arranges to ride in on a donkey to the acclaim of his followers, in fulfilment of the Messianic prophecy to this effect in Zechariah 9.9. This would simultaneously make the point of an unmistakable claim to Messianic kingship, yet in the status of a humble, non-violent, peaceful kind of Messiah (note Zech. 9.10). (This view is also reflected in his response to the question about paying tribute to Caesar, Mark 12.13–17 par.[23]) Jesus clearly appears to accept the Messianic acclamations of his followers, to the consternation of the religious leadership.

Once in Jerusalem, Jesus refers to himself obliquely as "Son of God" and as the last of the prophets in the Parable of the Wicked Tenants (Mark 12.1–12 par.), a provocation aimed squarely at the priestly establishment.[24] He was obviously

beginning to run into danger of a major confrontation with the
Jerusalem aristocracy.

Jesus' Demonstration in the Temple

In Mark and Luke, the final impetus for Jesus' arrest was given
by his demonstration in the Temple (Mark 11.15–17 par.; John
2 and other considerations make it likely that at least a threat
against the Temple was pronounced on an earlier occasion).
This action has traditionally been understood as a "cleansing" of
the Temple from the practice of selling sacrificial animals and
exchanging Roman for Tyrian coinage (which was required to
pay the Temple tax).   But Jesus seems to be aiming at more
than that: implicit in the synoptic accounts (and explicit in John
2.19) is Jesus' intention of a provocative demonstration
symbolizing the coming destruction of the Temple itself, as part
of the imminent appearance of judgement and the new age. As
we saw in Chapter Three, this may well have been based on his
outrage at the perceived corruption practised by the illegitimate
aristocratic families who not only controlled the High Priest-
hood but held a virtual monopoly over the sacrificial trading
practices. Jesus' demonstration in the Temple, then, symbolically expressed God's judgement over the present corruption,
and affirmed the imminent destruction of the Temple as part of
the restoration of the new age.   This contention would have
made Jesus odious and threatening in the eyes of the ruling
aristocracy. It would have added to their fear that Jesus might
cause a violent intervention of the Romans, and so it hastened
their formal decision to put him to death (John 11.47–53).
Clearly, Jesus' controversial convictions about the Temple were
integral to his aims and purposes, and the demonstration in the
Temple merely served to seal his fate.

The Last Supper

Jesus' last night of freedom was apparently spent in a private celebration with the inner circle of twelve disciples. The nature of this meal has been the subject of endless scholarly debate, the details of which cannot here be resolved. Some have argued on the strength of Mark 14.12–16 (par.) that it was a regular Passover meal.[25]   That suggestion, however, can only be sustained by discounting the Fourth Gospel's unambiguous assertion that Jesus was crucified *before* the day of Passover (John 13.1; 18.28; 19.14, etc.). John's date of the crucifixion of Jesus is also one of the few New Testament texts to find confirmation in Jewish sources.[26] The apparent chronology of Mark 14.12, by contrast, clashes with Jewish purity law prohibiting executions on feast days – a concern of which the Fourth Gospel shows some awareness (John 18.28).[27]

So the "passover" which Jesus held with his disciples on the night of his arrest was most likely an unofficial meal, whether or not a lamb was eaten.[28]   In explanation of the difficulty, it is sometimes suggested that Jesus may have celebrated the festival earlier because he followed the *solar* calendar of the Essenes.[29] However, aside from a lack of clear positive evidence, this proposal is weakened by the fact that Jesus and his disciples give every impression of participating in regular Temple worship.   In any case, even the Synoptic Gospels contain some evidence that Jesus was executed *before* the official Passover. Such, at any rate, is the stated intention of his adversaries (Mark 14.1f.), while Jesus' own words in Luke 22.15–16[30] may suggest a treasured but *unfulfilled* desire to eat the Passover with his disciples before his passion. Could it be that this meal was held *in anticipation* of the celebration which he knew he would not live to see?

In any case, whatever else we may wish to conclude about the chronology of the passion, the close proximity of this final meal and the subsequent events to the great Passover festival clearly impressed itself on Jesus' and his followers' consciousness as they anticipated (and later reflected back upon) his impending death.[31] And whether or not this meal was an actual

Passover, the synoptic evidence almost requires, and the rest of the New Testament allows, that the Last Supper would have been seen as closely linked both with his death and with the significance of the approaching festival. The crucifixion itself took place just as in the Temple the Priests began to slaughter the many thousands of Passover lambs in preparation for the evening's celebration.

Passover today is a traditional, joyful family affair with a set liturgical meal which symbolizes Israel's redemption from oppression in Egypt, and looks forward to the Messianic redemption to come. Much of this symbolism, and perhaps some of the form of the celebration, would already have been in place in the first century, even though the meal then was often celebrated by groups of between ten and twenty men (cf. Josephus, *War* 6.423). The head of each Passover "household" traditionally recites certain words for the different parts of the meal, explaining their symbolism: bitter herbs for the affliction the Israelites suffered in Egypt, parsley dipped in salt water for their tears, and so on. Four ceremonial cups of wine are part of the ceremony (note that Luke 22.17–20 mentions two, one before and one after the main meal); over each of them a benediction is pronounced. Passover is a meal of remembrance, in which the participants are to regard themselves as having personally participated in the redemption from Egypt.

Without finally identifying the form of the Last Supper, we can say that Jesus assigned special significance to his own imminent death in relation to this meal. It is interesting that he uses a similar kind of "this is that" language ("this is my body", "this is my blood of the covenant": Mark 14.22, 24 par.) as was perhaps already in use in the order of Passover. However we understand the setting of the Last Supper, it is clear that this provides us with Jesus' most profound and most explicit reflection on the significance of his impending death: his blood is the constitutive blood of the covenant, poured out on behalf of the redemption and forgiveness of God's people.[32]   For his disciples, this is to be part of their meal of remembrance. In the same context, Jesus himself takes a vow that he will abstain from wine until the Kingdom of God is established (Mark 14.25 par.). It is not unreasonable to see here an expectant desire that ← his very suffering will cause that Kingdom to come.

From Gethsemane to Execution

Later that night, after a third and final spiritual crisis in prayer at Gethsemane, an olive grove[33] in the Kidron valley between the Temple and the Mount of Olives, Jesus was arrested. Much has been said and written about the subsequent scenes of an informal hearing in place of a proper trial, sentencing (probably decided as early as John 11.53; cf. Mark 11.18), and crucifixion. We may offer a couple of final observations on Jesus' aims.

First, now that there is nothing left to lose, Jesus no longer hides his self-understanding. In all three Synoptic Gospels he openly admits his Messianic claim before the High Priest Caiaphas, and he seems to identify himself with the coming heavenly Son of Man "at the right hand of power" (Mark 14.62 par.). This assertion in turn evokes the High Priest's emotive charge of blasphemy, thus providing the officials of the Sanhedrin with convenient grounds for a guilty verdict which had already been decided on other grounds, and which for official Roman purposes was in any case based on the charge of sedition (John 19.21). Jesus' appearance before Pilate was then just a formality: he was sent off to execution almost immediately and without further delay.[34]

Beyond this, not much more needs to be said. Crucifixion was a horrible procedure, and it is moot to ask a man dying of torture about his aims and purposes. It is difficult to achieve a historically reliable reconstruction of Jesus' words on the Cross, but it seems certain that they included the words "My God, My God, why have you forsaken me?", hauntingly recorded in their original form[35] in Matt. 27.46 (cf. Mark 15.34). Such

testimony would not have been placed on his lips by his
followers.   First and foremost, these are the words of a
desperate man, abandoned by even his closest friends, and left
to die.   Taken at face value, they may also reflect the crushed
spirit of one who perhaps hoped that God would not ultimately
let him perish, that somehow at the very point of his innocent
death God would intervene and bring the Kingdom from heaven
with power (a possibility which, although impossible to prove,
might also be thought compatible with his Passover vow of
Mark 14.25 par.).[36] Instead, Jesus died in agony, and alone.

Conclusion

Resurrection and the Aims of Jesus

Had Jesus failed?   Clearly that was the obvious conclusion; it
was the one drawn by the Roman authorities, the Sadducean
leadership, and evidently even by the disciples.   The Gospels
record that even Peter denied him, and two days later Cleopas
on the road to Emmaus makes the telling comment, "But *we had
hoped* that he was the one to redeem Israel" (Luke 24.21).   To
all of them it seemed that Jesus had failed.   A disinterested
modern historian's frame of reference, too, might well come to
that conclusion, as did several ancient historians.

From a theological perspective it may seem natural at this
point to want to rush on to the resurrection as providing the
answer to all outstanding questions – as indeed it does, in one
sense.   One significant conclusion of this chapter is that
question of Jesus' own success or failure really does depend on
the resurrection, just as much as the question of whether he was
the Messiah (Chapter 2 above).   But there is another very
important point to make.   If belief in the resurrection is to be
more than a glossing over of facts which are otherwise thought
to be depressing, if it is to be a real endorsement of Jesus as the
Messiah and as one who achieved what he set out to do, then it
must uphold both the Jesus of faith *and* the Jesus of history.   It

must be able to confirm not only Christian convictions about God's eternal plan of salvation in his "only begotten Son" (a dimension with which Chapter Seven will deal), but also the purposes and expectations of the country carpenter from Galilee who was crushed by a power-hungry Jerusalem aristocracy in co-operation with the flawless machinery of the Roman imperial occupation forces. The resurrection can only establish that Jesus succeeded if it also confirms that the pre-Easter Jesus fulfilled his purposes.

[margin note: > his point/quest.]

Those purposes appear to have evolved and gained in clarity of definition over the course of Jesus' career. At his baptism by John, Jesus experienced a vision of divine affirmation and charismatic appointment in Messianic or near-Messianic terms. After working this through in the wilderness, his early ministry of healing and teaching focused on the announcement and symbolic enacting of the imminent Kingdom of God. Growing controversy and opposition led to a second crisis soon after the execution of John the Baptist, when it became clear that the Messianic dimensions of his ministry spelled danger ahead. This realization led him to the conscious reflection and affirmation of suffering as an integral part of his calling, increasingly moving him to interpret his likely death as a ransom and atonement for Israel, and as positively instrumental for bringing in the Kingdom of God. He saw this as fully compatible with his present Messianic role. At the same time, he continued to believe in a final, and perhaps imminent, vindication by the arrival of the heavenly Son of Man, with whom he may have associated himself (so especially in Mark 14.62 par.).

Seen in these terms, which are those of Jesus' own frame of reference, it is consistent to say that his death did not mean he failed. Indeed it is no accident that his very words of dying desperation, encountered earlier (p. 95; see also p. 134 below), are taken from Psalm 22: a Lament of the suffering righteous, which nevertheless ends in vindication (note v. 22–31).

Concluding his own extended discussion of the aims of Jesus, Ben F. Meyer writes,

> But what, in the end, made Jesus operate in this way, what energized his incorporating death into his mission, his facing it and going to meet it?
>
> The range of abstractly possible answers is enormous. And unless a satisfactory answer is forthcoming the inner intention of Jesus' life does remain ambiguous. We have referred to critical studies which substantially diminish the indeterminacy of the matter. But, as Kant observed of the central intention of a thinker, namely, that it comes to light slowly and reaches thematic status in the tradition he generates, so it is above all in the tradition generated by Jesus that we discover what made him operate in the way he did, what made him epitomize his life in the single act of going to his death: He 'loved me and handed himself over for me' (Gal. 2.20; cf. Eph. 5.2); 'having loved his own who were in the world, he loved them to the end' (John 13.1); he 'freed us from our sins by his blood' because 'he loves us' (Rev. 1.5). If authenticity lies in the coherence between word (Mark 12.28–34 parr.) and deed (Gal. 2.20; Eph. 5.2; John 13.1; Rev. 1.5), our question has found an answer.[37]

This is why, despite their initial surprise, his followers concluded that if indeed Jesus had been raised from the dead, this must mean his vindication and exaltation to be the Son of God in glory and with power.

Epilogue: Did Jesus' Future Hope Fail?

One final question. We may grant that Jesus' general aims and purposes were met in his ministry and death, and divinely ratified by his subsequent resurrection (about which more must be said in Chapter Seven). But what does that mean for his own ideas about the future, which come out most clearly in his private teaching to his disciples, for instance on the Mount of

Olives (Mark 13.3 par.)? He predicted the destruction of the Temple and envisioned a number of other cataclysmic events before the coming of the heavenly Son of Man and the consummation of history. He seems to have believed that all this would come to pass, if not within his own lifetime, then at any rate within the lifetime of his audience (Matt. 16.28 par.; Mark 13.30; Matt. 10.23; cf. 1 Thess. 4.15–17).

Did Jesus' time framework fail? Numerous explanations have been advanced to try and avoid this conclusion: the "coming of the Kingdom with power" has been seen as referring to the transfiguration, the resurrection, or (perhaps most plausibly) to Pentecost. The term "generation" has been generalized so as to give almost infinite flexibility to the statement that "this generation will not pass away before all these things take place" (Matt. 24.34 par.).

I do not wish to belittle these explanations. Some of them make good sense to me theologically. But the statements in view do seem to raise the question: did the historical Jesus *really* mean to suggest that the glorious arrival of the heavenly Son of Man and of the Kingdom of God was at least as distant from where he lived as he was from Abraham? I confess the historical facts and the witness of Scripture make that seem an improbable idea.

Must we therefore conclude that, although Jesus himself succeeded, his future expectations failed? If by that we mean that his statements about the time frame, taken as literal predictions, did not materialize, I think this conclusion is hard to avoid. Indeed the evidence is such that, as Ben F. Meyer puts it, "one wonders on what grounds (other than preference) an historical investigation might conclude that, unlike the Baptist and unlike his own disciples and other early Christians, Jesus did *not* expect the consummation of history in the near future."[38] And while there is little evidence that this problem particularly plagued the early Christians, it is not insignificant that the author of 2 Peter finds himself having to explain why the first generation of Christians have died and the promise of Christ's coming has yet to be fulfilled (2 Pet. 3.4; cf. also John 21.21–23). Some scholars, in fact, have concluded that because Jesus' expectation apparently failed, he himself failed – or at least, that his message therefore came to be fundamentally altered in early Christianity and in later theology.[39]

Even here, however, there are at least three good historical points to be made in understanding why the eschatology of Jesus may in fact have been rather more subtle – and, perhaps, why it has retained its power as a dynamic source of hope and encouragement throughout the many centuries of Christian history.

1. The Jesus of the Synoptic Gospels repeatedly stresses the need for watchfulness, since the "day or the hour" is known neither to his disciples nor even to him (Mark 13.32 par.). This kind of statement runs counter to the exalted christology of most later writers and thus further strengthens its claim to authenticity. Jesus recognized, as any good Jew would, that the time frame was ultimately in God's hands. This explains why, though the tenor of his language about the coming events is urgent, his statements about the schedule are remarkably restrained and *un*specific.[40]

2. Careful study reveals elements of a longer-term perspective in the very same passages which talk about the apocalyptic "coming" of the Son of Man (Mark 13.26f. par.)[41]: there will be wars, persecutions, apostasy, false Messiahs – and therefore, despite the urgency of the impending kingdom, the disciples must not be alarmed. The perspective of a wider missionary activity may also be present in the pre-Easter situation: the arrival of the Son of Man is near, but his followers will be occupied at least for a while with evangelizing the towns and villages of Palestine, even though they will not finish that task before he comes (Matt. 10.23). Indeed the notion that various other things must happen before the end can come is

commonplace in Jewish apocalyptic texts; and a similar co-existence of urgent eschatology and "Christian citizenship" is found in Paul's Thessalonian correspondence and elsewhere. The kingdom of God has come near and its proclamation is of pressing importance; but the end is not immediate (note especially Luke 21.7–9 par.).

3. Thirdly and most importantly, to understand the nature of apocalyptic texts it must be said that the re-interpretation and adaptation of prophetic promises had always been a staple of Jewish religion, indeed a positive theological asset rather than a liability.[42] So Jeremiah's prophecy of 70 years of exile (25.11f.; 29.10) is re-interpreted in Daniel 9.24–27 as 490 years; and 4 Ezra 12 reinterprets Daniel's vision of the fourth kingdom (2.40; 7.23) to apply to Rome. Similar re-interpretations would earlier have been required for Zechariah's apparent identification of the High Priest Joshua ben Jehozadak as the Messianic "Branch" (Zech. 4.10, 6.12). In later Jewish sources, the Dead Sea Scrolls affirm that the true meaning of the prophets has been revealed to the Teacher of Righteousness; Rabbinic Judaism could cope with and process the revered Rabbi Aqiba's mistaken identification of the second-century rebel leader Simon Bar Kochba as the Messiah. For all these cases, the revision of earlier views of prophetic fulfilment serves to express that the foundational faith in God's promises transcends any specific understanding of how and when they are to be fulfilled.

So also Christian tradition derived both encouragement and stimulation from the words of Jesus in each new generation. If the historical Jesus admitted that he did not know the divine schedule (Mark 13.32 par.), and perhaps expected the Son of Man would come sooner than in fact he did, that in no way diminishes the acute force of his message of the Kingdom, or its relevance for Christians. All it does is to affirm the integrity of the Christian view of incarnation: God the Son became fully human; even he did not know the day nor the hour.[43] In that state of incomplete knowledge he may have had a certain conception of the time frame, but this was not essential to the validity and permanence of his message.   Thus, a literalistic reading of apocalyptic gospel passages fails to do justice to either the letter or the spirit of Jesus' teaching.[44]

For Christian faith in subsequent generations, therefore, it was still arguably true and still urgent that the Son of Man would come with great power and glory, and gather his elect from the ends of the earth (Mark 13.26f.).   In arguing with Christianity's detractors on this subject, 2 Peter 3 concludes that God is not slow about his promise but is patiently trying to bring all to repentance, while believers are to live lives of godliness and holiness and thereby hasten the certain coming of the Lord.   In later centuries the hope of Christ's return continued among the Church Fathers,[45] and Christians continued to take courage in his assurance: "Stand up and raise your heads, because your redemption is drawing near" (Luke 21.28).

Chapter Five

Was Jesus a Christian?

In its major article on Jesus, the *Encyclopædia Britannica* includes the following statement:

> To say that Christianity "focuses" on Jesus Christ is to say that whatever else it comprehends, somehow it brings these realities together in reference to an ancient historic figure. ... The vast majority of Christians.... would not want to be nor would they be called Christian if they did not bring their eyes and attentions first and last to Jesus Christ.[1]

But was Jesus a Christian? That is to say, was Jesus not just the author and originator of that first-century Palestinian Jewish movement which eventually became known as the Christian church, but did he himself share or represent Christian beliefs, practices or experiences to the extent that one might rightly think of him as the first Christian?

Jesus the Jew and Jesus the Christian

First and foremost, clearly Jesus was a believing and practising Jew. He participated in synagogue and temple, and his teaching takes first-century Palestinian Judaism for granted. His brand of faith was at its core the covenant faith in the God of Israel. And despite all his controversy and disputes with the religious leadership, the Gospels (unlike some Christian theologians) do not give the impression that his purpose was to start a new and fundamentally incompatible religion.

To examine what it might mean for Jesus to have been a Christian, it is therefore important to begin by looking at where Jesus fits into the ambit of first-century *Judaism*. In the light of that we can then ask some questions about the areas in which he may or may not represent specifically *Christian* beliefs.

What Kind of Jew Was Jesus?
A Survey of First-Century Judaism

First, then, the question: What do we know about Jesus' Judaism? There is a lot that continues to be written about this question.[2] Here, I shall phrase my answer in a slightly roundabout way, beginning with a thumbnail sketch of Palestinian Judaism at the time of Jesus' ministry and stopping now and then to point out beliefs and practices which Jesus shared.

Judaism and the New Testament

First-century Judaism was not organized by strict canons of orthodoxy, but showed a great deal of diversity in both belief and practice. Some groups, like the Essenes and certain Pharisees, were very exclusive and maintained an exceptionally high standard of religious purity, although the Pharisees in particular evidently also had a great many sympathizers who, while practising a more lenient regime, were still generally observant. The extent of popular concern for purity has become evident in recent years through the discovery of large numbers of ritual baths in every part of the country. Of course the day-to-day observance of the masses (the `am ha'aretz`) will have varied quite considerably, and there is evidence for a good deal of Hellenization and syncretism.[3] Popular superstitions abounded, including magical and burial practices known from the wider Hellenistic religious world. A pagan religious presence is attested throughout the country, even in Jerusalem. And in regard to Jesus' ministry, it is interesting that the two leading cities of Galilee, Sepphoris and Tiberias, never feature in the Gospels[4] – perhaps because both had strong Hellenizing and pagan connections. Nevertheless, Judaism remained very much a religion of the people: Torah and Temple were shared values, and hundreds of thousands from around the country and abroad gathered in Jerusalem for the annual festivals. And despite Josephus's convenient fourfold classification of Judaism, it must be remembered that the majority of both Palestinian and Diaspora Jews would not have been formal members of one of the major sects. In that sense, then, it is appropriate to speak of a "common Judaism", consisting of "what the priests and the people agreed on".[5]

For the New Testament, the explicit relationship with contemporary Judaism seems, at least on the surface, largely strained and antithetical. For this reason, general statements about "the Pharisees" (in Matthew) or "the Jews" (in the Fourth Gospel) must be seen in the light of the early church's experience of being alienated and excluded from the much larger and more powerful mainstream Jewish communities.

Having said that, the New Testament does show Jesus interacting with a broad spectrum of Judaism. He converses with people called Pharisees, Scribes (legal and religious scholars), Sadducees (the Jerusalem aristocracy) and Herodians (most probably people who supported the Herodian royal family even though it was not ethnically Jewish).[6] One of Jesus' disciples is called "Simon the Zealot", suggesting that he may have come from the nationalist guerrilla movement or circles sympathetic to it (Luke 6.15; Acts 1.13). Thus, the religious variety which emerges from the description in Josephus, as well as from other sources including Philo and the Dead Sea Scrolls, is also reflected in the Gospels.

With this in mind, then both the New Testament and Josephus can help us understand a good deal about the nature and diversity of Palestinian Judaism.

Flavius Josephus on the Four Philosophies

In describing the character of first-century Judaism, Flavius Josephus discusses four Jewish "sects" or "philosophies".[7]

1. Pharisees

Name

The name "Pharisees" probably means "the separated ones" (*perushim*),[8] and basically refers to those who assigned particular significance to the Jewish purity laws with their stress on the separation of clean from unclean. For this reason it was necessary for them to distance themselves from "unclean" persons like non-observant Jews or Gentiles.

Historical Origin and Social Setting

The Pharisees were a popular conservative movement focused on a keen interest in the study of the Torah and in guarding the national traditions against pagan or secular trends. They emerged during the Maccabean period (mid-second cent. BC), as opponents of pagan secularization, and according to Josephus they enjoyed great religious popularity and influence among the masses (*Ant.* 13.288, 298; 18.15). They arguably emerge as the most important, if not the most powerful, of the Jewish religious movements at the time of Christ.

Religious Distinctives

The Pharisees were particularly distinguished for their emphasis on the accurate interpretation and observance of the Torah as God-given on Mt. Sinai. More specifically, they appear to have commended the observance of strict rules of temple purity at all times.[9] For some at least, this required living in special communities and the practice of an exclusive table fellowship. Among laypeople, at any rate, the Pharisees were arguably the spiritual and theological nucleus of Israel's mainstream religion, though only a small group within the nation. And thus, while they were by and large *not* in positions of political power, the general thrust of their theology nevertheless enjoyed majority support.[10]

As God's gift to Israel, the Torah reliably and precisely reveals God's will. For this reason the Pharisees placed great emphasis on study and scholarship. They carefully preserved the oral sayings of great "sages" like Hillel, Shammai, and others. They believed that tradition and interpretation should be a "fence" around the Torah to prevent its transgression, partly by making explicit what the Torah leaves implicit or unsaid. At the same time, the transmission of *oral law* concentrated on traditional interpretation and application of the Law, in a body of practical teaching known as the *halakhah*.[11] This was held to be equally binding, supplying the practical context of application for the legal ordinances contained in Scripture. It is a mainstay of later rabbinic Judaism, but its roots clearly are present before 70.[12] There is in all this a dialectical relationship between Scripture and tradition: in some statements tradition seems to have prior authority, in others Scripture.[13]

This background helps to understand a little of what the Gospels mean when they describe Jesus encountering those for whom in his view tradition and not Scripture was the final authority. The Sadducees and the community of the Dead Sea Scrolls were also in conflict with the Pharisees on the role of oral tradition. Nevertheless, in most other respects Jesus holds Pharisaic views, as we shall see.

The Pharisees believed in bodily resurrection and a final judgement involving rewards and retribution. In this they agree with the New Testament and with much of apocalyptic literature (beginning perhaps with Daniel 12.1–3). Denial of these truths was understood to be a key denial of the faith.[14] The Pharisees affirmed both divine providence and free will, countering both the Sadducees and Essenes in this regard. Rabbi Aqiba in the second century may have captured their doctrine in his famous dictum, "All is foreseen, but free will is given."[15]

While the Pharisees were not without varying political concerns and influence of their own (e.g. in their opposition to Alexander Jannaeus, Herod, and periodic Roman infringements against Jewish sensibilities), they were as a whole not in a position of political power. Some will have participated in the great revolt against Rome in AD 66–70 (Josephus suggests the zealots basically affirmed Pharisaic views); but at least after the year 70 there is a clear trend towards accepting religious without political freedom. Yohanan ben Zakkai and his followers voted with their feet when they abandoned the besieged city of Jerusalem and went on to found rabbinic Judaism in the academy at Yabneh. True, a Kingdom of God was ultimately the only political reality they could accept – and thus a Gentile government was in principle undesirable. The more lenient Pharisees, however, believed that any government was acceptable so long as it did not interfere with Torah observance.[16]

Impact on the New Testament

Jesus' disputes with the Pharisees were largely over his teaching and practice regarding the Sabbath and purity laws. The concerns of his opponents are exactly those we would expect from the strict groups of Pharisees (*haberim*), although no doubt also reflecting the animosity of anyone whose position of religious influence is threatened. One additional, but related dispute appears to have been over Jesus' association with "sinners", the irreligious and disreputable (Mark 2.16 par.).

The New Testament's "scribes" were probably largely Pharisaic (cf. especially Mark 2.16 "scribes of the Pharisees"). In any case, it is significant that the Pharisees were Jesus' main conversation partners during his ministry in Galilee. (In Jerusalem, as we saw in Chapters Three and Four, he ran afoul not of the Pharisees but of the priestly, and hence primarily Sadducean, aristocracy.[17]) Jesus himself was very close to the Pharisaic point of view on numerous issues. In fact, even where he criticizes his opponents he often takes a position which we know other Pharisees and rabbis held either at his time or later. Three important examples of this are (i) his belief that it is more important to save life on the Sabbath;[18] (ii) the idea that money promised as an offering to the Temple must not be withheld from support for one's parents;[19] (iii) his teaching that divorce is impermissible. The latter is parallel to Qumran teaching,[20] though with the added exception for adultery (as in Matthew 5.32; 19.9) it is also attributed to the first-century Pharisaic school of Shammai.[21]

On the subject of the oral law, Jesus shows himself opposed to many of the Pharisaic views he encounters, and more in keeping with the purist approach to Scripture favoured by Sadducees and Essenes (see especially Mark 7.1–13 par.). At the same time he takes the liberty to present his teaching in an unqualified, authoritative form which strikes his audience as being "not like the scribes" (e.g. Mark 1.22, 27).

It is surely also significant that Jesus dines with Pharisees and occasionally praises one of them for being not far from the Kingdom (Mark 12.34; Luke 14.1; we may also compare the story of Nicodemus in John 3.1–10; 7.50f.; 19.39). The Pharisees are clearly not all bad, and the strongly negative picture of them in the Gospel of Matthew may have more to do with the fact that Jesus' conflicts with them had particular relevance to a church that lived in increasing tension with the synagogue. Even Matthew has room for Jesus to acknowledge that the scribes and Pharisees sit in Moses' seat, and that one ought therefore to follow their teaching (23.2–3).

2. Sadducees

Name
The Sadducees (Greek *Saddukaioi*, Hebrew *tzaddukim*) were probably descendants of Zadok, the High Priest under David and Solomon. Since the Exile, they had become the nucleus of the priestly class (see 1 Chr. 27.17; 29.22; Ezek. 40.46, etc.).

Historical Origin and Social Setting
The Sadducees are much less well known, partly because they have left no literary remains: "all of the extant information about this sect must be culled from documents written by people

who were not members of the sect and who often opposed
them."[22] By and large they were the priestly aristocracy of
Jerusalem, living in fabulous cosmopolitan style in the upper
city, as recent archaeological evidence suggests. The Sadducees
were key players in the upper-class corruption, intrigue and
power play which goes on behind the scenes in the Gospels, in
Josephus and in the Mishnah. Responsible to the Romans for
law and order, the Sadducees had a vested interest in smooth co-
operation with the occupation forces – at least during the period
of Jesus' ministry.[23] Josephus also reports of much factionalism
and infighting; as we saw in Chapter Three, different groups
operated their own private armed guards which ruthlessly
implemented their political aims by force.

Nevertheless, the distinction between Sadducees and
Pharisees was probably a matter of class as much as of religion.
While Sadducees were almost by definition aristocrats, their
theological differences may have been a matter of emphasis
rather than of fundamentals.[24] The Pharisees were not necessarily hostile to priests, or vice versa; indeed some priests
apparently were Pharisees, and some Pharisees may have shared
positions of power in Jerusalem. But there were indeed different
emphases. What is more, the Sadducees mainly held political
clout in Jerusalem itself, with less popular support in the
provinces, such as in Galilee. Both Josephus and the Talmud
suggest that in matters of ritual practice the Sadducees were at
times forced to accept the more influential rulings of the
Pharisees.[25]

Religious Distinctives

According to Josephus, the Sadducees held an exclusive
emphasis on Scripture, rejecting Pharisaic oral tradition and all
interpretative additions to the Torah. It is possible that only the
Pentateuch was seen as strictly canonical: this might explain
their denial of the resurrection (which is affirmed in Daniel 12
and possibly a few other passages from the prophets and

writings).[26] We might note, too, how Jesus answers the Sadducees' query about resurrection *from the Torah* rather than from the prophets, as might have seemed more straightforward (Mark 12.18–26). We are told, moreover, that the Sadducees did not believe in predestination but only in free will; beyond that there were minor legal and attitudinal differences with the Pharisees, such as over stricter penalties or the freedom to criticize their teachers (Josephus *Ant.* 18.16). Rabbinic literature, by contrast, records disagreement between Pharisees and Sadducees mainly over issues of purity.[27] Overall, the Sadducees were often in agreement with Pharisaic interpretation – the real difference was over its authority.

Impact on the New Testament

Being from Galilee, Jesus and the disciples would have had relatively little to do with the Sadducees in the first part of his ministry. His interaction with them is negative without exception – as is the case between Pharisees and Sadducees in rabbinic literature. The people whom Judas approached about betraying Jesus (Mark 14.10) were almost certainly Sadducees. Jesus is said to have argued with some Sadducees from the Torah about their denial of the resurrection (Mark 12.18–27 par.), a point of view to which Paul later appealed to his own advantage (Acts 23.6–9).

Jesus agreed with what we know of the Sadducees in their opposition to the Pharisaic oral tradition; but since the sectarian Dead Sea Scrolls hold a similar view, this does not imply any relationship between Jesus and the Sadducees.

Because they were the ruling class, the Sadducees as a distinct group came to an abrupt end with the Jewish Revolt and destruction of Jerusalem in 70. Nevertheless, high-ranking priests at any rate contributed significantly to the formation of the rabbinic movement and continued to exercise influence, as is suggested by the role of people like R. Yose and R. Hanina in the first century, or the imprint "Eleazar the Priest" (possibly

R. Eleazar of Modiim) on coins from the time of the Bar Kokhba revolt, AD 132–135.

3. Essenes

Name
The derivation of the name "Essenes" is disputed. It possibly derives from Aramaic words either for "healers" or for "pious".

Historical Origin and Social Setting
Apparently the Essenes were a monastic desert group with tight community discipline including formal meals. Another branch also lived in Palestinian towns, and some of these married. They had a vested interest and particular skill in biblical interpretation, prophecy, healing, and knowledge of esoteric traditions. Because of a favourable prophecy, Herod liked them and bestowed favour on them (Josephus, *Ant.* 15.373ff.).

Near the shores of the Dead Sea, a Bedouin shepherd in 1947 accidentally discovered the first of eventually eleven caves containing numerous scrolls and fragments of scrolls. Although all the scrolls are now publicly accessible, many of them are still not available in official critical editions. And while no earth-shaking surprises are likely, there could still be some interesting discoveries ahead.

Eleven more or less complete scrolls were found, and thousands of fragments. We have in the Dead Sea Scrolls a wealth of Jewish material from the time immediately surrounding the time of Jesus, without later revision, adaptation, or censorship. There are biblical manuscripts in Hebrew (of different textual traditions) covering all books except Esther and Nehemiah, and parts of the Old Testament in Greek. The Hebrew manuscripts are a thousand years older than the earliest Old Testament manuscripts previously known. There are numerous non-canonical works, some previously known (like Sirach, Tobit, *1 Enoch, Testament of Levi*) and many previously unknown: commentaries on Isaiah, Hosea, Micah,

Nahum, Habakkuk, and the Psalms; non-canonical Psalms and Prayers; constitutional documents for an ascetic community; and legal and mystical texts.

There are many open questions about the identity and significance of these texts. While there is a degree of dissent, most Qumran scholars still believe that the community associated with at least a good many of the Scrolls was the desert branch of the Essene movement. This seems to fit with the evidence about their settlement and beliefs given in Josephus, in Philo of Alexandria and in the Roman author Pliny the Elder.[28] At the same time, that view also raises a number of serious questions. These include (1) what to do with the many documents which show no sign of being sectarian in character; (2) the problem of whether scrolls from caves which in one or two cases are several miles away from the settlement at Qumran really belong there; and (3) whether a small desert community could realistically be assumed to have needed and produced such a huge library of manuscripts.

An alternative suggestion is that we are simply dealing with precious manuscripts stored for safekeeping during the Jewish revolt, possibly by a wide range of different people.[29] Whether or not this theory is true, it does seem that the Dead Sea Scrolls may be an even more valuable resource than was once thought, since they quite probably represent a much wider cross-section of Jewish practice and belief than was supposed after the publication of the first few, mainly sectarian texts in the 1950s and 1960s.

Apparently the Essenes in the sectarian Scrolls were a priestly group originating in the Maccabean period, for whom the Sadducees were insufferably corrupt and the Pharisees were too lenient ("seekers of smooth things"). Led by the otherwise anonymous Teacher of Righteousness, an eminent priestly figure who opposed a non-Zadokite High Priest in Jerusalem (called the "wicked priest"), the community went to the desert and saw themselves as embodying the New Covenant promised in Jeremiah 31 (CD 6.19, 8.21, 19.33, 20.12; 1 QSb 5.21), as well as the true Temple (1QS 9; 1QpHab 12.3–4). The "Wicked Priest" may have been Jonathan Maccabeus, the second of the three Maccabean brothers.[30] Just before Qumran fell to the Romans in AD 68 during the Jewish Revolt, some community members may have joined the rebels' last stand at the fortress of Masada, where copies of a few of the Dead Sea Scrolls have been discovered.

Religious Distinctives

Strong priestly interests coincide with the rejection of the entire Temple as unclean because of its corruption. The Essenes thrived on careful interpretation of the Old Testament, producing special insights from both the law and the prophets which were secretly guarded as special revelation given to the Teacher of Righteousness and to his community. The subject matter of these revelations pertained especially to the practice of Judaism and to the end times, and this resulted in considerable differences over matters such as a solar versus the traditional lunar calendar, sacrifices, and purity regulations.

Among several other distinctives one might mention the Essenes' asceticism. The Qumran monks were apparently unmarried and led lives of simplicity and without private property, although some of the Essenes in the cities were married (and a few separate tombs of women and children have been found at the partly excavated burial ground of Qumran).

Impact on the New Testament

The last 45 years have seen a flood of publications on the many theological themes of striking relevance for the understanding of the New Testament. Even if some of the central religious beliefs and practices are decidedly different, there is nevertheless much here to help us understand how the teachings of Jesus and the New Testament writers would have been seen in the first century. Among the most relevant themes are the following.

The sectarian scrolls manifest a strongly dualistic cosmology. There is a universal warfare of light vs. darkness and a good vs. an evil spirit (cf. the Fourth Gospel, Ephesians, Colossians). This will lead to an imminent final conflagration in which the Children of Light will be victorious under their Messianic leader. The Essenes probably believed in resurrection, although only a limited number of texts have been found to refer to this doctrine (one example is 4Q521, the "Messianic Apocalypse").

Along with this cosmology goes an explicit determinism, which considers history and human life as entirely governed by divine sovereignty, with a seemingly reduced emphasis on free will. A belief in justification by God's grace co-exists with a strict obedience to the law (see 1QS 11). Not unlike the teaching of John the Baptist or of the early church (note Peter in Acts 2.38), Qumran's doctrine of baptism (see 1QS 3) teaches that a ritual washing combined with repentance from sins can remove both uncleanness and iniquity. The Essene community, like the early Christians (2 Cor. 6.16; 1 Pet. 2.4f., etc.), saw itself as a living Temple, as we noted earlier. In the mystical texts there is an emphasis on revelation and participation in heavenly worship (cf. 1 Cor. 11.10; 13.1; Col. 2.18; 3.1-3; Hebr. 12.22f.). Like Jesus and his followers, Qumran saw itself as a community of eschatological fulfilment, viewing the Old Testament prophecies as fulfilled and/or coming to fulfilment in their own history and experience. Important Messianic ideas include Melchizedek as the heavenly redeemer called *Elohim*, "God" (11QMelch); the doctrine of two Messiahs (one Davidic and one Aaronic, e.g. 1QS 9.11; CD 12.23; 4QBless); and the view of the Messianic Son of God (4QFlor 1.11) who is possibly also linked with the heavenly Son of Man in Daniel 7.[31]

Jesus may overlap with the Essenes on certain ascetic aspects of his teaching, and he agrees with their emphasis on the authority of Scripture over the watering-down effect of the Pharisaic oral tradition. Over all, however, there is no evidence that Jesus had any significant links with them,[32] although he possibly refers to them in passing (see Luke 16.10[33]) and there may have been some contact via John the Baptist. More specifically, Jesus does appear to agree with the Essene position against the Pharisees on the subject of forbidding divorce (CD 4.21; 11QT 57.17f.), but he takes a more lenient line on many other issues including the Sabbath (contrast CD 11.13f. with Matt. 12.11).

4. The "Fourth Philosophy"

Identification

Josephus lists a "fourth" philosophy, which he treats quite differently from the other three (*Ant.* 18.23; *War* 2.118). These have variously been identified with the Zealots (a group in the Jewish War named after their violent zeal for the national autonomy of Israel), Cananeans, and Sicarii, though these were probably different entities, united mainly in their violent pursuit of the religious and political struggle against the Roman regime and its collaborators.[34] During the siege of Jerusalem there were in fact opposing factions fighting each other. They seem to have been guerrilla groups of various kinds, with differing sponsors and political agendas. Some, moreover, may to outsiders have seemed indistinguishable from ordinary bandits.

Historical Origin and Social Setting

Although the picture given by Josephus tends to conflate the different groups grouped together under the "Fourth Philosophy", a few basic observations can nevertheless help to identify their place within first-century Judaism.[35] The origin of zealot perspectives (not just of the specific faction later known by that name) must be sought in the armed struggle against idolatrous foreign rule in the early second century BC. A conservative, "Pharisaic" type of theology became linked with the political agenda of ridding Israel of Gentile rule and defilement, by violent means if necessary. These sentiments probably continued to simmer in a variety of quarters. As a distinct group in the first century, the militants were first led by Judas the Galilean (cf. Acts 5.37) from Gamla above the Sea of Tiberias, and Zadok the priest around AD 6, in objection to the census of Quirinius. After an extended period of intermittent local unrest and growing tension, open war broke out in AD 66. Judas's family remained influential in the resistance for nearly 70 years. Among his descendants, Menahem briefly attained power in Jerusalem during the War against Rome, and Eleazar ben Yair then led the last stand at Masada in 70–73. Intriguingly, there was also significant upper-class influence, probably through the fact that rival aristocratic groups hired bands of militants to accomplish their own political purposes in and around Jerusalem.

Religious Distinctives
Zealots were theologically conservative (Josephus says they followed the opinions of the Pharisees), but politically radical and committed to freedom through violent means. This is a pattern which also applied in the Second Revolt of AD 132–135 under Bar Kokhba. They held a fervent expectation of God's kingdom, to be brought about by active human revolutionary co-operation; their motivation was a fanatical zeal for the law and the purification of the land. Only a free Jerusalem could offer pure worship: therefore no obedience and no taxes should be rendered to the Emperor. Messianism was important for them, though it is not clear whether primarily for theological reasons or as a political expedient to exploit the aspirations of the masses. The rabbis later condemned the political activists for "hastening the end". They were eminently ready for martyrdom, frequently choosing voluntary death rather than subservience to an evil and godless Empire.

Impact on the New Testament
The revolutionaries' direct impact on the New Testament is not

great. Jesus was evidently not in favour of violent revolution.
In Mark 12, the question about tribute to Caesar was obviously
a politically explosive one; Jesus' answer was an unmistakable
— rebuff to the zealot position. While he may have allowed that
his ministry would bring "not ... peace but a sword" (Matt.
10.34), he is also reported in Matt. 26.52 as saying that all
those who take up the sword shall perish by the sword (was this
a kind of prophecy?).[36] His intention was emphatically not that
of armed rebellion (Mark 14.48).

Nevertheless, Jesus certainly taught and practised an
undaunted life-and-death commitment no less radical than that
of zealots, calling people to "take up their cross" for the sake of
the Kingdom of God (Mark 8.34f. par.): in other words, to face
execution. It may be that Jesus' saying is in fact an adaptation
of a guerrilla slogan. He, too, had an unwavering commitment
to the rule of God, and evidently no great fondness of Gentile
overlords (Mark 10.42 par.). It is also significant that Simon
the Zealot was a disciple (Luke 6.15; Acts 1.13). In rejecting
violence, however, the ministry of Jesus thus shows at best a
negative impact of the Fourth Philosophy.

In summary: we have seen that Jesus' primary conversation partners were the Pharisees. He shared much in
common with them, but also disagreed with established opinion
in a number of important areas. The Sadducees are important
primarily as the main adversaries during his ministry, and
eventually his passion, in Jerusalem. Indirect contact with
Essenes is plausible, but their influence on Jesus probably
remained marginal; and the impact of the various violent
factions appears to have been largely that of a political
counterfoil to Jesus' own programme.

This brings us to the end of our rapid survey of Jesus'
place in Judaism. And so we return to the question with which
we began:

Was Jesus a Christian?

Very clearly Jesus was first and foremost a Jew, and he disputed with other Jews about what at the time were Jewish questions. Even the earliest Christians were called the "sect of the Nazarenes" (Acts 24.5): probably Christianity did look much like any other Jewish sect at the time (Josephus, *Ant.* 18.64 calls them a "tribe").

In fact, Jesus said and did very little which would suggest that he wanted to distance himself from Judaism. He fully participated in Jewish piety including circumcision and temple sacrifice, without the slightest hint of criticism of those divinely ordained institutions as such. He approved of tithing (Matt. 23.23 par.), sacrifice,[37] and voluntary gifts to the Temple (Mark 12.41–44 par.). Jesus said grace before meals (Mark 6.41 par.; 14.22 par.), appealed to biblical purity laws,[38] and apparently wore tassels on his garments (compare Matt. 9.20 par.; 14.36 with 23.5 and Num. 15.37–39). He explicitly stated that he was only interested in the "lost sheep of the house of Israel" (Matt. 10.6), and although the pro-Jewish Gentile centurion of Capernaum receives a favourable reply from him, this is such an exception that it is specially highlighted. His encounter with the Syro-Phoenician woman (Mark 7.25–30) further proves his reluctance to have contact with Gentiles, although the healing of a demon-possessed man in the Gentile region of the Decapolis (Mark 5 par.) may be particularly significant.

In all this, Jesus was very much a devout first-century Palestinian Jew. Does that mean he was not a Christian?

The classic 19th-century liberal views of Jesus regarded the essence of Christianity as being fundamentally in imitation of the *religion of Jesus*.[39] For these writers, Jesus' own religion and experience of God makes him *by definition* the first Christian. To practise Christianity meant to imitate the piety and morality of Jesus.

This understanding, while it admittedly reflects some typical concerns of 19th century idealism and romanticism, is probably not inappropriate as far as it goes. It takes into account some valid theological ideas about the relationship between Christ and the Christian, and encourages an attitude of imitation which the New Testament itself favours.

The major difficulties of the liberal view, however, are twofold. First, it ignores much of classical orthodox christology: those aspects, that is, which have to do with faith *in* Jesus rather than just the faith *of* Jesus. And secondly, its often sentimental picture of the piety and morality of Jesus looks uncannily like that of the 19th century liberal bourgeoisie, as Albert Schweitzer made clear in his famous book *The Quest of the Historical Jesus*.

In the 20th century we have not been immune from the danger of creating Jesus in our own image. Illustrations of this range from culturally imperialistic forms of evangelism to the giddy identification of the kingdom of God with political agendas of the right or the left.

Nevertheless, in the wake of dramatic literary and archaeological discoveries and rediscoveries in the 19th and 20th centuries, we are today in the fortunate position of being able to learn probably more about conditions at the time of Jesus than any generation of Christians since the first century.

In the light of this new information it seems possible to conclude that in several important respects Jesus was definitely *not* a Christian. First, being a Christian has historically also meant *not* being a Jew, and vice versa. For better or for worse (often the latter), the relationship between these two faiths has typically been defined as one of mutual exclusion and adversity. This of course has led to much needless ostracizing and persecution, at first of Christians by Jews and then of Jews by Christians. It is a strange but significant fact in this regard that to the day of his death the founder of Christianity by and large showed no appreciable interest in people who were not Jews. —> really?

What is more, it is indeed difficult to isolate areas in which Jesus stood *outside* or *over against* the Judaism of his day. True, his combination of a piety of intimate relationship with God, Messianic claims, and clear anti-establishment criticism makes it awkward to fit him comfortably into any of the groups Josephus describes. Nor does he agree well with later normative rabbinic Judaism. But he does not fall outside the much more broadly defined playing field of first-century Judaism.

There are other obvious ways in which Jesus was not a Christian. Christianity is concerned not only with faith in God but also with a cluster of beliefs about Jesus Christ as the Son of God, and about the New Testament as containing the authoritative revelation about him. What is more, the vast majority of Christians would subscribe to the ecumenical creeds of the Church which give further definition to the Christian faith. Clearly none of this is particularly useful in discussing Jesus of Nazareth, to whose thought world significant aspects of Christian practice and doctrine would have seemed foreign – as both journalistic and scholarly treatments of Jesus never tire of reminding us.[40]

For these and other reasons, therefore, our question probably must be answered in the negative: Jesus was not a Christian, in the ordinary sense of that term. The first Christians, then, would have to be either those who first formulated a separate religion (some scholars, especially Jewish ones, have suggested Paul); or his first followers (some Catholic theologians make the attractive suggestion that Mary the mother of Jesus was the first Christian); or else those who were first named after him.[41]

However, this is perhaps not the last word on the subject. It can be reasonably argued that *two* religions grew historically out of the same soil of first-century Judaism: Christianity and rabbinic Judaism. And although Jesus was not a Christian, it is here that we can identify ways in which Jesus is rightly regarded as the author of Christianity and stands in organic continuity with his followers to this day.[42] He was a first-century Jew, but several of his most central concerns have become key *Christian* concerns. This does not mean they might not also be Jewish, but merely that they are of key importance to Christianity, and can be shown to be in continuity with it.

Without going into detail, a list of these central concerns would surely include the emphasis on God's gracious forgiveness of sinners and an intimate relationship with God as merciful Father as well as Lord. Jesus taught the acceptance of the weak, the afflicted as well as the despised into the Kingdom of God, even before the strong and the righteous. His interest in the marginalized on occasion extended even to Gentiles; and although the early church fiercely debated *how* the Gentiles should be included, *that* they should be part of God's plan of salvation seems at least consistent with some of Jesus' beliefs and concerns (note his universalist affirmation that many will come from East and West, Matt. 8.11 par.).[43] Jesus, like Paul and (at least) the early Gentile church, showed a relative disregard for the externalism of established religion and in their interpretation of Scripture placed a higher priority on the command of love for one's neighbour.

One could further argue that Jesus' *view of himself* included the idea that he was the divinely appointed redeemer of Israel, the one through whom the Kingdom would come in. He spoke of the likelihood of his own suffering at the hands of the authorities; indeed he interpreted this suffering as necessary and somehow of redemptive significance. Given the Old Testament figure of the suffering righteous, as we saw in Chapter Four, even his belief in divine vindication seems plausible in its original setting – and in early Christianity it was understandably applied to his resurrection. Finally, he spoke of a heavenly Son of Man who would come as Judge and divine ruler, and according to the Gospels he may have subtly identified himself with that Son of Man. This, too, while not identical, is nevertheless fully compatible with what Christians believe about the exaltation and future return of Christ.

There are, moreover, several quite palpable *practices* of Jesus which had a kind of "institutional" significance, and therefore continuity, in the early church. One of these is a baptism of repentance, which Jesus both underwent (Mark 1.4, 9 par.) and administered (John 3.22, 26; contrast 4.1f.), and perhaps authorized (John 4.2; cf. Matt. 28.19). Secondly, he maintained and was remembered for a table fellowship which continued in the early church (1 Cor. 11.23–34; cf. Luke 24.30f., 35; John 21.12f.; Acts 2.42). This of course is particularly obvious in the Christian celebration of the Eucharist, which from the earliest extant documents appealed to the memory of the Last Supper (1 Cor. 11.23–25). There is, moreover, a significant personal continuity in that at least some of the Twelve whom he appointed became the leadership of the first Christian church. Jesus' attitude to existing institutions could also be cited as distinctively influential: the early Christian view of the nature of marriage and divorce appealed to his teaching, and at least one group of early Christians may have claimed his example in their radical attitude to the Temple (Acts 6.14; 7.48f.).

We might also add that although Jesus does not appear to have made his intentions unambiguous enough to avoid subsequent controversy, his followers clearly linked the proclamation of the gospel for Gentiles to their experiences with him after his resurrection. Both Matthew and Luke, as well as John and Paul, make it very clear that the risen Jesus was understood to have appointed his disciples to preach the gospel to the Jews and also to the Gentiles. However one may understand the resurrection appearances, there can be no doubt that the early Church was convinced that the mission to the Gentiles derived from the risen Jesus himself.

In the end, Jesus was not a Christian, but a Jew. Nevertheless, the Judaism of his time was the seedbed out of which grew two movements that ultimately became world religions: Christianity and Rabbinic Judaism. Although not identical, the Christian faith *in* Jesus is organically and inextricably linked to the Jewish faith *of* Jesus.

his point ⟨

How best can we characterize this ongoing connection with the life of the Church? One could argue that the surviving link between Jesus and Christianity consists primarily in Christian discipleship, the call to *follow* him; or in the continuity of Christian experience of the Spirit of God with that of Jesus.[44] Some will look in this context to the practice of baptism, which relates both to the Spirit and to discipleship, linking Jesus both with his Jewish predecessors (John the Baptist and possibly the Qumran sect) and with the subsequent practice of the Church. Similarly, it is possible to affirm that Jesus' interpretation of his Last Supper with the disciples finds its legitimate ongoing continuity and reality in the Christian celebration of the Eucharist. Chapter Six will serve as another kind of window on the path that leads from Jesus' own spirituality to that of the Church.

But however one perceives the vital link between Jesus and Christianity in view of this discussion, at the end of the day there is still good reason to identify Jesus of Nazareth, in the words of one early Christian, as "the pioneer and perfecter of our faith" (Hebrews 12.2).

Chapter Six

How Did Jesus Pray?

One of the ways in which we can examine the continuity between Jesus of Nazareth and the Church is by studying Jesus' own spirituality and assessing its influence on the Christians who claimed to follow him as Lord. In this chapter, then, we will focus on one illustration of this, taking as our example the basic elements of Jesus' prayer life and their impact on Christian spirituality in the Apostolic church.[1] In the New Testament's reflection on Jesus' theory and practice of prayer, we find a window of insight into one of the organic links between Jesus of Nazareth and the faith of the early Christians.

Central to the experience of the early church was an ongoing relationship with the exalted Jesus. This relationship is predominantly described by metaphors relating either to participation in Christ or to imitation of him. Participation affirms the present and continuing reality of salvation and is expressed (i) in terms of the body of Christ (Rom. 12; 1 Cor. 12), the vine and its branches (John 15), and the treasure or citizenship in heaven (Matt. 6; Phil. 3; Col. 3; Eph. 2; Heb. 12); and (ii) in the narrative metaphor of the believer's incorporation in the death and resurrection of Christ, both initially at baptism (Rom. 6; Col. 2) and continually in the afflictions and aspirations of the Christian life (2 Cor. 4.7–12; Col. 1.24; Heb. 13.12f.; 1 Pet. 4.13; cf. Mark 8.34; 10.39 par.).

The image of participation neatly dovetails with that of imitation, which was a practice deeply ingrained in the Jewish understanding of the teacher-disciple relationship.[2] Paul, the former Pharisee, repeatedly encourages his churches to "become imitators of me as I am of Christ" (1 Cor. 11.1 and passim). For a believer to be "in Christ" also implies an obligation to follow his teaching and example. Aspects of both participation and imitation are already present in Jesus' own teaching, and are actively encouraged in the Apostolic churches.

Perhaps the single most important practical expression of both participation in Christ and imitation of Christ was prayer. Prayer conveys most profoundly the openness, trust and dependence which characterize a true relationship with God. It is for this reason that the prayer life of Jesus will here be seen as an essential key to his own spirituality and, inasmuch as the influence can be demonstrated, to that of his disciples.

The material itself suggests an approach in three stages, reflecting the interpretation of Jesus' prayer life in the Synoptic Gospels, in the Johannine literature, and in the remainder of the New Testament.   Although redactional questions will be addressed as they present themselves, I do not intend in this chapter to distinguish sharply between the prayers of the historical Jesus and their re-formulation by the gospel writers. Instead, I want here to concentrate on the ways in which the remembrance of Jesus' prayer life left its impression on the New Testament church.

The Synoptic Gospels

Jesus' Experience of Prayer

The public ministry of Jesus begins with his baptism by John. As a symbol of personal and national repentance and restoration, it was evidently an experience of great spiritual significance for Jesus. This is true not least in view of the accompanying vision of the Spirit of God descending like a dove while a heavenly voice declared him to be the specially favoured "Son of God" (Mark 1.9–11 par.). This experience appears in turn to have precipitated the episode of Jesus' temptation in the wilderness. In Matthew and Luke this "temptation" takes the form of an identity crisis over his newly affirmed "Son of God" title (Matt. 4.3, 6 par.), with Satan already being cast as his main adversary. Although not explicitly concerned with prayer, these first two scenes of baptism and temptation are in fact highly suggestive of the basic orientation which characterizes Jesus' spiritual life, since they show his whole purpose and identity to be centred on his baptismal commissioning and relationship to God as Son. In the narrative of the Gospels, three crises precipitate a testing of this identity: the temptation in the wilderness, the questioning of his disciples at Caesarea Philippi, and the prayer at Gethsemane.

Perhaps more than any other part of the New Testament, the stories of Jesus manifest a dramatic, sometimes breathtaking spirituality of close familial intimacy with God and an external-ized, cosmic conflict with evil. Satan and his demons are the chief opponents of Jesus and the imminent kingdom of God (in addition to the healing miracles see Mark 4.15, 8.33 par.; Luke 13.16; 22.3, 31); his message and ministry have come to topple them from power (see especially Luke 10.18, Mark 3.27 par.).

Among the Synoptic evangelists it is Luke who develops the theme of Jesus' prayer most fully. Here, Jesus is praying when he receives his post-baptismal vision (3.21). He prepares for the selection of the Twelve by spending a night in prayer (6.12; cf. 5.16), and he thanks God for the successful mission of the Seventy (10.21f.). Both his question to the disciples at Caesarea Philippi (9.18) and his transfiguration (9.28–36) appear in the context of prayer. Luke makes prayer the repeated subject of Jesus' teaching (Ch. 11, 18) and he alone reports on Jesus' intercession for the disciples (22.31f.).[3]

According to all three Synoptic Gospels, Jesus nurtured his close relationship with God above all in frequent, extended periods of solitary prayer. He repeatedly withdraws from friend and foe alike to a lonely place at night or before daybreak (Mark 1.35, 45 par.). The location is often a mountain (Luke 6.12, 9.28), but in the end a quiet spot in the garden of Gethsemane, just beneath the city in the Kidron valley (Mark

14.32–42 par.).

Like his Jewish contemporaries, Jesus also assumed that the Temple was a place of prayer (Luke 18.9–14; Mark 11.17 par.). He undoubtedly prayed there himself, as indeed he joined in the customary forms of prayer associated with the annual Festivals in Jerusalem, including the Passover celebration which concluded with the singing of the second half of the *Hallel* (Psalms 116–18: cf. Mark 14.26 par.). Jesus will have participated in the daily recitation of both the *Shema* ("Hear O Israel", Deut. 6.5ff: note Mark 12.29f.) and possibly early versions of the *Amidah* (Eighteen Benedictions) or the *Kaddish*, synagogal prayers whose concerns are also present in his own teaching.[4]

While Jesus is often heard to stress the importance of *faith* for healing and deliverance (and to rebuke the disciples for their lack of it), he clearly also believed that the most difficult obstacles were only to be overcome by the kind of faith that is nurtured in persistent personal prayer (Mark 9.29 par.). That, it seems, is where he himself sought and found the strength to carry on his ministry. Above all else, the Gospels present Jesus' confident spirituality as rooted and anchored in the security of his relationship with God as Father (which, at least for Luke, begins long before his baptism: Luke 2.49).[5]

At the same time, it is in fact rare for Synoptic miracle stories explicitly to depict Jesus at prayer.[6] Exorcisms in particular are never said to be accompanied by prayer. This is possibly due to the preferred image of Jesus as the one who, fortified by the assurance of his sonship, appears in the role of the "stronger man" to assault and defeat Beelzebul (Mark 3.27; cf. Luke 11.22).

From the centrality of Jesus' relationship with God arose his deep conviction that all the circumstances of life, history and even nature were subject to the unstoppable advance of the Kingdom of God. This, clearly, is the consistent attitude in his personal encounters, where the call of God puts all human loyalties in their place (Matt. 8.21f. par., etc.). People came to recognize the extraordinary power and authority which emanated from Jesus' prayer life (Matt. 8.8f. par.; 19.13).

However, Jesus seems not merely to have claimed this closeness with God for himself. By his own example and teaching, especially in parables, he encouraged his followers to adopt the same sense of conscious expectancy and awareness of God's presence and care for them. Jesus took for granted *that* his disciples would pray (Mark 11.25 par.), and was more concerned with *how* they prayed: boldly, daringly, expectantly; with undaunted persistence and faith (Matt. 7.7 par.); privately and in secret (Matt. 6.6). Prayer addresses a *loving* Father and a *righteous* Judge who, far more than fallible earthly fathers and wavering unrighteous judges, will promptly act (Luke 11.11–13 par.; 18.1–8). Believers are to pray not in meaning-less, unthinking words (Matt. 6.7); not expecting God's mercy unless they themselves were merciful (Matt. 6.14f. par.). Humility and childlike candour are needed in approaching God (Luke 18.9–14, 15–17); but so is the sheer *chutzpah* of calling on a friend at midnight (Luke 11.5–8). Prayer protects against worry (Matt. 6.11, 25–33; cf. Phil. 4.7) and losing heart (Luke 18.1). It is a safe haven in the time of trial (Matt. 6.13; 26.41), and corporate prayer in particular is sure to be heard (Matt. 18.19f.). In view of the massive Kingdom harvest, the disciples are to ask God for workers (Luke 10.2 par.), which is in effect to ask him for the human resources needed that the Kingdom may come.[7]

Although the Synoptic Gospels do not offer much explicit evidence, what little we do know suggests that Jesus himself practised these same principles of prayer.

Jesus' Prayers

Six actual prayers are recorded and merit our attention; an additional one in Luke 22.31f. is merely reported and will be considered together with John 17 below.

1. First there is Jesus' thanksgiving for revelation in Luke 10.21, par. Matt. 11.25f. In Luke, not implausibly, the setting for this prayer is Jesus' joyful response to the successful mission of the Seventy:

> At that same hour Jesus rejoiced in the Holy Spirit and said, "I thank you, Father, Lord of heaven and earth, because you have hidden these things from the wise and intelligent and have revealed them to infants; yes, Father, for such was your gracious will."

The defeat of Satan and the demons in his name (Luke 10.17f.) causes Jesus to rejoice. He celebrates the mysterious work of God who has chosen to manifest the arrival of his Kingdom not to the theologians and the establishment, but to the simple people ("infants") who have become his disciples. Here, then, Luke presents a spontaneous, Spirit-filled expression of gratitude for God's work, which springs from Jesus' childlike, trusting identification with the Father's intentions: "Yes, Father, for such was your gracious will."

2. By far the most important passage is Luke 11.1–13, which contains the Lord's Prayer. This prayer, whether in its Lucan or Matthean version, strikingly encapsulates Jesus' own attitude to prayer and to God. In some ways the Church Father Tertullian (c. AD 160–225) was probably not amiss to regard it as the very essence of the gospel.[8]

In Matthew 6.9–13, the longer and more familiar version of the Lord's Prayer is presented as part of the Sermon on the Mount. It is one of very few passages in which Jesus speaks of *corporate* prayer (but cf. Matt. 18.19f.). In the Matthean context its form and brevity agree well with the gospel's criticism of both spiritual ostentation in the synagogue and meaningless wordiness among Gentiles (Matt. 6.5–8).

Luke, by contrast, has this text as the first of two passages specifically on prayer (18.1–13 being the second). His version is usually thought to be closer to the original, although Matthew's prayer shows signs of having been used liturgically in the primitive Aramaic-speaking church.[9]   Significantly for our purposes, the disciples' request, "Lord, teach us to pray" (Luke 11.1), arises *from their observation of Jesus at prayer*. Even allowing that part of their motive is a desire not to be outdone by John's disciples (11.1), they clearly admire and want to imitate their master in this regard.   Thus they ask him to show them his paradigm which they can follow.

For Luke, the prayer simply begins with "Father" – most likely "Abba" in Aramaic.   This word, which was a child's familiar address to a father or older man (although expressing a greater sense of respect and loyalty than "Daddy"[10]), was apparently Jesus' characteristic form of addressing God.[11]   Even the early Greek speaking church regarded this Aramaic term to be so significant that its use continued without translation (Mark 14.36; Rom. 8.15; Gal. 4.6).   Clearly it was thought to symbolize Jesus' own characteristically close relationship with the Father, in which Christians now participate.   His relationship with God here evokes and undergirds the childlike trust in which believers, too, can pray.

In substance, these verses display the manifest conviction that true prayer intends first and foremost to affirm this paternal will of God: it wants to contribute to his eternal glory by magnifying him in the temporal world.   There is no hint here of asking God to change his intended course of action, or of bending his will in keeping with human plans and desires.   That kind of prayer would betray a view of God which is too small and petty-minded.   Instead, the believer's will and needs are conceived as an integral and significant part of the larger concern for God's kingdom on earth.   As in contemporary Jewish spirituality, the relationship between God and his people in this prayer is such that when their will is transformed into God's will, God is glorified in providing the answer to their needs.   The third-century Rabban Gamaliel III is quoted as saying, "Do his will as your will, that he may do your will as his will" (Mishnah, *Aboth* 2.4).

The Lord's Prayer, then, has as its definitive concern the believer's trusting affirmation of the will of God. In the Synoptic tradition, Jesus' own prayer life and teaching were seen to indicate that one cannot in fact genuinely pray for the hallowing of God's name, the coming of his kingdom and the accomplishing of his purposes, without undergoing a profound re-alignment of one's own will with the will of God. All three Synoptic Gospels (as well as the Church Fathers) see Gethsemane as the place where Jesus most graphically demonstrated this.

Nevertheless, it would be a serious misunderstanding of Jesus' prayer to suppose that this affirmation of God's purposes simply implies a kind of spiritual sublimation of human needs and desires. Personal petitions do form an important part of the Lord's Prayer. They are best understood as the translation into the concrete personal realm of the first three requests. May God's name be hallowed, his will be done and his kingdom come – by his providing his people's material sustenance day by day, forgiving their sins in the context of human reconciliation, and protecting them from the coming Trial by which the Evil One wants to make them deny God's providential fatherhood and bully them into allegiance.[12]   And thus, in fact, the Lord's Prayer completes a full circle: as Jesus' own ministry makes clear, God's name is honoured and his kingdom comes precisely where his people are delivered from evil and their material and spiritual sustenance is supplied (see especially Matt. 10.7f. par.; 12.28 par.). Petition, then, has its rightful place in prayer: not as a plea that God may change his course of action, but as the concrete shape *on earth as it is in heaven* of "Hallowed be Your name; Your kingdom come".

3. The third recorded prayer of Jesus is set in the garden of Gethsemane. According to all four gospels, after the Last

Supper Jesus left the city with his disciples for the Mount of Olives. They appear, however, to have stopped in an olive grove or garden in the valley, just across the Kidron. Jesus went aside by himself to pray, in Mark's version (14.36): "Abba, Father, for you all things are possible; remove this cup from me; yet, not what I want, but what you want." Evident internal strife marks this final time alone with God (Matt. 26.38 par.; cf. John 12.27). Along with the discovery of Judas' betrayal, the events of the preceding days had made it quite clear that this must be the end. We saw in Chapter Four that Jesus had understood and affirmed God's will for him at least since Caesarea Philippi (cf. Mark 8.31 par.). Here, however, he comes closer than at any other time to a plea that God may change his purpose – a theme which lends the accounts a strong flavour of authenticity. This shows Jesus at his most human, the Jesus whom the writer to the Hebrews later upholds as the high priest subject to weakness (4.14–5.10, especially 5.7f.).

Even here, however, with a painfully burning request in view, Jesus is portrayed as drawing on an unquestioned trust in the providence of God. In spite of palpably desperate circumstances, his *cri de cœur* begins with "Abba" – Mark's account contains the only explicit use of this term in the Gospels. His task is harsh, but it is still the assignment of the same God whose paternal purpose he knows to be unchangingly providential, merciful, and all-powerful. This conviction allows him to affirm God's will as his – without thereby stifling his natural human desire of going only to the brim of the bitter cup, without having to drink it down to the dregs (Mark 14.36). The Lord's Prayer here becomes the prayer of Jesus in a very personal way. With his trust in man betrayed and all certainty eclipsed, Jesus' faith remains founded on the bedrock of the Fatherhood of God. Because God is Father, "Your will be done" still means "Your kingdom come". Even when it seems all but impossible to pronounce them, those words remain a prayer for salvation.

Job, in a somewhat different spirit, may have said, "Though he slay me, yet will I trust in him" (Job 13.15 KJV). Jesus' prayer, however, shows not righteous tenacity so much as a humble, obedient hope in the unchanging goodness of the Father's will.[13]

4. The last words of Jesus are reported differently in the four gospels. All three Synoptics show Jesus praying on the cross; but of the three traditional prayers, two appear only in Luke and one only in Mark and Matthew. The historical order and setting are difficult to recover; nevertheless, there are a number of consistent and recurring themes in these accounts.

Jesus, being nailed to the cross, asks: "Father, forgive them; for they do not know what they are doing" (Luke 23.34).[14] At least three significant observations can be made about this prayer. First, along with the promise to the repentant criminal, Jesus' prayer provides a kind of confirmation of the atoning and redemptive significance of his martyrdom on the cross (a theme which in Luke appears elsewhere only at 22.20 and 24.46f.). Secondly, it vividly illustrates the attitude of submission, mercy and fortitude for which the passion of Jesus was prominently remembered in the early church (see especially 1 Pet. 2.21–25). And thirdly, at the same time this request strikingly embodies his own (and early Christian) radical teaching about love and prayer for one's enemies (Luke 6.27–36 par.; Rom. 12.14; 1 Cor. 4.12).

5. Then there is Jesus' strongly attested cry of dereliction on the Cross: "My God, my God, why have you forsaken me?" We briefly discussed this earlier (see p. 95f.), but it is worth taking up once more in the present context. Quite apart from the historical questions of Jesus' success or failure, it is hard to exaggerate the literary and theological impact of this prayer. Its dramatic significance in Mark and Matthew is heightened all the more in that it represents Jesus' only words spoken from the

Cross. On the most obvious and literal level, this is the last outcry of a broken man, crushed in spirit as he feels abandoned by man and God. The bystanders, in a stroke of tragic irony, mistake Jesus' Hebrew address to God (*Eli, Eli*; Mark has Aramaic *Eloi, Eloi*) as a call for the expected end-time return of Elijah (*Eliyahu*). They are thus, it seems, completely blind to the remarkable transparency of these words. Here is a man, alone and in terrible agony in his dying moments, casting his desperate plight before a silent God.

And yet, as we saw, these very words explicitly recall Psalm 22, the quintessential prayer of the suffering innocent. Here is the bitterly forthright lament of the righteous believer who, bereft of every human consolation, holds on to the only certainty that remains: God's unchanging character as the Holy One who did not put his people's trust to shame in the past. What is more, lament (verses 1–21a) before long turns into thanksgiving and praise for deliverance obtained (21b–31), even in the face of imminent death (v. 29).

Whether the whole of Psalm 22 resonates in Jesus' words is of course unclear; the passion narratives, at any rate, clearly assign it pride of place in their interpretation of his experience (cf. also v. 7f. with Mark 15.29 par. and Luke 23.35; v. 18 with Mark 15.24 par.). Here the evangelists depict Jesus the righteous, shaken but unblemished, faithful to the last.

6. Jesus' final utterance, recorded simply as a loud cry in Matthew and Mark, is also rendered as a prayer in Luke: "Father, into your hands I commend my spirit" (23.46). Explicitly or implicitly, the bearing of this prayer from Psalm 31.5 typifies the death of Jesus in all four Gospels (cf. also John 19.30). Having drunk the bitter cup, true to his call even when this exacted the ultimate price, Jesus expires. For his enemies, this is the perfunctory but welcome seal of his failure; for the evangelists, the manner of his death shows his cosmic, crowning act of submission to the one who, nevertheless, is *Father*.

These last three prayers of Gethsemane and the cross had a profound impact on Christian spirituality in the New Testament and beyond. It seems that Luke, for instance, consciously formulated the prayers of the Church in Acts to reflect the prayers of Jesus.[15]

More particularly, the accounts of Jesus' struggle at Gethsemane became a natural illustration of the Lord's Prayer in the Church Fathers,[16] while the tradition of his prayers on the cross fed directly into Christian reflection on martyrdom. Luke's prayers of Jesus on the cross recur on the lips of the first Christian martyr in Acts,[17] and the attitude they exemplify is explicitly commended in 1 Peter 2.23: even in the midst of abuse and suffering, Christ "entrusted himself to the one who judges justly" (cf. Luke 23.46).

Martyrdom, it seems, came to be closely associated with participation in the suffering of Jesus. Thus we hear of the Apostles "being dishonoured for the sake of the Name" (Acts 5.41), and "filling up what is lacking in the sufferings of Christ" (Col. 1.24; cf. 2 Cor. 4.10f.). In the second century, Ignatius of Antioch looks forward to becoming "an imitator of the sufferings of my God" (*Romans* 6.3), while Polycarp rejoices that he may "share in the cup of Christ" (*Martyrdom of Polycarp* 14.2).   Christ, indeed, suffers in the martyrs to manifest his glory (*Passion of Perpetua* 6.2; Eusebius, *Ecclesiastical History* 5.1.23). In the light of this, the traditions about Jesus' prayer life were obviously of broad exemplary importance for the spirituality of the early church.

The Gospel of John

As in other respects, the Fourth Gospel differs markedly from the Synoptics in its view of Jesus' prayer life. There is no account of his baptism, and the post-baptismal vision is reported of John the Baptist rather than of Jesus (1.32). There is no temptation narrative, no teaching specifically on prayer, and no prayer on the cross. On the other hand, the Synoptic Gospels' description of Jesus' relationship to God as Father is now translated into a glorified relationship of the Son who is one with the Father (10.30). Jesus here is the Word become Flesh (1.14); he has life in himself, authority to judge, and his voice raises the dead (5.26–29; 6.39f.; cf. 11.43f.). Anyone who knows him knows the Father, and he and the Father make their dwelling with those who love them (14.7, 21, 23). Jesus speaks for the Father (12.50), so that whatever he says and does he has first seen or heard from him (3.11, 32; 5.19, 30; 8.26, 38, 40; 15.15). Jesus withdraws to the mountain by himself (6.15), but we do not explicitly hear of him spending long hours at prayer. John's picture of Jesus does not present his prayer life as a model to be followed by the believer, but instead portrays spiritual and mystical union with Christ as being in itself the way to the Father (14.6; 15.1ff.). The disciples are to pray in his name (14.13f.), but there is no implicit encouragement that they are to pray *like* him.

Aside from the grace before the miracle of the loaves and fishes (6.11), his first prayer occurs at the tomb of Lazarus (11.41f.). Here, however, is the utterance of the Son who is one with the Father, and hardly a prayer to be emulated by his disciples:

> Father, I thank you for having heard me. I knew
> that you always hear me, but I have said this for
> the sake of the crowd standing here, so that they
> may believe that you sent me.

The same spirit of oneness with the Father occurs in chapter 12, a parallel to the Gethsemane prayer set here at the beginning of the passion narrative. Jesus, clearly troubled by the events that lie ahead, considers the prayer "Father, save me from this hour" – but only to move beyond it and pray instead for the glorification of God's name, which of course is why he has come (12.27–28, 30):

> Now my soul is troubled. And what should I say?
> Father, save me from this hour. But it is for this
> reason that I have come to this hour. Father, glo-
> rify your name." Then a voice came from heaven:
> "I have glorified it, and I will glorify it again." ...
> Jesus answered, "This voice has come for your
> sake, not for mine."

The Johannine Jesus, though resolute in going to the cross,
nevertheless shares the anxiety described in the synoptic
Gethsemane accounts. Here as there, however, the will of the
Father is the higher concern. The Son for John is at one with
the Father and faithfully seeks to glorify him; immediate
confirmation of this is given from heaven.

One final text is of eminent significance in understanding
the early church's vision of Jesus' prayer life: John 17 presents
the most extensive prayer text of any of the Gospels. For
several centuries this has been known as Jesus' "high priestly
prayer", since one of its main themes is Jesus' representation of
his disciples before God. A term like "testamentary prayer"
may, however, be more descriptive.[18] We have here in any case
a powerful Johannine portrait of Jesus at prayer; and whether
the historical Jesus used such words or not, they do express to a
remarkable extent both the spirit and major themes of Jesus'
teaching and practice of prayer.

The prayer begins with Jesus asking to be glorified so that
he may in turn glorify the Father (17.1–5). This theme is
clearly a continuation of the previous prayer in 12.28, here
applied to his imminent crucifixion and exaltation in the "hour"
that has now "come". Indeed the whole passage can be read as
an elaboration of the request "Glorify your name", clearly in
close connection with the synoptic Gethsemane prayer "Your
will be done." In other words, Jesus here prays for the
glorification of the Father by his completion of the intended
design, including the return to his eternal glory.

A crucial part of Jesus', and thereby the Father's, glorification is the protection and sanctification of those who have been entrusted to him, who do not belong to the world but are sent into it. In a sense Jesus cannot be fully glorified if any of his people are lost, since he is glorified in them (17.10) and has given them the glory he received from the Father (17.22). This is in order that they may be completely one, may see Jesus' glory and be fully united with him (17.21–26). Thus the world will be able to know plainly both Jesus' and God's love for his people (17.23).

Two important conclusions follow for the understanding of Jesus' spirituality in the Gospel of John. The first was intimated earlier: unlike the Synoptic Gospels, the Fourth Gospel presents Jesus' prayer life not primarily as an example to imitate, but as indicative of the Son's mystical union with the Father, in which believers come to *participate*.

Secondly, more than any other text in the Gospels, John 17 highlights Jesus' role in effective *intercession* for his disciples both now and as they continue their lives in the world. Here, as elsewhere (especially in the Farewell Discourses, John 13–17), the evangelist's presentation anticipates and almost fuses the transition from the earthly to the heavenly ministry of Jesus. The opposition of the Evil One continues after Jesus' victory on the cross; and the world, for which Jesus emphatically does *not* pray (v. 9), is Satan's domain (cf. 12.31; also 1 John 5.19). Nevertheless, believers now have a powerful advocate with the Father whose continuing intercession is sure to be heard, so that the adversary cannot prevail.[19] Through Jesus' intercession, they are assured of their participation in the love of God and the union of the Father and the Son: "I in them and you in me, that they may become completely one, so that the world may know that you have sent me and have loved them even as you have loved me" (John 17.23).

At this point it is worth briefly retracing our steps to the

Synoptic Gospels, where Jesus' intercession is not a major theme. True, there are several sayings of the form "Whoever is ashamed of me.../denies me before others, I also will deny before my Father in heaven" (Mark 8.38 par. Luke 9.26; Matt. 10.33 par. Luke 12.9; cf. Rev. 3.5). This implies that, at least in regard to the final judgement, Jesus' advocacy is of crucial importance. Nevertheless, Luke 22.31f. is the only explicit Synoptic reference to Jesus' intercession on behalf of others[20]:

> Simon, Simon, listen! Satan has demanded to sift all of you like wheat, but I have prayed for you that your own faith may not fail; and you, when once you have turned back, strengthen your brothers.

Faced by the impending tribulation of his arrest and the likely scattering of his followers, Jesus perceives Satan's antagonism to this small band of disciples and confidently entrusts Peter's (and through him the disciples') continuing faithfulness to God. Jesus once again is stronger than Satan; his prayer therefore must be superior to that of the adversary (who, it appears, must also *request* to "sift" the disciples; cf. Job 1f.). Like John 17, these verses occur in the context of the passion narrative, quite possibly pointing to the Lord's continuing post–resurrection role of intercession with the Father.

This theme is one which also comes to prominence in Romans, Hebrews, and 1 John.

The Rest of the New Testament

Although there are a large number of potentially relevant texts about the exalted Christ or the activity of the Spirit, I want here to concentrate specifically on a few New Testament passages which allude directly to Jesus praying. This will serve further to indicate the influence of the spirituality of Jesus in the early church.

Romans 8 celebrates the believers' liberation from sin and death by "the Spirit of life in Christ Jesus" and their adoption as children of God. Throughout the passage, "Christ" and "Spirit" are apparently interchangeable: as "Christ is in you", so the Spirit dwells in you (vv. 9–11). This Spirit of Christ comes to the aid of Christians who, in their weakness and longing for their future glory, may not know how to pray as they ought; so the Spirit, who is intimately known by God, "intercedes with sighs too deep for words" (v. 26f.). It is the same Spirit who was earlier said to confirm and bear witness to their adoption as children of God who may boldly address him with the prayer of Jesus, "Abba!" (v. 15f.; cf. Gal. 4.6). The identification is completed in v. 34, where the same Christ Jesus who died and was raised is now at the right hand of God and "intercedes for us". For Paul, then, Christians' imitation of Jesus' own prayer goes hand in hand with participation in the benefits of his heavenly intercession for them. Christ's position at the right hand of God is here not simply an expression of his exalted power, but enables him uniquely to win the Father's favour on behalf of his people, the Church. It is through him, and presumably by the power of his intercession, that Christians have inalienable access to the love of God in Christ (vv. 31–39; cf. Eph. 3.12).

Jesus' prayer is not the explicit subject of attention elsewhere in Paul's writings. Nevertheless, other texts about Christ's being at the right hand of God (Col. 3.1; cf. Eph. 1.20; 1 Pet. 3.22) are at least compatible with, if not indeed suggestive of, the theme of his intercession for believers.[21] Similarly, what Paul says about sharing in the sufferings of Christ (2 Cor. 4.10f., Phil. 3.10, Col. 1.24; cf. 1 Pet. 4.13) is quite plausibly in keeping with the "Gethsemane spirituality" we discussed earlier. The related (but more general) theme of Christ's self-humbling obedience, even to the point of death on a cross, is specifically endorsed as the paradigm of Christian conduct in the well-known christological passage of Phil. 2.5–11.

Some of the most evocative language about Jesus' prayer life occurs in the anonymous letter to the Hebrews. Here the

primary emphasis of the theme of Christ's sitting at God's right
hand is to distinguish him from angels and lesser beings (1.13).
Such "high" christology notwithstanding, in chapter 5.7–9 the
author wields powerful words about the humanity of Jesus,
highlighting what appears to be the struggle at Gethsemane:

> In the days of his flesh, Jesus offered up prayers
> and supplications, with loud cries and tears, to the
> one who was able to save him from death, and he
> was heard because of his reverent submission.
> Although he was a Son, he learned obedience
> through what he suffered; and having been made
> perfect, he became the source of eternal salvation
> for all who obey him, having been designated by
> God a high priest according to the order of
> Melchizedek.

Taking the humanity of Jesus seriously, this New Testament
writer regards Jesus' anxious Gethsemane prayer and his
attitude of submission as both exemplary (cf. Heb. 12.2) *and*
contributing to the redemption in which Christians participate.
Because Jesus experienced weakness and testing as they do, he
can sympathize and deal gently with them (cf. 4.15).

But conversely, Hebrews goes on to say, Jesus has
"passed through the heavens" (4.14) and entered behind the
curtain of the heavenly Holy of Holies (6.19f.; 9.25) as sinless,
eternal high priest on behalf of his people. As such he is the
guarantor of their salvation and their effective intercessor:
"Consequently he is able for all time to save those who
approach God through him, since he always lives to make
intercession for them" (7.25). Once again it is clear how both
the motif of exemplary submission at Gethsemane and that of
intercession for his disciples are taken up from the traditions
about the prayer of Jesus.

We come then, finally, to 1 John 2.1f., where Jesus once
again appears as the heavenly advocate:

> My little children, I am writing these things to you

so that you may not sin. But if anyone does sin, we
have an advocate with the Father, Jesus Christ the
righteous; and he is the atoning sacrifice for our
sins, and not for ours only but also for the sins of
the whole world.

In many ways the first Letter of John closely reflects the
theology of the Fourth Gospel. But unlike John 17, and more as
in Hebrews, the subject of Christ's intercession here is not
general protection but specifically atonement for sin: it is his
sacrifice which intervenes with the Father for the sin of the
believer. This sacrificial atonement not only represents a once-
and-for-all forgiveness, but in the person of Christ our advocate
(*paraklétos*) it is still continually present before the Father and
"cleanses us from all sin" (1 John 1.7).

Conclusion

The prayer life of Jesus profoundly influenced early Christian
spirituality. He taught and practised the habit of taking frequent
times alone with God. He encouraged his disciples to pray as he
did: boldly, trustingly, persistently, and yet always having God's
greater glory as his chief concern. Next to the Lord's Prayer,
which majors on this theme and came to be said thrice daily
(e.g. *Dîdache* 8.3), the most influential accounts of Jesus'
prayers were those of his passion, chiefly at Gethsemane and on
the cross. His spirit of guileless submission, even in the midst
of profound anxiety, became a pattern of the Christian life in
times of adversity or persecution. Moreover, it may well be that
the intensity of Jesus' prayer for the kingdom of God finds
another counterpart in the early Christian prayer for his return
(cf. *Marana tha*, 1 Cor. 16.22; Rev. 22.20).[22]

Similarly, Jesus' earthly and exalted intercession for the
disciples, mentioned in the Synoptics and profiled in John and
several epistles, became a powerful source of encouragement to
the early Christians. It greatly bolstered their assurance of the

Father's undivided love and favour to know that by his Spirit Christ himself, their friend, high priest, and advocate, was always praying with them and on their behalf.[23]

The life of prayer, therefore, proved to be a link of living continuity between the religion of Jesus and that of the early Christians.

Chapter Seven

Why Was Jesus Exalted to Heaven?

This chapter concludes our series of studies on Jesus with another somewhat provocative sounding title. The subject, in a nutshell, is the question of the historical fallout: given what we have discovered about Jesus of Nazareth, how did the early Church arrive at its credal acknowledgement and worship of the exalted Christ of faith? For an answer we must look at the nature of early Christian experience as well as the apostolic testimony about the resurrection, interpreting this against the background both of contemporary Judaism in general and of the life and work of Jesus in particular.

From Jesus to the Creeds: Three Reasons for the Development

Many Christians are familiar with the Creeds from their daily and weekly worship. Here is what the Apostles' Creed says about Jesus, whom it acknowledges as "Christ, [God's] only Son, our Lord":

> He was conceived by the power of the Holy Spirit
> and born of the Virgin Mary. He suffered under
> Pontius Pilate, was crucified, died and was buried.
> He descended to the dead. On the third day he
> rose again. He ascended into heaven, and is seated
> at the right hand of the Father. He will come
> again to judge the living and the dead.

Up to now we have been concentrating on a very human Jesus, the Jesus about whom we can confidently affirm with the Creed that he was born of Mary and suffered and died at the time of Pontius Pilate. How, then, did the Christians come to claim a continuity between those past tense statements and the present tense assertion that Jesus is not only Christ, but "our Lord" and "seated at the right hand of the Father"?

It is telling testimony to the schizophrenic state of much contemporary New Testament scholarship that while there are plenty of treatments of christology proper, most recent books on *Jesus* prefer to banish such questions from their scope of relevant historical inquiry to the fertile fields of ancient Mediterranean imagination – from the historical to the hysterical, so to speak. The idea that historical questions might be asked of the genesis of beliefs, or that real historical personalities and experiences might engender theological convictions, never seems to arise for these authors.[1]

Of course it is true that statements like "Jesus rose from the dead" or, "Christ ascended into heaven" *are* theological affirmations which are not *as such* subject to historical verification. And of course we must be prepared to recognize that the New Testament texts or the Apostles' Creed lend themselves to different interpretations of the events underlying the early Christians' experience of the risen Lord. Nevertheless, it is surely a naïve and blinkered view of history which refuses to perceive connections between admittedly theological affirmations and the real and hence historically investigable experiences, however understood, which gave rise to them. To assert that the resurrection appearances of Jesus and their significance cannot be related to a historical perspective, is much like claiming that Karl Marx and the rise of Marxism are incompatible objects of study that bear no historical relation to each other. It seems odd that in so many books on Jesus we should be required to choose between two flavours of discourse: either history or christology, but not both.

Fortunately, that curious bifurcation may now be closer to being corrected than has been the case for a very long time. This is due largely to scholars working "from the other side", as it were: recent years have seen the publication of a number of significant studies showing that the origins of christology must in fact be located within the thought world of first-century Jewish wisdom and apocalypticism with its interest in divine mediator figures, angels and exalted patriarchs.[2] The surprisingly large area of compatibility between first-century Jewish and Christian Messianic ideas has made it possible to trace what were once thought to be later christological accretions down to a very primitive stage in the experience of the early Christians. This quite considerable reassessment of first-century Messianic expectations (e.g. regarding the Son of Man[3]) has meant that in some cases scholars have once again become willing to take the search for the beginnings of christology back into the life of Jesus himself.[4] While continuing methodological vigilance is still called for, this new trend towards a less disjointed view of Christian origins lends support to the argument for the kind of continuity between history and faith which I have been advocating.

To return to the question we raised earlier: three fundamental facts, I believe, account above all for the astonishing transition from the historical Jesus of Nazareth to his followers' veneration of him as seated at the right hand of God. First, the early Christians' unequivocal belief in the resurrection and exaltation of Jesus. Secondly, the early Christian proclamation in which the preacher became the message, without in the process being stripped of the central emphases of his own teaching. And thirdly, the worship of Jesus in formative parts of the Early Church. Let us now look at each of these in turn.

The Resurrection and Exaltation of Jesus

Dozens of books have of course been written on this subject alone; once again, our brief discussion here will have to concentrate on essentials.

Introductory Observations

It is useful to start with a few largely self-evident observations.

1. If everyone concerned had thought that Jesus of Nazareth had simply lived and taught and died, the New Testament Gospels would never have been written, and we might well know no more about him than what is contained in one passing reference in the first-century Jewish historian Josephus (see p. 11 above). What is more, it is indeed quite arguable that a short passage like that would not have been an unfair representation of his relative importance for the world stage in the first century.

2. Unlike all other world religions, most of Christianity's truth-claims depend in a strangely one-sided way on an unparalleled event that is believed to have happened *after* the death of its founder: that is, his resurrection from the dead. There is obviously some breadth of scope and variation in emphasis here. But one can make a strong case that to a significant extent the whole of the apostolic faith in Christ depends on that event. Arguably, all writers of the New Testament either presuppose or refer explicitly to the resurrection, regardless of other differences between them. The Apostle Paul brings this perspective to its clearest expression in 1 Corinthians 15: "If Christ has not been raised, then our preaching is in vain and your faith is in vain. ... If Christ has not been raised, your faith is futile and you are still in your sins." (vv. 14, 17). Many of the apostles went on to stake their lives on this conviction.[5]

3. The Gospels have been written with the resurrection in mind, back to front in some ways. What they intend to tell us about Jesus, and how they tell it, only ultimately makes sense if one accounts for their belief in the resurrection. Although the authors do want to describe the life and work of Jesus of Nazareth, and use some early and much simpler sources, all of

them (including Mark, with his lack of resurrection appearances) write as people who have a hindsight, after-Easter perspective. A narrator who knows the outcome of the story will clearly tell it differently from someone who has only fragments of a tale with a depressing end. If Jesus was not raised, he may still have been an impressive religious teacher, but there is no point in thinking that he was in any sense uniquely important. But if he *was* raised, everything changes.[6]

It is therefore to this complex question of the resurrection that we must now turn.

What Were the Facts of the Resurrection?

A majority of scholars follow the chronology of John's gospel in believing that Jesus died on Friday afternoon, the 14th of Nisan (7th April) in the year 30 AD, though significant arguments in favour of AD 33 or 36 continue to be advanced.[7] The location is now generally held to have been an abandoned quarry under the present Holy Sepulchre Church in Jerusalem. Since the Sabbath starts at sunset (and this evening began the day of Passover, a high holiday), Jesus had to be buried very quickly. His disciples feared for their safety and were nowhere to be found, but a wealthy sympathizer by the name of Joseph of Arimathea looked after the burial. He owned a freshly hewn shaft tomb nearby (John 19.42) in the same old quarry, of the distinctive first-century design that is closed by a rolling stone. (Several of these can still be seen in the Holy Sepulchre Church and around Jerusalem.) Joseph placed the body of Jesus there in the antechamber, wrapped in linen and spices, but apparently ran out of time for the full procedure of embalming. Some of Jesus' women disciples watched the proceedings, while the Twelve had scattered. Then the tomb was sealed by the circular stone rolled in front of it.

Nothing very significant happened on Saturday, the Passover feast day; Luke suggests the disciples "rested according to the commandment" (Luke 23.56).

None of the Gospels actually describe the resurrection itself (though Matthew more elaborately reports an earthquake and the appearance of an angel to roll away the stone; the second-century apocryphal *Gospel of Peter* uses this lack of description to construct a most ornate and fantastical account).

Nevertheless, all four canonical gospels (and by clear implication 1 Cor. 15.4, the earliest written testimony to the resurrection) agree on the fact of the tomb being found empty on Sunday morning, and on the message that Jesus had risen from the dead as he himself had hinted. In fact, the discovery of the empty tomb can be accepted as one of the more assured historical data about Jesus; it is possible to establish "an originally pre-kerygmatic, pre-apologetic tradition on the tomb."[8] The accounts in all four gospels and in 1 Corinthians 15 agree on very few *other* specifics; but this discovery called for interpretation, one way or another.[9]

The original version of Mark's gospel ends quite suddenly here, with the disciples being stunned and afraid by these developments and by the announcement of resurrection (16.8). In the other three gospels, several encounters with the risen Jesus now follow, beginning with Mary Magdalene who meets him outside the tomb itself (John 20.11–18). Matthew, Luke and John each describe various experiences of Jesus which his followers had in the weeks that followed. It is difficult to date these appearances or to give a coherent synopsis of what took place. Even the information about the geographic location is not easily reconciled between Jerusalem (Luke 24.49; Acts 1.4), Galilee (Mark 16.7), or both (Matthew, John).[10] Furthermore, it is not clear exactly what kind of experiences we are dealing with: were these the sorts of encounters that a journalist could have recorded on videotape and in interviews? The evangelists describe them quite differently: sometimes Jesus is difficult to recognize, enters through closed doors, or suddenly disappears from sight. At other times he seems quite physically present and even eats with the disciples: Luke (24.36–43; Acts 10.41) and to some degree John (20.24–29) are eager to emphasize Jesus' concrete, tangible presence. Terms like "appearance", "encounter", "vision" and "revelation" all seem to capture something of these inexplicable experiences.

Nevertheless, in all the Gospels it is clear that this presence of Jesus is not a resuscitation of a dead body, or even of a merely comatose person, as has sometimes been suggested. Jesus is unlike people who merely "come back to life", such as Lazarus in John 11. And his resurrection presence is in any case different from the pre-crucifixion Jesus, who did *not* walk through closed doors or disappear at will, and who was not difficult to recognize.

The earliest written discussion of the resurrection of Jesus is found in Paul's first letter to the Corinthians (1 Cor. 15.3–8). Paul takes pains to quote a Christian tradition about the appearances to Peter and the other apostles, and he includes his own call vision on the Damascus Road with these apostolic resurrection appearances. The language used is that of seeing (*ôphthê* = "was seen by, appeared to"), as also more directly in 1 Cor. 9.1: "Am I not an apostle? Have I not seen the Lord?" On the other hand, the same terminology of 1 Cor. 15 is in the Greek Old Testament used specifically in contexts of revelation, for instance in the case of Moses and the burning bush (Exod. 3). Elsewhere, Paul himself describes the resurrection appearance as a revelation (Gal. 1.12, 16), though he seems to distinguish carefully between this and other "visions and revelations of the Lord" (2 Cor. 12.1–7).[11]

In discussing what resurrection is like, Paul goes out of his way to show that the believer's resurrection body will be like that of Jesus: *not*, however, a resuscitated physical body, but an immortal, spiritual and glorious body (1 Cor. 15.35–49). Paul's image is that the mortal "puts on" the imperishable like a garment (v. 54). Despite an important qualitative discontinuity, therefore, there is at the same time an essential continuity between the body that is "sown" (v. 44) and the one that is raised. Thus, although Paul does not match the emphasis in Luke or John on the material aspects of the resurrection encounters, his general perspective does tally with another aspect of the gospel accounts: there, it is definitely the real Jesus whom the disciples meet, but he does not appear in public, he does not stay with them, and these appearances eventually stop. Luke seems to describe him as physically ascending into the sky (Acts 1.9f.), while Paul and other early Christian preachers speak more metaphorically and theologically of Jesus having been exalted as the Judge and Son of God with power (Rom. 1.3f; Eph. 1.20; Heb. 12.2; 1 Pet. 3.21f.), who will come from heaven to judge the world and redeem his people.[12]

What exactly, then, is the empirical significance of the resurrection? What physically happened? The New Testament documents do not really give us that information, nor do they seem ultimately interested in it. What is of decisive significance for them is the *fact* that Jesus – the same Jesus who had died consciously giving his life as a ransom for his people – was the first to be raised from the dead, thereby being fully vindicated and approved by God as both Messiah and as Lord. "Jesus is Lord" (Rom. 10.9; 1 Cor. 12.3): that is the unequivocal content of the earliest Christian confessions. The earthly Jesus and the exalted Lord were one and the same.

Whatever else Jesus' resurrection may have been like, there was an empty tomb followed by a series of extraordinary experiences which a significant number of early disciples independently understood as real and historical encounters with Jesus.[13] To be sure, their master now was different from his earlier self, not merely "come back to life". Nevertheless, he also was not a ghost or a phantom, but undeniably the same Jesus and the real person whom they knew. These experiences are attested by Paul and three of the four gospels (the earliest form of Mark ends abruptly, giving only the angels' *message* of resurrection and promise of an appearance in Galilee).

Some theologians have argued that questions of factual history are irrelevant to the reality of the resurrection: Rudolf Bultmann spoke of Jesus rising only "in the faith of the disciples", while the Bishop of Durham created a stir a few years ago with his widely reported statement that it did not matter to his faith if the bones of Jesus were still in a tomb somewhere in Palestine. And indeed, the earliest New Testament evidence (St. Paul) could be taken to suggest that although the *fact* of the resurrection is crucial, Jesus' bones themselves might not have to be. We have seen that 1 Cor. 15 clearly emphasizes the ways in which the resurrection body is *different* from the mortal body (see vv. 35–50, especially 42–49).

Nevertheless, it is important that the New Testament's argument for the resurrection, both of Christ and of the believer, is one of essential *continuity*. And thus, while 1 Cor. 15 by itself may suggest that the bones of Jesus as such are not *in principle* a part of the risen Christ, the fact that the tomb was empty became an important and powerful symbol of the personal *continuity* of the person who died with the one who was raised.[14] It has the same function in that regard as John's account of the nail prints in Jesus' hands (20.26–28), those "wounds yet visible above"[15] which Thomas encountered. The assertion of an empty tomb in all four gospels need not perhaps be understood to indicate a strictly material continuity. But it certainly does symbolize a continuity of the embodied human person. This is crucial to the proclamation of the early church: "This Jesus God raised up, ... this Jesus whom you crucified" (Acts 2.32, 36). That is why it is right to disagree with those who take a phantom-like, docetic view of the resurrection. It *does* matter that the tomb was empty. Had they really thought that the bones of Jesus were in fact still in a tomb somewhere, no first-century Jews would have spoken about his resurrection.[16] The earliest Christians affirmed that the incarnation and death of Jesus were in a body, and that in fundamentally important respects his was also a bodily resurrection.

What, then, is the New Testament witness of the resurrection of Jesus? Two days after Jesus' death, the disciples found themselves face to face with Jesus, to their great shock and surprise. The New Testament writers telling of these experiences use the strongest and most emphatic terms they know to assure their readers of the reality of these encounters. Here they saw God invading their own familiar world – unexpectedly, but palpably and undeniably.

History as Fact and Interpretation

The authors of the New Testament are all firmly agreed that Jesus was raised from the dead, and that this makes all the difference. How can we appropriate this conviction? Historical judgements today as much as in the Bible always pertain to *interpreted events*. Something happens, and we interpret that it must mean thus and so. The relationship between event and interpretation is always complex and dependent on many different factors, but in the study of history we never relate to uninterpreted events. Sometimes the interpretations are obvious if you are on the scene but much less clear if you are far removed. The sight of two women walking hand in hand in public is likely to mean something very different in San Francisco from what it might mean in Istanbul or Kathmandu.

Given the first-century Jewish setting and what Jesus had taught about suffering, death and vindication, the shock of the empty tomb followed by startling appearances beginning two days after Golgotha could only mean one thing. This post-Easter Jesus was neither resuscitated nor a ghost or figment of the imagination, and yet was very concretely present. His own teaching had been that his death would be instrumental to the redemption of Israel and the coming of the Kingdom of God. Against that eschatological backdrop, these new developments could only mean his powerful vindication, indeed his resurrection.[17]

Greeks or Romans would never have used such Jewish language, and one wonders what Roman observers (like those possibly envisioned in Matt. 27.66; 28.11) might have made of these events.   Similarly, it must be doubtful how even the disciples would have understood this notion at the time: Jewish expectation had, after all, been of a *general* resurrection, not an individual one.[18]   But in the context of Old Testament and Jewish thought they found themselves able to conclude only one thing after Easter: Jesus had become the first to be raised from the dead.   The general resurrection was expected at the end of the present world order, and by raising Jesus from the dead God had inaugurated this final phase of history, which must now be imminent.   This was heaven breaking in to earth.   God had vindicated Jesus and exalted him to the highest place in heaven.

The Gospel of Jesus: From the Preacher to the Message

Just as Jesus during his lifetime had sent his disciples out to preach his message of the Kingdom, so his resurrection appearances appear to have had the very practical purpose of commissioning his apostles among those who saw him.   This is clear from the New Testament use of the word "apostle", which applies to those (including Paul, 1 Cor. 9.1; 15.8) who saw the Lord after the resurrection and were thereby commissioned to preach the gospel.   Paul justifies his apostleship by the revelation of Christ to him (Gal. 1.15f.) and by the fact that he has "seen the Lord" (1 Cor. 9.1).

The first sermons preached by Peter in Acts are striking in what they reveal about the content of early Christian preaching.   The resurrection has meant that the message *of* Jesus, who proclaimed the Kingdom of God inaugurated in his own teaching and ministry, has become much more explicitly the message *about* Jesus, whom by his resurrection God has endorsed as both Messiah and Lord of the Kingdom.   Luke's account of Pentecost (Acts 2) crystallizes how the presence of Jesus came to be experienced in the outpouring of the Spirit. Here Jesus himself has become the clear centre of the message.

This is indeed a shift, but one which is precipitated by the events of Easter and of Pentecost. Even before Easter, however, this emphasis has roots in Jesus' claim that the Kingdom had arrived in his person: as we saw in Chapters Four and Five, even the earthly ministry in a real sense was already *about* Jesus. With all due historical restraint, the likely impact of pre-Easter claims to the effect that Jesus' kingdom ministry represented "something greater than Solomon" (Matt. 12.41f. par.) must over time have been very considerable.[19]

In the early Christian message, there is therefore a traceable continuity between (i) the Jesus of Nazareth who healed and preached the Kingdom and died on a cross, (ii) the Jesus of the resurrection who appeared to his disciples, and (iii) the Jesus of faith who was experienced as present by the Holy Spirit given to all believers.

The same continuity is further affirmed by another aspect of early Christian teaching. Jesus had spoken of discipleship as taking up one's cross and following him. Those who followed him were to be servants as he had been a servant. As we noted in Chapter Six, the teaching of the early church variously described the Christian experience as an identification with Jesus. St. Paul expressed this in terms of baptism as the participatory experience of *dying and rising with Christ*. Living the life with Christ, for Paul as for other New Testament writers, included a call to imitate his humility and become conformed to him.[20] Imitation of Christ meant to follow the *pattern* of the historical Jesus – the one who accepted poverty and humility, and even suffering, in obedience to the will of God and for the sake of Israel's redemption. In this way Jesus the preacher easily and quite naturally became central in the message as both the Redeemer to be trusted and the Lord to be followed.

The Worship of Jesus

We come now to the third important factor which profoundly shaped the way the early church continued to relate to Jesus. Revelation 5.6–14 contains the following description:

> Then I saw ... a Lamb standing as if it had been slaughtered.... The four living creatures and the twenty-four elders fell before the Lamb.... Then I looked, and I heard the voice of many angels surrounding the throne and the living creatures and the elders; they numbered myriads of myriads and thousands of thousands, singing with full voice, "Worthy is the Lamb that was slaughtered to receive power and wealth and wisdom and might and honour and glory and blessing!" Then I heard every creature in heaven and on earth and under the earth and in the sea, and all that is in them, singing, "To the one seated on the throne and to the Lamb be blessing and honour and glory and might forever and ever!" And the four living creatures said, "Amen!" And the elders fell down and worshipped.

While the language here is highly symbolic, the context makes it clear that the Lamb is the triumphant Messiah of David who with his blood redeemed people from every people and nation. In this vision of heaven it is the crucified and exalted Christ who is associated with God on the throne and is jointly worshipped with him in heaven and on earth. Jesus himself is now not only risen from the dead and preached as Messiah and Lord, but he himself shares in the worship given to God.

Although this is perhaps the most graphic and powerful New Testament image of the worship of Jesus, it is compatible with a number of other significant New Testament texts. In Matthew's Great Commission the risen Jesus has been given "all power in heaven and on earth" (28.18). Philippians 2 talks about Jesus after his crucifixion being given "the name above every name" (i.e. the divine name), to whom every knee shall bow in adoration. Similarly, Hebrews 1–2 stresses that Jesus is worshipped by the angels and crowned with honour and glory, seated at God's right hand. Perhaps second only to the Lord's Prayer, the most widely used Christian prayer since the very early days of the Church was *Marana tha*, "Come, Lord Jesus" (1 Cor. 16.22; Rev. 22.20), which both acknowledges the Lordship of Jesus and prays for the coming of the Kingdom in connection with his return.

It is clear from this sampling of texts that apostolic Christianity commonly believed the events of Easter amounted to a great deal more than just a few visionary appearances. If indeed the resurrection had confirmed Jesus as Messiah, as Son of God with power, and as the exalted heavenly figure of whom he himself had spoken, then that must have lasting implications for how his followers should relate to him.

Reflection on the meaning of these developments might appear to raise enormous questions for the unshakeable Jewish belief in one God. How could Christianity affirm Jesus as exalted judge on the throne of God and even worship him, without denying the very foundations of monotheism and the faith in the God of Israel? At least by the late first or early second century, Jewish and Gentile Christian views of the exalted Jesus had begun to seem suspect to many Jewish observers.

But how did Christianity arrive at the worship of Jesus? Recent studies of this question have pointed out that the idea of an earthly figure being exalted to heaven to sit on the throne of God as judge and mediator is repeatedly found in Jewish literature both before and after the time of Jesus. This is above and beyond Old Testament and apocryphal texts that speak about the heavenly figure of Wisdom as the one who existed with God before creation, through whom God created the world and is now present in it (Proverbs 8, Philo's *Logos*; cf. Sirach 24; Wisdom 7, John 1).

Among these exalted human figures is Enoch, who according to the Bible was taken up by God (Gen. 5.24). In various apocalyptic and mystical works he is perceived as having become the heavenly scribe who records human deeds; the one who is the heavenly Messiah, who sits on God's throne in his presence, who receives the acclamations of angels, and who in one document is even called the "little Yahweh" (*3 Enoch* 48.7; cf. *1 Enoch*). Another document has an angel called Yahoel, who looks like a man and like the description of God in Daniel, bears the name and power of God, destroys the power of evil, and who in the end is included in the worship offered to God (*Apocalypse of Abraham* 17). One of the Dead Sea Scrolls speaks of Melchizedek as a heavenly Redeemer who is called "El" and "Elohim", "God" (11QMelch). The philosopher Philo of Alexandria believed that God accomplishes his purposes in the world through one manifestation of himself, that is his "word", his Logos, who is variously referred to as his firstborn Son (*Confusion of Tongues* 146), and in one place even as a kind of "second God" (*Questions on Genesis* 2.62).

These and other Jewish texts show that, although Jewish theology in the first century was firmly and without compromise committed to the worship of one God, there were some highly varied attempts to affirm both God's almighty transcendent power above all human affairs and his intimate involvement in the lives and sufferings of his people. One very common way in which this concern found expression was through the description of exalted Biblical figures exercising a kind of mediating function between the majesty of God and the straits of human experience. The shape of first-century Jewish monotheism, then, was in no way monistic; it should instead be seen as concerned with divine "monarchy" (the sole *rule* of God) and "monolatry" (the sole *worship* of God).[21]

It is not difficult to see how this breadth of Jewish belief might have stimulated the early Christians who came to affirm that Jesus had been raised from the dead and thereby exalted to the position of Messiah and "Son of God in power" (Rom. 1.3f.). In view of the resurrection and exaltation of Jesus, the early Christian communities could draw on solid Jewish precedent as they increasingly conceived of their risen master in the highest and most intimate relationship with God. It was in the Palestinian Jewish context that Christians first began to include Jesus in their worship of God, without intending to compromise for a minute their fierce loyalty to monotheism: they continued their firm belief in "one God..., and one Lord" (1 Cor. 8.6).

Although versatile in their monotheistic beliefs, Jews nevertheless tended to be cautious in transferring such flexibility to their *worship* of God.[22] Christians would therefore encounter a degree of resistance and censure, especially with the emergence of an increasingly normative rabbinic Judaism after AD 70. At the same time, this also means that the "parting of the ways" between Christianity and Judaism can only be understood against the backdrop of changes within Judaism as well as of the developments within the Church.[23]

Larry Hurtado, one recent writer on this subject, has argued that in a first-century Jewish setting all the necessary theological concepts were already in place for a conception of Jesus being exalted to the throne of God; the only addition (he calls it a "mutation") was when Christians drew the conclusion, at an early stage, that even worship of Jesus was fully appropriate. Texts of the kind we have discussed suggest that this mutation may not have transpired entirely out of the blue.[24] That the Holy Spirit eventually came to be discussed in the same context has to do with the view in Paul and other New Testament writers that the Spirit is in fact the Spirit of Jesus (e.g. Acts 16.7; 2 Cor. 3.17 "the Lord is the Spirit").

However, any argument in favour of continuity between Jesus and Christian faith must also consider that in the course of time this Doctrine of Christ came to be more explicitly located within the Doctrine of the Trinity. It is important to recognize in the first instance that orthodox Christian discussion of the Trinity represents an attempt to reaffirm the essential *unity* of God, while allowing for differentiation corresponding to the ways in which he has revealed himself. As such, this endeavour is not fundamentally unlike certain theological developments within Second-Temple Judaism, as we saw.

Thus, it is perhaps an unfortunate but fateful accident of history that later christological controversies tended to be conducted in formulaic language taken not from that Jewish background against which the spiritual reality originally made sense, but from Greek philosophy. And thus, while the pronouncements of the Nicaean and Chalcedonian Councils do fall emphatically within the bounds of monotheism, careless use of their christological terminology has clearly contributed to a history of miscommunication both within the Church and between Christianity and Judaism (as well as Islam).

Without surrendering the reality to which Christians have held fast through the ages, the time may have come for a public moratorium on the technical talk of divine "natures" and "persons", in order to reaffirm in clear and communicable language the fundamental relational truths of historic Christian faith – beginning with the Jewish creed of Jesus and the Apostles that "the LORD our God is one" (Deut. 6.4; cf. Mark 12.29).[25] Our starting point must be to recall that all good christology is no more nor less than an expression of faith in the God of Israel. Only then can faith in the exalted Christ claim to stand in any kind of substantial continuity with Jesus the Jew and his first followers. Anything less than that leaves Christians open to the charge of corrupting monotheism, as it has long been raised by Jews and Muslims.[26] If the divinity and worship of Jesus are not understood against a clearly monotheistic setting as suggested above (and too frequently they have *not* been so understood in the public mind), then Christianity is indeed in grave danger of turning Jesus "from Jewish prophet to Gentile god", as one recent book title has it.[27]

In a church concerned – as the Church must always be – with discipleship of the earthly and now exalted Jesus, the doctrine of the Trinity also begins and ends with the one "God and Father of the Lord Jesus" (to quote the Apostle Paul[28]). Belief in the Trinity is then most appropriately seen as a move not towards the worship of a "Blessed and Holy Three"[29] but of the Holy One, God alone, who has decisively revealed himself as Father, Son, and Holy Spirit.[30]

Conclusion

We have seen, therefore, how the preacher inspired and became the message, and how the apostolic church would have moved from following Jesus of Nazareth to worshipping the one God of Abraham as Father, Son and Holy Spirit. Who Jesus was had to do with what God had done through his life, death and resurrection. What happened over the next four centuries is a process of continuing reflection and interpretation about the meaning of the gospel and the person and work of Christ. In this context, the creeds are the formulations which were found most helpful in describing how and why for Christians the Jesus of History is also the Christ of Faith, for all time. Here, too, the resurrection is key.

Philippians 2.5–11 is one early description of how this process was perceived. This is an appropriate passage with which to close this chapter. It emphasizes what Jesus did, who and where he is now, and his presence and example for the life of Christians:

> Let the same mind be in you that was in Christ Jesus, who, though he was in the form of God, did not regard equality with God something to be exploited, but emptied himself, taking the form of a slave, being born in human likeness. And being found in human form, he humbled himself and became obedient to the point of death – even death on a cross. Therefore God also highly exalted him

and gave him the name that is above every name, so that at the name of Jesus every knee should bend, in heaven and on earth and under the earth, and every tongue should confess that Jesus Christ is Lord, to the glory of God the Father.

This Jesus

We conclude in two short sections, first a summary and then a suggestion of implications for different readers. A brief Epilogue will serve as a final reflection.

Summary

On our tour of issues relating to the life and significance of Jesus we have covered a lot of ground in a short time.

In the Introduction we examined the road map and tried to get our bearings in the crowded traffic of Jesus research. I suggested that the time is ripe for us to reconsider the possibility that historical study of Jesus of Nazareth can be compatible and continuous with faith in the risen Christ as Lord.

Chapter One took us back to the very beginnings of Jesus' life, examining something of the historical and theological meaning of the infancy narratives. From an open viewpoint of intelligent faith, the traditional Christmas stories still present a sound and authentic way of appropriating Jesus' humble personal origins in their proper significance for his life's story – the story of one who, for those with "ears to hear", was uniquely sent by God.

The nature of that mission concerned us in Chapter Two, where we began by surveying Jewish Messianic expectations in the first century. We then discovered that Jesus' life and work almost certainly *did* have Messianic connotations, but also that a number of key Messianic expectations were evidently *not* fulfilled. Given Jesus' own future expectations, this led to the conclusion that he himself did not foresee the Messianic redemption being completed until the final revelation of the heavenly "Son of Man coming with the clouds" envisioned in the

164

book of Daniel. A closer look at the early Christian preaching revealed that the early Church did not in any case take an "all-or-nothing", "once-and-for-all" approach to the question of Jesus' messiahship: rather, they fully affirmed that his job was not yet completely done, but was still coming to fruition in the present work of the Spirit and would finally be complete at his return in power as redeemer and judge.

From there we took a more specific look in Chapter Three at the background and meaning of Jesus' attitude to the Temple, concluding that his criticism of a corrupt religious establishment and prediction of the Temple's destruction and reconstruction were founded in a rich tradition of Biblical interpretation, which he shared with a variety of Jewish contemporaries.

Closely connected with this issue was the question of Jesus' aims, the subject of Chapter Four. We found his purposes to be intimately concerned with his proclamation and inauguration of the Kingdom of God, with a growing emphasis on his own death as redemptive and instrumental to the arrival of that Kingdom. In that light, his appearances to his followers after three days were seen as powerfully expressing God's vindication of those purposes.

Against the background of first-century Judaism, Chapter Five asked whether Christians are right to see Jesus as the founder of their faith. The evidence shows that Jesus was first and foremost a Jew, and yet that his ministry in that first-century soil has vital and organic links with the faith of his followers, both Jewish and Gentile. In that sense Jesus was indeed the pioneer of the Christian faith.

A more particular "snapshot" illustration of this continuity came to light in Chapter Six, where we discovered a key link between Jesus and the Church in his prayer life – as both an example for his followers and an expression of his ongoing intercession on their behalf.

Finally, we surveyed some of the difficult issues relating to the development of christology, the move from Jesus of

Nazareth as teacher and leader to Christ as the object of
Christian preaching and worship. We found that much of the
early Christian reflection arose directly from convictions about
the reality and significance of the resurrection of Jesus. When
read against the background of Jewish monotheism and mystical
reflection about God's immanence in mediator figures, the
emergence of christology can be seen as an authentic and
consequential expression of the Apostolic faith in the risen
Jesus.

"So What?" Some Implications

This book has argued that it can be both valid and plausible to
regard Jesus of Nazareth as giving rise to the faith of the
Church. If our discussion may have served as something of a
Let's Go guide (cf. p. 9), it has admittedly provided no more
than a whirlwind tour of the subject. Some readers will have
seen and learned all or more than they expected; others will feel
a need to go back and cover in greater detail some of the issues
raised, perhaps beginning with the suggestions for further
reading at the end of the book. For all my readers, however, I
sincerely believe that those who do go further will nevertheless
find the fundamental thesis of these pages borne out: that,
although the questions inevitably multiply and interpretations
abound, faith in the apostolic gospel of Christ remains an
intellectually viable and profoundly appropriate response to
Jesus of Nazareth. And from this perspective it continues to be
true, even a hundred years after Martin Kähler, that the question
of who Jesus was cannot be fully answered without the question
of who Jesus *is* – and vice versa.[1]

There is one other point which I must raise especially
with a view to those readers who may be biblical scholars in
their own right, and yet who maintain an interest in the
theological subject matter. The limitations of my argument will
be most obvious to them, as indeed some are apparent to me.

However, regardless of the degree to which my particular formulation of the case may be judged to have succeeded, it hardly needs stressing that an authentic link between Jesus of Nazareth and the exalted Christ is in fact *theologically indispensable* for Christianity. If there are no reasonable grounds for a personal continuity between "crucified under Pontius Pilate" and "seated at the right hand of God"; if the Apostles' Creed could really be shown to be the greatest of insults to the historical Jesus, as some argue[2]: then Christian faith would indeed be a travesty. A Christianity demonstrably without Jesus would finally justify the claim that "subjectivity is the *only* criterion of Gospel truth"[3]. For good or ill, the creed and credibility of Christianity remain irrevocably bound up with the person of Jesus of Nazareth. That is why the study of his life can never become dispensable.

My argument in these pages has been that orthodox Christian faith, properly understood, is indeed a plausible and legitimate interpretation of that person. In other words, it is possible to join with integrity in the early church's conviction that "God has made *this Jesus* both Lord and Messiah".

Open Questions

To ask questions is a uniquely human privilege and predicament. Some queries can find answers, and I firmly believe the basic thesis of this book to be one of these. Nevertheless, as long as we know only in part, there are going to be open questions even in the most important areas of life and faith. Many of our unresolved problems about Jesus will remain so.

This is itself significant in two different ways, pertaining to the questions and to the questioner. To say that questions are open means, first, that the answer might be in more than just one place; and many of our questions about Jesus Christ are indeed of that kind. Some have tried to force closure, by denying either the reality of the questions or the possibility of answers. Both stances, the obscurantist and the sceptical, have surprisingly flourished in our supposedly scientific, post-enlightenment era. This is peculiar in that both the denial of doubt and the denial of faith are in the end impoverished attempts to explain the world by contradicting a part of it.

At the same time, it must be said that theological scholarship in the twentieth century has suffered more from the demise of faith than that of doubt. Open historical and philosophical questions about Jesus and Christianity have too often been declared closed in ways which amputate the former from the latter and in effect *preclude* faith. Hatched in ivory towers and reared in theological colleges, these ideas have sometimes seemed to lay observers to show the academics fiddling while the Church burns.[1]

Against this background, I want here to commend the thesis of a legitimate compatibility of faith and history in the study of Jesus: not only because it is academically defensible but also because I consider it to be profoundly appropriate to the subject under investigation.

Finally, however, we are confronted with that second implication of affirming useful "open questions": the need for an openness in the questioner. Anselm of Canterbury (c.1033 – 1109) is rightly famous for his definition of the Christian intellectual stance as "faith seeking understanding". But the reverse must surely also be valid: indeed Christian inquiry is itself a spiral of faith seeking understanding which in turn seeks faith. In the study of Jesus, no less than in other areas of human exploration, to acknowledge open questions means at the same time to allow ourselves to be found by the answers. To search genuinely is to be open to discovery, and to listen means to be ready to be addressed by the Other.

And there are times when that Other addresses us not in the form of a packaged conclusion. Some of our open questions about Jesus must remain "unanswered" because we are dealing with realities which defy description in rational discourse. Perhaps more than anywhere else it is at these points of human silence that our quest for analysis is ultimately met by the divine call to faith.

Christian faith in this sense is faith in a Messiah whose identity in fact is not to be found in the past or present alone, but who always also meets us as the One who is to come. To accept and affirm that Jesus of Nazareth is also the exalted, coming Christ is thus at the same time in a profound sense to accept and affirm that classic Jewish confession, "I believe with perfect faith that the Messiah will surely come; and though he tarry, yet I will daily wait for him."[2]

Further Reading

General

De Jonge, Marinus. *Jesus, the Servant-Messiah*. New Haven/ London: Yale University Press, 1991.

Dunn, James D. G. *The Evidence for Jesus*. London: SCM, 1985.

Hoskyns, Sir Edwyn, and Davey, Noel. *The Riddle of the New Testament*. London: Faber & Faber, 1931.

Moltmann, Jürgen. *The Way of Jesus Christ: Christology in Messianic Dimensions*. London: SCM, c1990.

Sanders, E. P. *The Historical Figure of Jesus*. London: Allen Lane/ Penguin, 1993

Stanton, Graham N. *The Gospels and Jesus*. Oxford: Oxford University Press, 1989.

Theissen, Gerd. *The Shadow of the Galilean: The Quest of the Historical Jesus in Narrative Form*. Translated by J. Bowden. London: SCM, 1987.

Major Ancient Sources in English Translation

Flavius Josephus, Philo of Alexandria, the Apostolic Fathers, Pliny the Younger, Tacitus, Suetonius, Dio Cassius and Eusebius can be found in the Loeb Classical Library.

Danby, Herbert, trans. *The Mishnah*. Oxford: Oxford University Press, 1933; repr. 1985.

Epstein, I., ed. *Hebrew-English Edition of the Babylonian Talmud*. 20 vols. London: Soncino, 1972–1984.

McNamara, Martin, et al., eds. *The Aramaic Bible*. Edinburgh: T&T Clark, 1987–. [Multi-volume translation of the Targums.]

Neusner, Jacob, trans. *The Tosefta*. 6 vols. New York: Ktav, 1977–1986.

Neusner, Jacob. *The Talmud of the Land of Israel: A Preliminary Translation and Explanation*. Chicago/ London: University of Chicago Press, 1982–. [Multi-volume translation of the Palestinian Talmud; 35 volumes have appeared to date.]

Schneemelcher, Wilhelm, ed. *New Testament Apocrypha*. ET edited by R. McL. Wilson. Vol. 1: *Gospels and related writings*. Rev. edn. Cambridge: J. Clarke & Co.; Louisville, KY: Westminster/John Knox Press, 1991.

The Old Testament Pseudepigrapha. Edited by James H. Charlesworth. 2 vols. Garden City: Doubleday, 1983–1985.

Vermes, Geza. *The Dead Sea Scrolls in English*. 3rd edn. Harmondsworth: Penguin, 1987. This should now be supplemented with Robert H. Eisenman & Michael Wise, *The Dead Sea Scrolls Uncovered* (Shaftesbury, etc.: Element, 1992).

Introduction: Which Jesus?

History of Jesus Research

Evans, Craig A. *Life of Jesus Research: An Annotated Bibliography*. New Testament Tools and Studies 13. Leiden, etc.: Brill, 1989.

Hagner, Donald A. *The Jewish Reclamation of Jesus: An Analysis and Critique of Modern Jewish Study of Jesus*. Grand Rapids: Academie/Zondervan, 1984.

Kümmel, Werner Georg. *The New Testament: The History of the Investigation of Its Problems*. Translated by S. McLean Gilmour and Howard C. Kee. London: SCM, 1973. See also his extensive survey articles "Jesusforschung seit 1981", in *Theologische Rundschau* 53 (1988) – 56 (1991).

Neill, Stephen, and Wright, Tom. *The Interpretation of the*

Testament: 1861–1986. Oxford/New York: Oxford University Press, 1988.

Wright, N. T. "Quest for the Historical Jesus." *Anchor Bible Dictionary* 3 (1992): 796–802.

General Problems in the Study of Jesus

Bowden, John. *Jesus: The Unanswered Questions.* London: SCM, 1990.

Harvey, A. E. *Jesus and the Constraints of History.* London: Duckworth, 1982.

Meyer, Ben F. *The Aims of Jesus.* London: SCM, 1979.

Sources for the Historical Jesus

Mason, Steve. *Josephus and the New Testament.* Peabody, MA: Hendrickson, 1992.

Meier, John P. *A Marginal Jew: Rethinking the Historical Jesus.* Vol. 1. New York, etc.: Doubleday, 1991.

Bruce, F. F. *Jesus and Christian Origins outside the New Testament* (2nd edn. London: Hodder & Stoughton, 1984).

Chapter One: Where Did Jesus Come From?

Bauckham, Richard. *Jude and the Relatives of Jesus in the Early Church.* Edinburgh: T&T Clark, 1990.

Brown, Raymond E. *The Birth of the Messiah: A Commentary on the Infancy Narratives in Matthew and Luke.* New York, etc.: Doubleday, 1977. Brown evaluates subsequent scholarship in "Gospel Infancy Narrative Research from 1976 to 1986", *Catholic Biblical Quarterly* 48 (1986) 468–483, 660–680.

Cranfield, C. E. B. "Some Reflections on the Virgin Birth." *Scottish Journal of Theology* 41 (1988) 177–189.

Laurentin, René. *The Truth of Christmas Beyond the Myths: The Gospels of the Infancy of Christ.* Translated by Michael J. Wrenn et al. Petersham, MA: St. Bede's

Publications, 1986.

Articles on Bethlehem, Nazareth, and Capernaum in the *Anchor Bible Dictionary*.

Chapter Two: Was Jesus the Messiah?

The Messianic Hope in Ancient Judaism
De Jonge, Marinus. "Messiah." *Anchor Bible Dictionary* 4 (1992) 777–788.
Klausner, Joseph. *The Messianic Idea in Israel from Its Beginning to the Completion of the Mishnah.* Translated by W. F. Stinespring. London: Allen & Unwin, 1956.
Neusner, Jacob, et al., eds. *Judaisms and their Messiahs at the Turn of the Christian Era.* Cambridge, etc.: Cambridge University Press, 1987.
Scholem, Gershom. *The Messianic Idea in Judaism.* New York: Schocken, 1971.
Schürer, Emil. *The History of the Jewish People in the Age of Jesus Christ (175 B. C. – A. D. 135).* A New English Version Revised and Edited by G. Vermes et al. Vol. 2, pp. 488 – 554. Edinburgh: T&T Clark, 1979.

Was Jesus the Messiah?
Hengel, Martin. *The Cross of the Son of God.* Translated by J. Bowden. London: SCM, 1986.
Witherington, Ben, III. *The Christology of Jesus.* Minneapolis: Fortress, 1990.

Chapter Three: Why Did Jesus Predict the Destruction of the Temple?

Goodman, Martin. *The Ruling Class of Judaea: The Origins of the Jewish Revolt against Rome A. D. 66–70.* Cambridge, etc.: Cambridge University Press, 1987.

Jeremias, Joachim. *Jerusalem in the Time of Jesus: An Investigation into Economic and Social Conditions during the New Testament Period.* Translated by F. H. & C. H. Cave. Philadelphia: Fortress, 1969.

Saldarini, A. J. *Pharisees, Scribes and Sadducees in Palestinian Society: A Sociological Approach.* Wilmington: Glazier, 1988.

Sanders, E. P. *Judaism: Practice and Belief 63 BCE – 63 CE* London: SCM, 1992.

Chapter Four: Did Jesus Fail?

General

Borg, Marcus. *Jesus: A New Vision.* San Francisco: Harper & Row, 1987.

Harvey, A. E. *Jesus and the Constraints of History.* London: Duckworth, 1982.

Meyer, Ben F. *The Aims of Jesus.* London: SCM, 1979.

The Kingdom of God

Beasley-Murray, G. R. *Jesus and the Kingdom of God.* Exeter: Paternoster, 1986.

Chilton, Bruce, ed. *God in Strength.* Sheffield: Sheffield Academic Press, 1987.

Viviano, Benedict T. *The Kingdom of God in History.* Wilmington: Glazier, 1988.

Parables

Blomberg, Craig L. *Interpreting the Parables.* Leicester: Apollos, 1990.

Jeremias, Joachim. *The Parables of Jesus.* Translated by S. H. Hooke. 3rd edn. London: SCM, 1972.

Westermann, Claus. *The Parables of Jesus in the Light of the Old Testament.* Translated and edited by F. W. Golka and A. H. B. Logan. Edinburgh: T&T Clark, 1990.

The Transfiguration

McGuckin, John. *The Transfiguration of Jesus in Scripture and Tradition*. Lewiston, NY: Mellen, 1986.

Jesus' View of his Own Suffering

Bayer, Hans F. *Jesus' Predictions of Vindication and Resurrection*. Tübingen: Mohr (Siebeck), 1986.

Hengel, Martin. *The Cross of the Son of God*, 221–263. Translated by J. Bowden. London: SCM, 1986.

Stuhlmacher, Peter. *Reconciliation, Law, and Righteousness: Essays in Biblical Theology*. Translated by E. R. Kalin. Philadelphia: Fortress, 1986. [Especially the first three chapters.]

The Last Supper

Jeremias, Joachim. *The Eucharistic Words of Jesus*. Translated by N. Perrin. London: SCM, 1966.

Marshall, I. Howard. *Last Supper and Lord's Supper*. Exeter: Paternoster, 1980.

Jesus' Future Hope

Beasley-Murray, George R. *Jesus and the Last Days*. Peabody, MA: Hendrickson, 1993.

Borg, Marcus J. *Jesus: A New Vision*, especially pp. 150–171.

Caird, G. B. *The Language and Imagery of the Bible*, chapter 14. London: Duckworth, 1980.

Cranfield, C. E. B. "Thoughts on New Testament Eschatology." *Scottish Journal of Theology* 35 (1982) 497–512.

Harvey, A. E. *Jesus and the Constraints of History*, chapter 4. London: Duckworth, 1982.

Meyer, Ben F. "Jesus' Scenario of the Future." *Downside Review* 109 (1991) 1–15.

Tiede, David L. *Jesus and the Future*. Cambridge: Cambridge University Press, 1990.

Chapter Five: Was Jesus a Christian?

First-Century Judaism

Grabbe, Lester L. *Judaism from Cyprus to Hadrian.* 2 vols. Minneapolis: Augsburg Fortress, 1992.

Hengel, Martin. *Judaism and Hellenism: Studies in their Encounter in Palestine during the Early Hellenistic Period.* 2 vols. in 1. London: SCM, 1974.

Hengel, Martin. *The 'Hellenization' of Judaea in the First Century after Christ.* Translated by J. Bowden. London: SCM; Philadelphia: TPI, 1989.

Sanders, E. P. *Judaism: Practice and Belief 63BCE – 66CE.* London: SCM; Philadelphia: TPI, 1992.

Was Jesus a Christian?

Dunn, James D. G. *The Partings of the Ways Between Christianity and Judaism and their Significance for the Character of Christianity.* London: SCM; Philadelphia: TPI, 1991.

Jeremias, Joachim. *Jesus' Promise to the Nations.* Translated by S. H. Hooke. London: SCM, 1958.

Rowland, Christopher. *Christian Origins: An Account of the Setting and Character of the Most Important Messianic Sect of Judaism.* London: SPCK, 1985.

Sanders, E. P. *Jesus and Judaism.* London: SCM, 1985.

Vermes, Geza. *Jesus the Jew.* 2nd edn. London: SCM, 1983. And *The Religion of Jesus the Jew.* London: SCM, 1993.

Chapter Six: How Did Jesus Pray?

Barton, Stephen. *The Spirituality of the Gospels.* London: SPCK, 1992.

Cooke, Bernard J. *God's Beloved: Jesus' Experience of the Transcendent.* Philadelphia: TPI, 1992.

Dunn, James D. G. *Jesus and the Spirit*. London: SCM, 1975.

Jeremias, Joachim. *The Prayers of Jesus*. Translated by John Bowden et al. London: SCM, 1967.

Petuchowski, Jakob J., and Brocke, Michael, eds. *The Lord's Prayer and Jewish Liturgy*. Translated by E. Petuchowski. London: Burns & Oates, 1978.

Turner, M. M. B. "Prayer in the Gospels and Acts." In *Teach Us to Pray: Prayer in the Bible and the World*, 58–83. Edited by D. A. Carson. Exeter: Paternoster; Grand Rapids: Baker, 1990.

Chapter Seven: Why Was Jesus Exalted To Heaven?

The Resurrection and Exaltation of Jesus

Brown, Raymond E. *The Virginal Conception and Bodily Resurrection of Jesus*. London: Chapman, 1973.

Goergen, Donald. *The Death and Resurrection of Jesus*. Wilmington: Glazier, 1988.

Harris, Murray J. *Raised Immortal: Resurrection and Immortality in the New Testament*. London: Marshall, Morgan & Scott, 1983.

Lapide, Pinchas. *The Resurrection of Jesus: a Jewish Perspective*. Translated by Wilhelm C. Linss. London: SPCK, 1984.

Moule, C. F. D., ed. *The Significance of the Message of the Resurrection for Faith in Jesus Christ*. London: SCM, 1968.

The Worship of Jesus

Bauckham, Richard. "The Worship of Jesus." *Anchor Bible Dictionary* 3 (1992) 812–819.

Dunn, James D. G. *Christology in the Making*. London: SCM, 1980.

Hurtado, Larry W. *One God, One Lord: Early Christian Devotion and Ancient Jewish Monotheism*. Philadelphia: Fortress, 1988.

Notes

Introduction: Which Jesus?

[1]Albert Schweitzer, *The Quest of the Historical Jesus*, trans. W. Montgomery, 2nd edn. (London: Black, 1922), 4f. and *passim*. Bruce Chilton reformulates Schweitzer's insight for the twentieth century as follows: "The result is that the ideologies of yesterday are uncovered within lives of Jesus, and that today's ideologies are triumphantly invoked at the end..." (*The Temple of Jesus: His Sacrificial Program Within a Cultural History of Sacrifice* (University Park, PA: Pennsylvania State University Press, 1992), 93.

[2]Using a broader brush, John Bowden paints an intriguing picture of the "kaleidoscopic" variety of Christ images ancient and modern, in his important work *Jesus: The Unanswered Questions* (London: SCM, 1988), 51–71 and *passim*.

[3]E.g. *Church Dogmatics* IV.3, trans. G. W. Bromiley (Edinburgh: T&T Clark, 1958), 165. Note, too, his famous exchange of letters with Adolf von Harnack in 1923: H. Martin Rumscheidt, *Revelation and Theology: An analysis of the Barth-Harnack correspondence of 1923* (Cambridge: University Press, 1972), 35 and *passim*. See also Eberhard Busch, *Karl Barth: His life from letters and autobiographical texts*, trans. J. Bowden (London: SCM, 1976), 448 and *passim*.

[4]Dietrich Bonhoeffer, e.g. *Christology*, trans. John Bowden (London: Collins, 1966), 75: "The confirmation of historical investigation is irrelevant before the self-attestation of Christ in the present." This despite his earlier admission that "dogmatics needs to be certain of the historicity of Jesus Christ, i.e. of the identity of the Christ of preaching with the Jesus of history" (p. 73).

[5]See the classic statement in Rudolf Bultmann, *Jesus and the Word*, trans. L. P. Smith & E. Huntress (London: Collins Fontana, c1962), 12–14 and *passim*. Bultmann's student Willi Marxsen concurs as recently as 1990: *Jesus and Easter: Did God Raise the Historical Jesus from the Dead?*, trans. V. P. Furnish (Nashville: Abingdon, 1990), 13ff.

[6]Docetism was an early Christian, and especially Gnostic, tendency to consider the human life and sufferings of Jesus as merely apparent rather than real.

[7]The image of 19th-century liberal Jesus scholarship contemplating its own reflection at the bottom of a deep well was made famous by George Tyrrell, *Christianity at the Cross-Roads* (London: Longmans, Green & Co., 1909),

44. His tongue firmly planted in his cheek, Tyrrell describes the presuppositions of this quest as follows (p. 40): "No sooner was the Light of the World kindled than it was put under a bushel. The Pearl of Great Price fell into the dustheap of Catholicism, not without the wise permission of Providence, desirous to preserve it till the day when Germany should rediscover it and separate it from its useful but deplorable accretions. Thus between Christ and early Catholicism there is not a bridge but a chasm."

[8]An example of this is Norman Perrin, *Rediscovering the Teaching of Jesus* (London: SCM, 1967), 39–47.

[9]A criticism most influentially made in E. P. Sanders, *Paul and Palestinian Judaism* (1977); *Jesus and Judaism* (1985).

[10]See e.g. John Dominic Crossan, *The Historical Jesus: The Life of a Mediterranean Jewish Peasant* (San Francisco: Harper, 1991); also Helmut Koester, *Ancient Christian Gospels: Their History and Development* (London: SCM; Philadelphia: Trinity, 1990); John S. Kloppenborg, *The Formation of Q: Trajectories in Ancient Wisdom Collections* (Philadelphia: Fortress, 1987); and most recently Burton L. Mack, *The Lost Gospel: The Book of Q and Christian Origins* (Shaftesbury etc.: Element, 1993).

[11]To date, two volumes of results in the Jesus Seminar Series have been published: Robert W. Funk et al., *The Parables of Jesus: Red Letter Edition* (Sonoma, CA: Polebridge, 1988) and *The Gospel of Mark: Red Letter Edition* (1991).

[12]A useful anthology of current perspectives in this school of thought can be found in *Semeia* 55 (1991), with contributions by leading advocates (John S. Kloppenborg & Leif S. Vaage, pp. 1–14; Burton L. Mack, pp. 15–39). Richard A. Horsley, "Q and Jesus: Assumptions, Approaches, and Analyses" (pp. 175–209) argues for a more moderate position involving the consideration of *clusters* of Q logia rather than just individual sayings; this leads him to allow a more prophetic picture of Jesus. (For a sociological critique see further Horsley's important book *Sociology and the Jesus Movement* (New York: Crossroad, 1989), 108ff. and *passim*.)

In the same volume Harold W. Attridge offers a useful and circumspect criticism of the "Q" school ("Reflections on Research into Q", pp. 223–234). After surveying the field he criticizes the elaborate assumptions and hypotheses involved, for instance, in the multiplication of redactional layers in Q. He highlights the tendency of Q scholarship to ignore christological titles, the death and resurrection theme, the deeds of Jesus, and in general the evidence for the widespread nature of kerygmatic-apocalyptic Christianity in the earliest church – which often co-existed side by side with a more wisdom-oriented strain. Attridge concludes (p. 233), "A focus on Q, particularly Q[1] [Kloppenborg's first layer], as the surest path to the origins of Christianity is methodologically flawed. ... The originating figure himself was a much more complex individual than Q^1 gives him credit for being."

From a somewhat different angle, another leading advocate of the idea of Jesus as a Cynic philosopher is F. G. Downing, e.g. in *Cynics and Christian Origins* (Edinburgh: T&T Clark, 1992).

[13]Kloppenborg, *Formation of Q*, 244–245, does allow for early and possibly dominical elements even in the secondary (apocalyptic) compositional phase of Q. Another somewhat more cautious approach is that of David Catchpole, *The Quest for Q* (Edinburgh: T&T Clark, 1993).

[14]This point is repeatedly made in N. T. Wright's light-hearted satire of J. D. Crossan's approach, "Taking the Text with Her Pleasure", *Theology* 96 (1993) 303–310.

It is of course true that all of us bring our own presuppositions to the task of interpretation. Circularity of reasoning, therefore, should not as such occasion surprise or necessitate outright dismissal. Instead, we always face the problem of distinguishing more or less appropriate circularities. The problem lies not in the *fact* of circular or "spiral" reasoning but in unacknowledged starting points and unexamined presuppositions.

[15]Crossan, *The Historical Jesus*, 237f., 282–292 explicitly argues in such terms, suggesting that at an early stage in his career Jesus radically changed his mind regarding John the Baptist.

[16]On this point cf. also J. L. Houlden's review of Crossan in *Times Literary Supplement*, 25 September 1992, p. 27; and see E. P. Sanders, *The Historical Figure of Jesus*, 176–187. Even if one agreed to swallow the redactional manoeuvres within the supposed Q document, one would still be left with a massive presumption to reconstruct the theology of a "Q^1-Christianity" *solely and sufficiently* on the basis of one hypothetical list of sayings. (N.B. Crossan's reconstruction thrives precisely on the lacunae which he discovers in relation to eschatology, Kingdom of God, the death of Christ, etc.) This procedure is all the more remarkable in view of the universally acknowledged importance of story and narrative, midrash and *haggadah*, for the culture of first-century Palestinian Judaism.

[17]Thus N. T. Wright, e.g. in Stephen Neill & Tom Wright, *The Interpretation of the New Testament: 1861–1986* (Oxford/New York: Oxford University Press, 1988), 379–403. See also Wright's survey of Jesus research in "Quest for the Historical Jesus", *Anchor Bible Dictionary* 3 (1992) 796–802. A fuller survey (in German) of the last decade of Jesus research is offered in a series of articles by Werner Georg Kümmel, "Jesusforschung seit 1981", *Theologische Rundschau* 53 (1988) 229–249 [history of research, methodology]; 54 (1989) 1–53 [comprehensive

182

This Jesus

accounts]; 55 (1990) 21–45 [Jesus' teaching]; 56 (1991) 27–53 [parables], 391–420 [Jesus' personal claim, his trial and death on the cross].

[18]John Dominic Crossan, Helmut Koester, Burton L. Mack, James M. Robinson, et al. On the basis of a primarily sayings-based approach, this latter school prefers to view Jesus as an itinerant Cynic sage with little or no interest in prophetic or apocalyptic concerns.

[19]The most important recent authors in this vein include James H. Charlesworth, *Jesus within Judaism* (New York: Doubleday, 1988); Ben F. Meyer, *The Aims of Jesus* (London: SCM, 1979); E. P. Sanders, *Jesus and Judaism* and now *The Historical Figure of Jesus*; Geza Vermes, *Jesus the Jew* (2nd edn. London: SCM, 1983), *Jesus and the World of Judaism* (London: SCM, 1983), and *The Religion of Jesus the Jew* (London: SCM, 1993). Comparable continental authors might be said to include Martin Hengel, *The Charismatic Leader and His Followers* trans. J. C. G. Greig & ed. J. Riches (Edinburgh: T&T Clark, 1981); *The Cross of the Son of God*, trans. J. Bowden (London: SCM, 1986); Marinus de Jonge, e.g. *Jesus the Servant-Messiah* (New Haven/London: Yale University Press, 1991); Rainer Riesner, *Jesus als Lehrer* (2nd edn. Tübingen: Mohr (Siebeck), 1984); as well as Gerd Theissen, *The Shadow of the Galilean*, trans. J. Bowden (London: SCM, 1987); *The Gospels in Context: Social and Political History in the Synoptic Tradition*, trans. L. M. Maloney (Edinburgh: T&T Clark, 1992). N. T. Wright, having commented extensively on what he calls the "Third Quest", is currently preparing a major book for publication.

[20]See e.g. Gaalyah Cornfeld (ed.), *The Historical Jesus: A Scholarly View of the Man and His World* (New York: Macmillan; London: Collier Macmillan, 1982); David Daube, *The New Testament and Rabbinic Judaism* (London: Athlone, 1956); David Flusser, *Judaism and the Origins of Christianity* (Jerusalem: Magnes, 1988); Pinchas Lapide, *The Resurrection of Jesus*, trans. W. C. Linss (London: SPCK, 1984); Geza Vermes, see n. 19 above; Paul Winter, *On the Trial of Jesus*, trans., rev. and ed. T. A. Burkill & G. Vermes, 2nd edn. (Berlin: de Gruyter, 1974).

[21]Earlier important Jewish contributors included C. G. Montefiore, Israel Abrahams and Joseph Klausner; Alfred Edersheim as a Jewish Christian is also worth noting.

[22]Donald A. Hagner offers a critical survey of this trend in *The Jewish Reclamation of Jesus: An Analysis and Critique of Modern Jewish Study of Jesus* (Grand Rapids: Academie/Zondervan, 1984). See also Anton Wessels, *Images of Jesus: How Jesus Is Perceived in non-European Cultures*, trans. J. Vriend (London: SCM; Grand Rapids: Eerdmans, 1990), 21–37.

[23]Ben F. Meyer, *The Aims of Jesus* (London: SCM, 1979), 252 (ital. mine). Cf. Marinus de Jonge, *Christology in Context: The Earliest Christian Response to Jesus* (Philadelphia: Westminster, 1988) and *Jesus, the Servant-Messiah* (New Haven/London: Yale University Press, 1991); Ben Witherington III, *The Christology of Jesus* (Minneapolis: Fortress, 1990), *passim*; Peter Stuhlmacher, *Jesus von Nazareth – Christus des Glaubens* (Stuttgart: Calwer, 1988); Eduard Schweizer, *Jesus Christ: The Man from Nazareth and Exalted Lord*, ed. H. Gloer (Macon: Mercer University Press, 1987).

[24]A more complete guide to Jesus research up to 1988 can be found in Craig A. Evans, *Life of Jesus Research: An Annotated Bibliography*, New Testament Tools and Studies 13 (Leiden etc.: Brill, 1989).

[25]Chrestus was a common slave name (which in Hellenistic Greek was liable to be pronounced "Christus"); if Suetonius had intended Jesus, a religious leader who had been dead for quite a long time, one might have expected a word or two of explanation. See also J. Mottershead, *Suetonius: Claudius* (Bristol: Bristol Classical Press, 1986) 149–57.

[26]The same is true for another Roman reference: a letter of Pliny the Younger to Trajan from Asia Minor around AD 112 discusses the persecution of Christians and mentions their worship of Christ "as if a god", *quasi deo* (*Letter* 10.96). On Greek and Roman sources in general see the useful discussion by Murray J. Harris, "References to Jesus in Early Classical Authors", in David Wenham (ed.), *Gospel Perspectives*, vol. 5 (Sheffield: JSOT Press, 1985), 343–68.

[27]E.g. G. A. Wells, *Who Was Jesus? A Critique of the New Testament Record* (La Salle, IL: Open Court, 1989); John M. Allegro, e.g. *The Dead Sea Scrolls and the Christian Myth* (2nd edn. Buffalo, NY: Prometheus, 1992), 190–203.

[28]E.g. Hugh Schonfield, *The Passover Plot: A New Interpretation of the Life and Death of Jesus* (New York: Geis, 1966); cf. Barbara Thiering, *The Qumran Origins of the Christian Church*, Australian and New Zealand Studies in Theology and Religion (Sydney: Theological Explorations, 1983), 156–226; she has now expanded this argument in *Jesus the Man: New Interpretation from the Dead Sea Scrolls* (New York/London: Doubleday, 1992).

[29]*Peregrinus* 11; on Lucian as well as Celsus see Robert Wilken, *The Christians as the Romans Saw Them* (New Haven: Yale University Press, 1984), 96f.

[30]Cf. John P. Meier, *A Marginal Jew: Rethinking the Historical Jesus*, vol. 1 (New York etc.: Doubleday, 1991), 61; also pp. 56–88. Meier's omission

of any reference to the Christ leaves him with the awkwardness of an unexplained statement about Christians being "named after him". See also Ernst Bammel, n. 31 below.

[31]See e.g. Ernst Bammel, "Zum Testimonium Flavianum", in idem, *Judaica: Kleine Schriften I* (Tübingen: Mohr (Siebeck), 1986), 183.

[32]See p. 33 and n. 22 below.

[33]B.T. *Sanhedrin* 43a; *Shabbat* 116a-b.

[34]On this interesting document see e.g. Günter Schlichting, *Ein jüdisches Leben Jesu: Die verschollene Toledot-Jeschu-Fassung Tam û-mû'âd* (Tübingen: Mohr (Siebeck), 1982).

[35]Recurring themes include the name Pantera (in Celsus and the Talmud), charges of Jesus' sorcery and leading Israel astray (B.T. *Sanhedrin* 43a; *Abodah Zarah* 27b; P.T. *Abodah Zarah* 2, 40d–41a, etc.; cf. already Mark 3.22 par.), and death on the eve of Passover (agreeing with the Johannine but not the Synoptic chronology); also the curious assertions, in Celsus and the *Toledot Yeshu*, of Jesus' escape after his arrest and his execution together with John the Baptist. I am grateful to Dr. William Horbury for drawing my attention to these correlations, which are discussed and documented e.g. by Ernst Bammel, "Christian Origins in Jewish Tradition", in his *Judaica*, 220–238, especially pp. 230ff. Ethelbert Stauffer, *Jesus and His Story*, trans. R. & C. Winston (London: SCM, 1960), 162 claims that independent Jewish tradition about Jesus may have survived until around AD 500.

[36]Cf. similarly John P. Meier, *A Marginal Jew*, 1.93, interacting with important earlier studies by Joseph Klausner and Johann Maier.

[37]The brief text of the *Secret Gospel* is contained in a letter discovered by Morton Smith and published in *Clement of Alexandria and a Secret Gospel of Mark* (Cambridge, MA: Harvard University Press, 1973). A circumspect discussion and appraisal is offered in Meier, *A Marginal Jew*, 1.120–122 and notes; his conclusion is critical of the exaggerated claims sometimes advanced for the significance of this text: "To use such a small fragment of dubious origins to rewrite the history of Jesus and the Gospel tradition is to lean on a reed" (p. 121).

[38]See John Dominic Crossan, *Four Other Gospels: Shadows on the Contours of Canon* (Minneapolis etc.: Winston Press, 1985); idem, *The Historical Jesus: The Life of a Mediterranean Jewish Peasant* (San Francisco: Harper, 1991); also Helmut Koester, *Ancient Christian Gospels: Their History and Development* (London: SCM; Philadelphia: Trinity, 1990).

[39]The Ebionites were an early sect of Jewish Christians known from Justin Martyr (*Dialogue* 47), Irenaeus (e.g. *Against Heresies* 1.18.2) and Hippolytus, among others. Their characteristics included observance of the Mosaic law and a belief in the human descent of Jesus from Joseph and Mary.

[40]Christopher M. Tuckett, "Thomas and the Synoptics", *Novum Testamentum* 30 (1988) 132–157 has demonstrated a degree of dependence on redactional elements in all three of the synoptic gospels. The shift away from an originally synoptic-like orientation is also demonstrated by N. T. Wright, *The New Testament and the People of God* (London: SPCK, 1992), 435–443. He points out in particular that the term "kingdom of God", which is found in an altered, non-eschatological sense in the *Gospel of Thomas*, is overwhelmingly likely to have originated in "an overtly Jewish movement which used it in a sense close to its mainline one.... If there has been a shift in the usage, it is far more likely to have been *from* this Jewish home base into a quasi-Gnostic sense..." (p. 440). See further Meier, *A Marginal Jew*, 1.124–139 and notes.

[41]Meier, *A Marginal Jew*, 1.123.

[42]Raymond E. Brown, "The *Gospel of Peter* and Canonical Gospel Priority", *New Testament Studies* 33 (1987) 321–43. Similar assessments abound.

[43]For a recent treatment of the subject of dominical teaching in Paul cf. e.g. Michael B. Thompson, *Clothed with Christ: The Example and Teaching of Jesus in Romans 12.1–15.13* (Sheffield: Sheffield Academic Press, 1991).

[44]Thus also e.g. Chilton, *The Temple of Jesus*, 115f.

[45]See p. 4 above. Crossan, *The Historical Jesus*, 424f. attempts to defend the Jesus Seminar's "majority vote" principle by citing comparable procedures used by the United Bible Societies in their edition of the Greek New Testament. Four major advantages of the UBS team, however, make this an improper comparison. (i) The UBS team was arguably composed of international experts occupying a recognizable middle ground in text critical methodology. (ii) With only very few exceptions (text included in square brackets), UBS produced a clear text without shades of pink and grey. (iii) "Dissenting opinions", i.e. variant readings together with supporting evidence, were neatly included in the apparatus included with every edition. (iv) Perhaps most importantly, UBS dealt in virtually every case with variations (however early) on an assumed single original text, rather than with gospel-like documents that arise out of a multiplicity of parallel traditions, more than one of which might be authentic at any given point.

[46]Compare also the moderate and circumspect list of criteria offered by Ben F. Meyer, "Jesus Christ", *Anchor Bible Dictionary* 3 (1992) 776f. In the same work John Riches, "The Actual Words of Jesus", endorses a

methodological emphasis on "those sayings which, taken together, can be seen to have a coherent sense and to offer an explanation both of Jesus' relationship to his contemporary world and its beliefs and to the subsequent history of the early Church and its beliefs" (ibid., p. 804).

[47]See e.g. Joachim Jeremias, *New Testament Theology*, trans. J. Bowden (London: SCM, 1971); Birger Gerhardsson, *The Gospel Tradition* (Lund: Gleerup, 1986); Rainer Riesner, *Jesus als Lehrer* (2nd edn. Tübingen: Mohr (Siebeck), 1984).

[48]Thus e.g. Riesner, *Jesus als Lehrer*, 491–498; from a different perspective see now Gerd Theissen, *The Gospels in Context: Social and Political History in the Synoptic Tradition*, trans. L. M. Maloney (Edinburgh: T&T Clark, 1992).   Theissen's argument is particularly persuasive on the connection between the written composition of the Synoptic Apocalypse (Mark 13 par.; note 13.14) and the Judaean crisis under Caligula in AD 39–40 (pp. 151–165).

[49]For example, both Mark and Matthew show themselves keen to include the Gentiles within the scope of Christian mission (e.g. Mark 7.19; 14.9; Matt. 8.5–13; 28.19).   Against the background of this redactional interest, we can affirm an increased likelihood of authenticity in passages like Jesus' rebuke of the Syro-Phoenician woman (Mark 7.27 par.) or his instructions that the twelve disciples are to "go nowhere among the Gentiles" on their Galilean mission (Matt. 10.5).

[50]See also Peter Stuhlmacher, *Jesus von Nazareth – Christus des Glaubens* (Stuttgart: Calwer Verlag, 1988).   Drawing on A. E. Harvey, *Jesus and the Constraints of History* (London: Duckworth, 1982), N. T. Wright makes a compatible point: Jesus' life, teaching and death cohere, and the very fact of his crucifixion suggests "that the events which led up to that moment must have been substantially as the four canonical gospels record them" (*Who Was Jesus?*, 15; cf. his "'Constraints' and the Jesus of History", *Scottish Journal of Theology* 39 (1986) 189–210).   A significant related point is raised by Eugene E. Lemcio, *The past of Jesus in the gospels* (Cambridge etc.: Cambridge University Press, 1991), who shows that far from conveniently making Jesus address the concerns of their own Christian experience (e.g. circumcision, kosher laws, mixed marriages), the evangelists consciously distinguish between the past story of Jesus and their own time. This serves as a methodological restraint on their treatment of the Jesus of history and the Christ of faith.

[51]*Der sogenannte historische Jesus und der geschichtliche, biblische Christus* (1892; 2nd edn. Munich: Kaiser, 1956); E.T. trans. & ed. Carl E. Braaten (Philadelphia: Fortress, 1964).

[52]Compare Ben Witherington III, *The Christology of Jesus* (Minneapolis: Fortress, 1990); and on the problem of history and interpretation note the important methodological discussion in N. T. Wright, *The New Testament and the People of God* (London: SPCK, 1992), 81–120.

[53]A similar point was made by G. K. Chesterton in a fascinating article on the separation of Jesus from Christ. Allowing for the possibility of a *nuance* of functional difference between the names Napoleon and Bonaparte, Chesterton nevertheless concludes, "If there were no life of General Bonaparte there would... be no legend of Napoleon; his public life may have been more glorious than his private, but it is essential... that they should both have happened to the same man" ("Jesus or Christ? A Reply to Mr Roberts", *Hibbert Journal* 7 (1909) 746).

Chapter One: Where Did Jesus Come From?

[1]P.T. *Megillah* 1, 77a.

[2]See J. B. Pritchard, *Ancient Near Eastern Texts Relating to the Old Testament*, 3rd edn. (Princeton: Princeton University Press, 1969), pp. 483–90, No. 290 (EA).

[3]Prior to this time, St. Jerome suggests that from Hadrian until the fourth century the cave of Jesus' birth had been turned into a pagan shrine of Tammuz/Adonis (Letter 58.3 to Paulinus).

[4]John 7.40f.: "Surely the Messiah does not come from Galilee, does he? Has not the Scripture said that the Messiah is descended from David and comes from Bethlehem, the village where David lived?" It is unclear whether this is an example of Johannine irony or of the author's genuine unfamiliarity with the Synoptic tradition.

[5]Note, however, the obscure 4th century tradition regarding the birth in Bethlehem of one Menahem ben Hezekiah, the son of Judah and grandson of Hezekiah of Gamla, who was a Messianic pretender and for a while led the Revolt against Rome in AD 66: P.T. *Berakhot* 2.4, 5a18; *Lamentations Rabbah* 1.51; cf. Josephus, *War* 2.433ff.; also Jeremias, *Jerusalem*, 277. See further *Targum Pseudo-Jonathan* Gen. 35.21; and of course the account of Herod's inquiry in Matt. 2.4–6.

[6]Thus e.g. John P. Meier, without reference to the works of Benoit or Laurentin (cited below), in a recent full-scale treatment of Jesus: "Jesus was born in the hill town of Nazareth" (*A Marginal Jew*, 1.350; more cautiously on p. 407). Even so circumspect a scholar as Raymond E. Brown concludes

that the evidence for Jesus' birth in Bethlehem is "much weaker than the evidence for Davidic descent or even... the evidence for virginal conception" (*The Birth of the Messiah: A Commentary on the Infancy Narratives in Matthew and Luke* (New York etc.: Doubleday, c1977), 516. Others are less diplomatic, e.g. Fergus Millar: he allows that Matthew's account of events around the nativity *could* be true at least in outline, even if Luke's is "wholly impossible"; nevertheless, "in fact neither is true" ("Reflections on the Trials [*sic*] of Jesus", in *A Tribute to Geza Vermes: Essays on Jewish and Christian Literature and History*, ed. P. R. Davies & R. T. White (Sheffield: Sheffield Academic Press, 1990), pp. 356–359). Although such assessments must be taken very seriously, it may be significant to note that they rest more on the *lack* of corroborating data than on cogent evidence to the contrary.

[7]A census is conceivable at the time of the oath of allegiance to Herod and the Emperor (c. 7 BC), when Augustus had a documented desire to take stock of the entire empire, and Rome was mounting efforts to tighten control over Palestine and the Eastern frontier. Although Saturninus and not Quirinius was legate to Syria at this time (9–6 BC; see also Tertullian, *Against Marcion* 4.19), in a general sense Luke's mention of the latter refers to the census which was the culmination of a process that had been going on for some time. While the specific reference to Quirinius may, like that to Theudas in Acts 5.36, be an excusable oversight (Josephus, too, on occasion appears to confuse some of the remarkably similar circumstances of AD 6 with those around 4 BC), the remainder of Luke's reference on the census can be satisfactorily explained. Thus the argument of P. Benoit in his remarkable but by and large ignored article, "Quirinius", *Dictionnaire de la Bible: Supplément* 9 (1979) 696–699, 705, 715. [He also cites A. Schalit to the effect that Herod may have conducted a census every six years, p. 696.] An older work still useful in some respects is W. M. Ramsay, *Was Christ Born at Bethlehem? A Study on the Credibility of St. Luke* (London: Hodder & Stoughton, 1898).

[8]I.e. *prôtos* with the genitive (=*proteros*), as e.g. in John 1.15, 30; 15.18. So e.g. Nigel Turner, *Grammatical Insights into the New Testament* (Edinburgh: T&T Clark, 1965), 23f.; more recently John Nolland, *Luke 1–9:20* (Dallas: Word, 1989), 101f.; see also N. T. Wright, *Who Was Jesus?* (London: SPCK, 1992), 89. Critics of such a rendering (e.g. G. Ogg, "The Quirinius Question Today", *Expository Times* 79 (1967–68) 233) point out that this sense of *prôtos* followed by a genitive absolute would be highly unusual. Nolland (*Luke*, 102), however, replies that Luke's Greek remains awkward on *any* reading. Later scribes repeatedly tried to put things right,

some evidently reading "first" (so the majority text) and others, it seems, "before" (so e.g. *Codex Sinaiticus*, changing the word order).

[9]Note Benoit, "Quirinius", 700: contrary to the assertions of most commentators, Luke does *not* say that Joseph was from Nazareth, merely that he was there with his fiancée, possibly to get married or to work. Indeed, one could take the redactional summary of 2.39f. to be referring only with hindsight to Nazareth as "their" city. Luke 1.26–56, moreover, when taken at face value, does not even require permanent residence in Nazareth for Mary: 1.39 is sufficiently vague to allow a more plausible, shorter trip to Elizabeth to have taken place *after* the (return) journey to Bethlehem in 2.4. Residence in Bethlehem also best accounts for Mary's accompanying Joseph. It is worth noting that Matthew's Joseph leaves Bethlehem only for fear of Herod (2.13) and moves to Nazareth only for fear of Archelaus (2.19–23).

[10]This translation is preferable to the traditional reading "inn": see e.g. A. J. Kerr, "No room in the kataluma", *Expository Times* 103 (1991–92) 15f.

[11]*Protevangelium of James* 18–19; Justin Martyr, *Dialogue* 78; Origen, *Against Celsus* 1.51. Cf. the LXX of Isa 33.16, which, in a messianic context (v. 17ff.), speaks of the righteous man's refuge in a cave. The presence of animals at the birth of Jesus, suggested in the *Protevangelium* and familiar from icons and folklore, is sometimes thought to be conditioned by Christian reflection on Isa. 1.3: "The ox knows its owner, and the donkey its master's crib; but my people Israel does not know, my people do not understand." Joan B. Taylor, *Christians and the Holy Places* (Oxford: Clarendon, 1993), 99–112 argues that the traditional Christian identification of the specific cave of Jesus' birth cannot be shown to predate the third century.

[12]St. Jerome and other patristic sources claim that Mary is descended from David, but there is little NT evidence for this. The possibility of Mary's youth near the Temple is also entertained by Bargil Pixner, *Wege des Messias und Stätten der Urkirche*, ed. R. Riesner (Giessen/Basel: Brunnen, 1991), 54, citing D. Flusser, S. Safrai and F. Manns.

[13]Luke 3.23; 4.22; John 1.45; 6.42. Note, too, that the frequency of death in childbirth in the ancient world would have meant a much greater number of widowers than is the case today. Remarriage for this reason was common-place until the 19th century.

[14]Davidic descent was also claimed for figures like Zerubbabel (1 Chr. 3.19; Matt. 1.12; Luke 3.27), Hillel (P.T. *Ta'anit* 4.2, 68a; *Genesis Rabbah* 98.10), and later R. Hiyya bar Abba and the Babylonian exilarchs. A burial cave in Jerusalem has yielded a first century BC or AD ossuary identifying its occupant as "belonging to the house of David" (*shel bê[t] David*): see

David Flusser, *Judaism and the Origins of Christianity* (Jerusalem: Magnes, 1988), 721f. and pl. 7, with additional references. Vespasian, Domitian and Trajan all persecuted the family of David as a political threat; see further the discussion in Joachim Jeremias, *Jerusalem in the Time of Jesus*, trans. F. H. & C. H. Cave (Philadelphia: Fortress, 1969), 276f. Jesus' Davidic descent is ably defended in R. E. Brown, *Birth of the Messiah*, 505–12; Bargil Pixner offers an intriguing (if somewhat idiosyncratic) treatment of related matters in *Wege des Messias*, 47ff.

[15] The virginal conception and the doctrine of Mary's perpetual virginity are technically different. While the New Testament affirms only the former, the latter is not only the stated doctrine of the Roman Catholic church, but may find expression as early as Ignatius of Antioch (*Ephesians* 19) and possibly in the Apostles' Creed. It was developed in the fourth century by Hilary of Poitiers, Didymus, and later Ambrose. Note also *Protevangelium of James* 19.3–20. It may come as a surprise to Protestant readers to find that this doctrine was endorsed e.g. by the confessional writings of the Lutheran church: Schmalkaldic Articles (1537) 1.3 [Latin]; Formula of Concord (1580) *Solida Declaratio*, 8 (*Die Bekenntnisschriften der evangelisch-lutherischen Kirche*, 8th edn. (Göttingen: Vandenhoeck & Ruprecht, 1979), 1024).

[16] Ignatius, *Letter to the Ephesians* 19.1; see also Justin's *Dialogue* 105.1, Aristeides' *Apology* 15.1, Melito of Sardis, and the *Infancy Gospel of James*.

[17] This is a point also made in the interesting but little known work of René Laurentin, *The Truth of Christmas Beyond the Myths: The Gospels of the Infancy of Christ*, trans. Michael J. Wrenn et al. (Petersham, MA: St. Bede's Publications, 1986), 416 and *passim*.

[18] Thus e.g. Laurentin, *Truth of Christmas*, 406–408. He also accepts the argument that 1.13 in the Prologue may reflect an awareness of the virginal conception when it refers to the Christian's adoption and rebirth as being "not of blood or of the will of the flesh or of the will of a man, but of God." (Note, however, his questionable text critical reading of *hos* for *hoi* (supported only by Irenaeus and Tertullian), assuming that the subject of the clause is in fact Christ rather than the believers.)

[19] While it is true that none of the seven biblical references are positively identified as married women, several evidently refer to a lover (Prov. 30.19; Song 6.8). Arguably the "young woman" for Isaiah is the prophetess who bears his son (8.3f.; cf. 7.14–16).

[20] Philo, in a passage of allegorical comment on the matriarchs as virtues, does conclude from Gen. 21.1; 29.31; 25.1 and Exod. 2.22 that the holy women received "divine seed" directly from God and conceived through no

human agency (*Cherubim* 45–47). However, Philo does not deny that the matriarchs were married, and there is no question here of *virginal* conception. His argument, moreover, unlike the Gospel infancy narratives, occurs in a context of allegorical interpretation of the Bible.

Geza Vermes, *Jesus the Jew*, 2nd edn. (London: SCM, 1983), 218–22 attempts to account for the idea of a "virgin birth" against a Jewish background, but in doing so he seems to travel rather a long way from the plain meaning of the gospel texts. David Daube, after a somewhat tenuous and not altogether germane discussion about Moses' birth, is nevertheless right to conclude that "the narrative of Jesus's birth originated in a properly Jewish rather than Hellenized milieu" (*The New Testament and Rabbinic Judaism* (London: Athlone, 1956), 9).

[21]See Irenaeus, *Against Heresies* 1.26.1–2; 4.33.4. This view has repeatedly been espoused, most recently e.g. in Geoffrey Parrinder, *Son of Joseph: The Parentage of Jesus* (Edinburgh: T&T Clark, 1992).

[22]Cf. *Acts of Pilate* 2.3; Origen, *Against Celsus* 1.28, 32, 69; Epiphanius *Refutation of all Heresies* 78.7; also Tosefta, *Hullin* 2.22–23; B.T. *Shabbat* 43a (Baraita); P.T. *Abodah Zarah* 2.2, 40d73ff.; *Shabbat* 4.4, 14d70ff., etc. An inscription found in Germany mentions one Tiberius Julius Abdes Pantera, an archer from Sidon in Phoenicia who was transferred to Germany in AD 9. (Cf. full documentation in Brown, *Birth of the Messiah*, 535–537). Jane Schaberg, in a recent discussion of these texts from a different perspective, *accepts* the charge of illegitimacy (*The Illegitimacy of Jesus: A Feminist Theological Interpretation of the Infancy Narratives* (San Francisco: Harper & Row, 1987), 145–194 and *passim*); similar, if more muddled, is John Shelby Spong, *Born of a Woman: A Bishop Rethinks the Birth of Jesus* (San Francisco: Harper, 1992).

[23]Deut. 23.2 stipulates that a *mamzer*, more precisely defined in Rabbinic thought as the offspring of either adultery or incest (cf. Mishnah, *Kiddushin* 3.12; *Yebamot* 4.12f. etc.), "shall not enter the congregation of the LORD." Note that intercourse with a woman betrothed to another man constitutes adultery (Deut. 22.23f.). (On the other hand, sexual intercourse by a betrothed couple before marriage, although generally frowned upon, would not render their child illegitimate.)

[24]This continues to include more than a few mainstream biblical scholars. See e.g. the cautious treatment offered by Brown, *Birth of the Messiah*, 517–533 (with full bibliography); also his earlier treatment *The Virginal Conception & Bodily Resurrection of Jesus* (London/Dublin: Chapman, 1973), along with his clear assessment of more recent discussion in *Catholic Biblical Quarterly* 48 (1986) 675–680. Other significant recent contributions include C. E. B. Cranfield, "Some Reflections on the Subject

of the Virgin Birth", *Scottish Journal of Theology* 41 (1988) 177–189; Ben Witherington III, "Birth of Jesus", in *Dictionary of Jesus and the Gospels*, ed. Joel B. Green & Scot McKnight (Leicester/Downers Grove: InterVarsity, 1992), 60–74.

[25]See 4Q318, especially fragment 2, 2.6–9 (now accessible in Robert H. Eisenman & Michael Wise, *The Dead Sea Scrolls Uncovered* (Shaftesbury etc.: Element, 1992), 258–263); also 4QMessAr: once generally thought to apply to the Messiah, the latter document probably pertains to Noah. See the English translation in Geza Vermes, *The Dead Sea Scrolls in English* (3rd edn. London: Penguin, 1987), 305–307; and note "fragment 3" of 4Q534–536 in Eisenman & Wise, 33–37. Cf. further Joseph A. Fitzmyer, "The Aramaic 'Elect of God' Text from Qumran Cave IV", in his *Essays on the Semitic Background of the New Testament* (London: Chapman, 1971), 158–159 and *passim*.

[26]Another (?) "Conon, Deacon of Jerusalem", is honoured in a fourth-century mosaic inscription in what may be a Jewish Christian synagogue at Nazareth. See James F. Strange, "Nazareth", *Anchor Bible Dictionary* 4 (1992) 1050f.; contrast Joan B. Taylor's more sceptical view in *Christians and the Holy Places* (Oxford: Clarendon, 1993), 243. Two grandsons of Jude, the brother (?) of the Lord, were farmers (in Nazareth?). As descendants of David they were nevertheless considered politically risky and had to appear before the Roman authorities during the reign of Domitian: thus Hegesippus in Eusebius, *Ecclesiastical History* 3.20.4f. See further Richard Bauckham, *Jude and the Relatives of Jesus in the Early Church* (Edinburgh: T&T Clark, 1990).

[27]M. Avi-Yonah, "A List of Priestly Courses from Caesarea", *Israel Exploration Journal* 12 (1962) 137–39; the text is also cited in Schürer/Vermes, *History of the Jewish People*, 2:248. Some have suggested that the reference in *Ecclesiastes Rabbah (Midrash Qohelet)* 2.8.2 to pepper grown at "Nitzhanah" may be a textual corruption of "Nazareth": see the note to this effect in the Soncino translation.

[28]See James F. Strange, "Sepphoris", *Anchor Bible Dictionary* 5 (1992) 1091.

[29]Similarly Jerome Murphy-O'Connor, *The Holy Land: An Archaeological Guide from Earliest Times to 1700* (3rd edn. Oxford/New York: Oxford University Press, 1992), 411.

[30]B. Bagatti, cited in Bargil Pixner, *With Jesus through Galilee according to the Fifth Gospel*, trans. C. Botha & D. Foster (Rosh Pina: Corazin, 1992), 17.

[31]Thus Strange, "Nazareth", 1050.

[32]On the likely education of Jesus, see Rainer Riesner, *Jesus als Lehrer* (2nd edn. Tübingen: Mohr (Siebeck), 1984), 206–245; cf. further H. L. Strack & G. Stemberger, *Introduction to the Talmud and Midrash*, trans. M. Bockmuehl (Edinburgh: T&T Clark, 1991), chapter 2.

[33]It is sometimes suggested (e.g. by Murphy-O'Connor, *The Holy Land*, 413) that Jesus' scathing criticism of insincere religious leaders as *hypokritai* ("stage actors", Mark 7.6 etc.) reflects Jesus' personal acquaintance with the spectacular Roman theatre that Antipas had built at Sepphoris. Although easily conceivable, that possibility must be balanced generally against the opposition to pagan theatre in conservative circles at this time, and more specifically against the well-established Jewish use of Greek acting terminology to denigrate dissembling and wickedness. In other words, Jesus need not have attended the theatre at Sepphoris in order to develop an antipathy for "actors". Compare Josephus' description of John of Gischala as a *hypokritēs* in *War* 2.586f.; cf. Ulrich Wilckens, *"hypokrinomai ktl."*, *Theological Dictionary of the New Testament* 8 (1972) 563–566.

[34]The city of Tiberias was unacceptable to devout Jews because it was built over tombs and animal statues were on public display there. See James F. Strange, "Tiberias", *Anchor Bible Dictionary* 6 (1992) 547.

[35]On this figure see Robert L. Webb, *John the Baptizer and Prophet* (Sheffield: Sheffield Academic Press, 1991).

[36]Virgilio C. Corbo, "Capernaum", *Anchor Bible Dictionary* 1 (1992) 868.

[37]See the reports in *Excavations and Surveys in Israel* 3 (1984) 64; 4 (1985) 59; 7–8 (1988–89) 109.

[38]Cf. Bargil Pixner's suggestion of a "Bay of Parables" with remarkable acoustic qualities near Tabgha: *With Jesus through Galilee*, 41f.

[39]In the Byzantine period we begin to find evidence of Christian pilgrimage along with considerable rivalry between sizeable Jewish and Christian communities. By the Middle Ages, however, the town was dying out.

Chapter Two: Was Jesus the Messiah?

[1]See also p. 105 and note 5, below.

[2]See 1 Chr. 3.17–24; cf. p. 29 and n. 14, above.

[3]Thus Mark 12.18 par.; Acts 23.8; *Abot deRabbi Nathan* A 5. Sirach and 1 Maccabees, which reflect priestly and perhaps Sadducean concerns, make no mention of the resurrection: 1 Macc. 6.44 and Sir. 44.13–15 speak instead of winning for oneself "an eternal name".

[4]See Markus Bockmuehl, *Revelation and Mystery in Ancient Judaism and Pauline Christianity* (Tübingen: Mohr (Siebeck), 1990), 124–26 and *passim*.

[5]For a fuller example of this kind of synthetic survey see e.g. Schürer/Vermes, *History of the Jewish People* 2:514–47.

[6]See already Hos. 13.13; Dan. 12.1; more specifically e.g. *Sibylline Oracles* 3.795–807; 4 Ezra 5.1–13; 6.17–28; *2 Baruch* 70.2–8; 1QM 12.9; 19.1f.; Mishnah, *Sotah* 9.15; and in the New Testament Mark 13.8; Matt. 24.8; etc.

[7]On the Messianic Son of Man (especially common in *1 Enoch*) see below, p. 147 and n. 3.

[8]See Dan. 9.25f. and 4 Ezra 7.28. *Pesiqta deRab Kahana* 5.8 speaks of the Messiah being hidden for a time after his first appearance, while B.T. *Sanhedrin* 99a mentions his death.

[9]Cf. further the Targum's (limited) Messianic interpretation of Isa. 53; the Messianic use of Zech. 9.9 in B.T. *Berakhot* 56b, *Pirqe deRabbi Eliezer* 31 and *Yalkut Shim'oni* 575 (435d); Zech. 12.10, 12 in B.T. *Sukkah* 52a, *Targum Jonathan* (variant reading), and *Yalkut Shim'oni* 581 (436c); and generally the later Rabbinic doctrine of the warlike Messiah son of Joseph or Ephraim who dies in battle (see note 10 below). Early Christian *Adversus Iudaeos* literature makes massive use of an "argument from prophecy" in support of this kind of expectation. In addition to New Testament evidence like Matt. 26.24, 64; Luke 24.26f.; Acts 3.18–21, the argument that Christ had to come in humiliation before he could come in glory is taken up in the *Epistle of Barnabas* (5.12–6.7), the *Pseudo-Clementine Recognitions* (1.49), Tertullian (*Against the Jews* 10), and especially in Justin Martyr: e.g. *Dialogue* 14.8 (with reference to Hosea [*sic*: read Zech. 12.10] and Daniel), 32.2 (Isa. 53; Zech. 12.10–12), 52 (Gen. 49.8–12), 97 (e.g. Isa. 53; Psa. 22), 110; cf. also *Apology* 1.32–35; 50–52. Interestingly, Trypho the Jew concedes in *Dialogue* 89 and 90 (cf. 68) that the Messiah was indeed to suffer according to the Scriptures – though not to be crucified. See further Markus Bockmuehl, "A 'Slain Messiah' in 4Q Serekh Milhamah (4Q285)?", *Tyndale Bulletin* 43.1 (1992) 168 n.34.

[10]This idea is apparently based on Gen. 49.22ff. See the references cited in P. S. Alexander, "Enoch", *The Old Testament Pseudepigrapha*, ed. J. H. Charlesworth, vol. 1 (Garden City: Doubleday, 1983), 298 n. *t*; also Hippolytus, *Against Heresies* 9.30 cited in Schürer/Vermes, *History*, 2:513; and E. G. King, *The Yalkut on Zechariah* (Cambridge: Deighton, Bell, 1882), 85–108). Note further the useful discussion in W. D. Davies, *Paul and Rabbinic Judaism* (3rd edn. Philadelphia: Fortress, 1980), 274–84; and

cf. *Yalkut Shim'oni* 499, 404d on Isa. 60 (Psa. 22.8); *Sefer Zerubbabel* (A. Jellinek, *Bet ha-Midrasch* 2:54–57).

[11]E.g. Luke 4.24 par.; 7.16, 39; 13.33; 24.19; John 4.19; 6.14; 7.40; 9.17. Note also the possible allusion in Mark 9.7 par. to the promise of a prophet like Moses to whom Israel shall listen (Deut. 18.15).

[12]See e.g. Philo, *On Rewards and Punishments* 116–18; *2 Baruch* 73.2f.; 74.1; and a Qumran fragment published as "A Messianic Vision" by Robert H. Eisenman in *Biblical Archaeology Review* 17 (November/December 1991) 65. On the latter text see further Markus Bockmuehl, "Recent Discoveries in the Dead Sea Scrolls", *Crux* 28.4 (December 1992) 14–21.

[13]James D. G. Dunn, *Christology in the Making* (London: SCM, 1980), argues forcefully against the presence of "pre-existence" language in Paul; but critics have pointed out that passages like 1 Cor. 8.6; 2 Cor. 8.9; Phil. 2.6–11 appear to cast doubt on this argument. See e.g. C. F. D. Moule's review of Dunn in *Journal of Theological Studies*, N.S. 33 (1982) 258–263.

[14]The meaning of the "Son of Man" language in the Gospels has been widely discussed in scholarship. For recent surveys and further bibliography see George W. E. Nickelsburg, "Son of Man", *Anchor Bible Dictionary* 6 (1992) 137–150; John J. Collins, "The Son of Man in First-Century Judaism", *New Testament Studies* 38 (1992) 448–466.

[15]See e.g. Craig A. Evans, "Life-of-Jesus Research and the Eclipse of Mythology", *Theological Studies* 54 (1993) 3–36.

[16]See most conveniently the discussion of the relevant texts in Geza Vermes, *Jesus the Jew*, 2nd edn. (London: SCM, 1983), 69–80.

[17]See e.g. Douglas J. Moo, *The Old Testament in the Gospel Passion Narratives* (Sheffield: Almond Press, 1983), 392–395.

Chapter Three: Why Did Jesus Predict the Temple's Destruction?

[1]Meir Ben-Dov, *In the Shadow of the Temple: The Discovery of Ancient Jerusalem*, trans. Ina Friedman (New York etc.: Harper & Row, 1985), 77.

[2]Josephus, *Antiquities* 20.219.

[3]Ben-Dov, *Shadow*, 88.

[4]B.T. *Sukkah* 41b (*Baraita*); B.T. *Baba Bathra* 4a.

[5]A point well argued by C. H. Dodd, "The Fall of Jerusalem and the 'Abomination of Desolation'", in *More New Testament Studies* (Manchester: Manchester University Press, 1968), 72ff. Cf. also John A. T. Robinson, *Redating the New Testament* (London: SCM, 1976), 26ff.

[6]The *Gospel of Thomas* appears to place this threat explicitly on the lips of Jesus in an isolated saying (logion 71). At the same time, it is difficult to know the extent to which this reflects the document's generally anti-Jewish flavour (14a [contrast 27], 43, 53) and possibly Gnostic influence (e.g. 2, 22, 37, 67, 77, 114). E. P. Sanders offers the plausible compromise that Jesus "threateningly predicted" the destruction of the Temple: *The Historical Figure of Jesus* (London: Allen Lane/Penguin, 1993), 258–260.

[7]Josephus, *War* 6.301. The importance of this oracle is accentuated by Anna Maria Schwemer, "Irdischer und himmlischer König: Beobachtungen zur sogenannten David-Apokalypse in Hekhalot Rabbati §§122–126", in M. Hengel & A. M. Schwemer (eds.), *Königsherrschaft Gottes und himmlischer Kult im Judentum, Urchristentum und in der hellenistischen Welt* (Tübingen: Mohr (Siebeck), 1991), 352–58.

[8]In another place he reports, "The Jews... had it recorded in their oracles that the city and the sanctuary would be taken when the Temple should become four-square" (6.311; I have not come across any satisfactory explanation of this supposed Scriptural oracle).

[9]The reference in view would appear to be Dan. 9.26–27. It is not in-significant that this passage contains the term "abomination of desolation" which Jesus quotes in the Synoptic apocalypse. Both Mark and Matthew affix a gloss, quite conceivably predating the year 70, "Let the reader understand" (Mark 13.14; Matt. 24.15; cf. Rev. 13.18). Gerd Theissen links this passage with the crisis of AD 39–40 under Caligula: *The Gospels in Context: Social and Political History in the Synoptic Tradition*, trans. L. M. Maloney (Edinburgh: T&T Clark, 1992), 151–165.

[10]Eusebius, *Ecclesiastical History* 3.5.3; the reliability of this tradition has been disputed.

[11]*Aboth deRabbi Nathan* A 4.41ff. (ed. Schechter, p.11b); par. B.T. *Gittin* 56a.

[12]Geza Vermes, *Scripture and Tradition in Judaism: Haggadic Studies*, Studia Post–Biblica 4, 2nd edn. (Leiden: Brill, 1983), 26–39. For the early Christian use of the metaphor cf. H. F. D. Sparks, "The Early Christian Interpretation of *Lebanon* in the Fathers", *Journal of Theological Studies* N.S. 10 (1959) 264–279.

[13]This is the explanation given by R. Isaac b. Tablai in B.T. *Yoma* 39b; see also *Sifre Deuteronomy* 1.6 (ed. Finkelstein, p. 15); and the *Targum* to Song of Songs 5.15.

Determined to find this identification of Lebanon and Temple even in the Torah, rabbinic literature resorted to a less obvious passage, viz. Deut. 3.25: "Let me, I pray, cross over and see the fair land, that good hill country and Lebanon." See B.T. *Gittin* 56a; *Targum Onkelos* Deut. 3.25;

Mekhilta on Exod. 17.14 (ed. Lauterbach, 2:151.) This is because, of the three Pentateuchal passages mentioning *Lebanon*, Deut. 3.25 provides the most plausible proof text for a symbolic interpretation. See further Vermes, *Scripture*, 36.

[14]1QpHab 12.3–5. Cf. 1 Cor. 3.16f.; 2 Cor. 6.16; Eph 2.19–22; 1 Pet. 2.5.

[15]D. R. A. Hare in James H. Charlesworth (ed.), *Old Testament Pseudepigrapha* 2:381 n.11 (Garden City: Doubleday, 1985) also takes this as a pre–70 statement.

[16]B.T. *Yoma* 39b (*Baraita*); cf. *Mekhilta* on Exod. 17.14 (ed. Lauterbach 2:151).

[17]E.g., *Testament of Judah* 23.3; *Testament of Levi* 14.1–15.1; *1 Enoch* 89.72f., 90.28f., 91.13; *Sibylline Oracles* 3.665; 11QTemple 29.9 and *passim*; etc. One might also argue that the episode of Acts 6 makes consistent sense only in light of a contested but pre–70 expectation of the temple's destruction. John 4.21, if reflecting an early tradition, may also be significant.

[18]Thus also Sanders, *Jesus and Judaism*, 88.

[19]Thus Lloyd Gaston, *No Stone on Another: Studies in the Significance of the Fall of Jerusalem in the Synoptic Gospels*, Supplements to *Novum Testamentum* 23 (Leiden: Brill, 1972), 113. Cf. further *Testament of Moses* 6.1.

[20]Cf. Joachim Jeremias, *Jerusalem in the Time of Jesus*, trans. F. H. & C. H. Cave (London: SCM, 1969), 193f., 377f.

[21]See e.g. Mishnah, *Sheqalim* 5.1–4; 6.5; 7.7; Tosefta, *Sheqalim* 3.2–4, 9; B.T. *Menahot* 21b etc. on the established sale of tokens ("seals") by which the worshippers then arranged for wood, bird and drink offerings. Note further Jeremias, *Jerusalem*, 48–49, 166–167.

[22]We are told that 40 years before the destruction of the Temple (i.e. c. AD 30) the Sanhedrin was expelled (presumably by the landlord, i.e. the chief priesthood) from its headquarters in the Temple's Chamber of Hewn Stone and moved to *Hanut*, possibly the trading halls in the three-storied Royal Portico on the South side of the Temple Mount (an alternative theory has them moving to the shops of the "sons of Hanan" on the Mount of Olives). Possibly some traders were displaced from their previous location and set up stalls in the Court of the Gentiles itself; or some other permutation of previous trading practices took place. In any case a number of scholars have argued that Jesus may have been among those who were offended and reacted to a relatively *recent* change in commercial activity. This case was made by Victor Eppstein, "The Historicity of the Gospel Account of the Cleansing of the Temple", *Zeitschrift für die neutestamentliche*

Wissenschaft 55 (1964) 48f., 55; and has been accepted in various forms e.g. by W. L. Lane, *The Gospel According to Mark* (Grand Rapids: Eerdmans, 1974), 403f.; Benjamin Mazar, *The Mountain of the Lord* (Garden City: Doubleday, 1975), 126; Gaalyah Cornfeld (ed.), *The Historical Jesus: A Scholarly View of the Man and His World* (New York: Macmillan; London: Collier Macmillan, 1982), 146–155; Bruce Chilton, "Caiaphas", *Anchor Bible Dictionary* 1 (1992) 868 and see his *The Temple of Jesus*, 107f.

[23]Mishnah, *Keritot* 1.7; cf. Jeremias, *Jerusalem*, 33f.

[24]B.T. *Pesahim* 57a (*Baraita*). See Jeremias, *Jerusalem*, 98. Martin Goodman, *The Ruling Class of Judaea* (Cambridge etc.: Cambridge University Press, 1987), 94–96, 212–214 suggests that prior to AD 66 such measures were probably limited in scope.

[25]Acts 4.1ff., Mark 14.43, John 18.3, etc. See further Jeremias, *Jerusalem*, 98.

[26]Josephus, *Antiquities* 20.181, 206f.

[27]B.T. *Pesahim* 57a; Tosefta, *Menahot* 13.21; cf. Josephus, *Antiquities* 20.206. Note also the interesting observations of Craig A. Evans ("Jesus' Action in the Temple: Cleansing or Portent of Destruction?", *Catholic Biblical Quarterly* 51 (1989) 268f.), following C. T. R. Hayward, regarding the anti-priestly bias of the Jeremiah Targum. Compare also Hab. 2.17LXX, which envisions a judgement due to the godlessness (*asebeia*) of Lebanon and the city. The widely perceived corruption of the post-Maccabean Temple hierarchy is further attested in the Dead Sea Scrolls (CD 5.6–8; 6.12–17; 1QpHab 8.11; 9.3–5; 9.16–10.1; 12.2–10; also 4QMMT B 75–77 and *passim*); and see *Testament of Moses* 5.5f.; *Testament of Levi* 14.1, 4–6; 17.11. Much of this material is usefully compiled in another study by Craig A. Evans, "Jesus' Action in the Temple and Evidence of Corruption in the First-Century Temple", *Society of Biblical Literature Seminar Papers* 28 (1989) 522–39.

Incidentally, Sanders's stated unawareness (*Jesus*, 367 n.39; a claim also addressed by Evans, "Jesus' Action", 263) of any evidence of high priestly fraud and theft is curiously confirmed by the fact that most of the ancient texts here quoted do not appear in his index. In his impressive work *Judaism: Practice and Belief 63BCE–66CE* (London: SCM; Philadelphia: Trinity Press International, 1992), Sanders does now discuss some of this evidence, even allowing that "of the high priests during the period 6–66CE, some were corrupt" (p. 323; cf. 324–332; 185f.) and that the illegitimacy of the high priestly families was a matter of concern to ordinary Jews (p. 327). Nevertheless, he still declines to relate this to the issue of the Temple trade (pp. 85–92), paradoxically asserting on the one hand that the priests had no monopoly (pp. 185, 90f.); and on the other hand that they were in a position to control the (low) price of sacrifices (p. 91).

Another curious aspect of Sanders's discussion is his emphatic denial that bulls and sheep (John 2.14f.) were ever sold in the Temple; "they did not ascend the steps to the Holy Mountain" (p. 87f.). Aside from the fact that Rabbinic literature clearly *does* attest at least the periodic availability of sacrificial sheep on the Temple Mount (e.g. Tosefta, *Hagigah* 2.11; P.T. *Betzah* 2.4, 61c13ff.), it is strange that Sanders's argument should be largely based on the problem of impurity due to excrement and the possibility of blemish due to broken limbs in negotiating the steps. Would not this same concern apply in the case of *any* animals waiting to be sacrificed, not least the 30,000 annual Passover lambs (p. 136) which surely ascended the Temple Mount with their owners and thus via the steps? (Cornfeld, *Jesus*, 151, 154f. offers the plausible suggestion that the large vaulted halls now known as Solomon's Stables, *under* the Royal Portico, may have served for gathering and readying the animals and other supplies for the regular sacrifices.)

Be that as it may, it is surely an unfair caricature to intimate that scholars who use the evidence in question as part of the setting for Jesus' demonstration are thereby declaring such vices to be "*the* failings of official Judaism" (p. 91). All that is required for my interpretation of the "cleansing" is a stark socio-economic dichotomy between a pious rural proletariat and a cosmopolitan priestly aristocracy who *in the public perception* were associated with even just a handful of well-known, notorious incidents of corruption.

[28]Nahman Avigad, *Israel Exploration Journal* 20 (1970) 7; Yigael Yadin & Joseph Naveh, *The Aramaic and Hebrew Ostraca and Jar Inscriptions*, in *Masada I: The Yigael Yadin Excavations 1963 1965, Final Reports* (Jerusalem: Israel Exploration Society, 1989), no. 405.

[29]Thus also Millar, "Reflections on the Trials [*sic*] of Jesus", 379.

[30]The inscription "Joseph bar Qayyapha" was published in *Atiqot* 21 (1992): Ronny Reich, "Ossuary Inscriptions from the 'Caiaphas' Tomb", 72–77 (the identification *Qatros=Qaiapha* is argued on p. 75f. and endorsed in David Flusser's "Caiaphas in the New Testament", ibid. p. 83); also Zvi Greenhut, "The 'Caiaphas' Tomb in North Talpiyot, Jerusalem", 63–71. Popular illustrated versions of both articles appear in *Biblical Archaeology Review* 18 (Sept.–Oct. 1992) 38–44, 76; 28–36, 76.

Note, however, the alternative reading "*Joseph bar Qopha*", now advanced e.g. by William Horbury in "The 'Caiaphas' Ossuaries and Joseph Caiaphas", forthcoming in *Palestine Exploration Quarterly;* Horbury also cites Émile Puech for a similar view (see "A-t-on redécouvert le tombeau du grand-prêtre Caïphe?", *Le monde de la Bible* 80 (1993) 42–47).

[31]See the excellent summary in Jeremias, *Jerusalem*, 92–99; and cf. Goodman, *The Ruling Class*, 51ff.

[32]Cf. further the sociological studies of Gerd Theissen, e.g. "Die Tempelweissagung Jesu: Prophetie im Spannungsfeld von Stadt und Land", *Theologische Zeitschrift* 32 (1976) 144–158; and more generally Goodman, *The Ruling Class of Judaea*.

[33]Mishnah, *Sheqalim* 1.3.

[34]E.g. Jacob Neusner, "The Absoluteness of Christianity and the Uniqueness of Judaism: Why Salvation is Not of the Jews", *Interpretation* 43 (1989) 22–26; idem, "Money-Changers in the Temple: The Mishnah's Explanation", *New Testament Studies* 35 (1989) 287–290. The demonstration in the Temple must have been incomprehensible, Neusner argues rather implausibly, because Jesus' purpose can only have been to deny the validity of cultic expiation altogether and, in place of the money-changers' tables, to establish his own new table of the Eucharist.... Opposition to perceived abuse seems to me a better clue to Jesus' intention.

Accepting Neusner's view, David Seeley ("Jesus' Temple Act", *Catholic Biblical Quarterly* 55 (1993) 263–283) takes matters one step further in a remarkable exegetical vanishing act: 1. Jesus' action makes no historical sense to Jacob Neusner, but 2. Mark puts it to good narrative effect; *ergo*, despite its attestation in all four gospels the entire event must be Mark's literary creation. The conclusion, however, does not follow. What is more, the first premise is doubtful evidence, while the second merely confirms that good history often makes for a good story.

[35]Richard Bauckham, "Jesus' Demonstration in the Temple", in Barnabas Lindars (ed.), *Law and Religion: Essays on the Place of the Law in Israel and Early Christianity* (Cambridge: James Clarke, 1988), 73f.

[36]Cf. Horbury, "The Temple Tax", in Ernst Bammel & C. F. D. Moule (eds.), *Jesus and the Politics of His Day* (Cambridge etc.: Cambridge University Press, 1984), 282f.

[37]Mishnah, *Berakhot* 9.5. In light of this passage it is puzzling to find Sanders confidently asserting that Mark must have "had in mind some other temple than the one in Jerusalem", where the issue of shortcut through the Temple could not have arisen (*Judaism*, 503 n. 9).

[38]John 2.16 might seem to read otherwise, as indeed this evangelist's interpretation of the incident is a different one (2.21). Even for John, however, the original point of Jesus' displeasure may well be the crassly commercial *nature* of the sacrificial trade in the Temple precinct, rather

than the *fact* that such transactions pertaining to the Temple took place at all.

[39](This might help explain Jesus' reported annoyance with sellers *and* buyers: Mark 11.15 par.) I am again in disagreement here with Sanders, who denies that any notion of judgement is present, but who argues instead that Jesus is symbolically attacking the divinely ordained sacrifices themselves in order to point to the imminent establishment of the new Temple (Sanders, *Jesus and Judaism*, Chs. 1–2 *passim*, especially pp. 75–76). Bauckham and others have rightly criticized Sanders for ruling out the note of *judgement* in Jesus' action (allowing merely that of eschatological replacement), and because he does not plausibly explain why Jesus would have been executed for what would really amount to the expression of a common Jewish *hope*. (Sanders, *Jesus and Judaism*, 296–306 believes that Jesus was probably executed because his demonstration was perceived to be a threat which would be *offensive* to most Jews (p. 302).) See Bauckham, "Jesus' Demonstration", 86f.; Morna D. Hooker, "Traditions about the Temple in the Sayings of Jesus", *Bulletin of the John Rylands Library* 70 (1988) 17; N. T. Wright, "Jesus, Israel and the Cross", *Society of Biblical Literature Seminar Papers* 24 (1985) 79f. Evans, "Jesus' Action", 269 and *passim* has mounted a strong case for the retention of the term "cleansing" as a proper description of Jesus' action; see also Morna D. Hooker, *A Commentary on the Gospel According to St Mark* (London: Black, 1991), 264f.

[40]See the arguments cited by Sanders, *Jesus and Judaism*, 66 and 367 n. 40.

[41]Thus e.g. Bauckham, "Jesus' Demonstration", 81–86; Marcus J. Borg, *Conflict, Holiness & Politics in the Teaching of Jesus*, Studies in the Bible and Early Christianity 5 (New York/Toronto: Mellen, 1984), 173; Hooker, "Traditions"; and see the commentaries on the passage, e.g. Taylor and Pesch. If this were a fabricated saying, it is not easy to see why Zech. 14.21 should have been left out in the context: "There shall no longer be a trader in the house of the LORD of hosts on that day."

[42]1QpHab 10.1: the beams of the Temple are robbery. Robbery is the possessions of the priests in Jerusalem, 4QpNah 1.11.

[43]Gaston, *No Stone*, 117 concludes from the use of Jer. 7.34 that Jesus ben Ananias specifically objected to a *defilement* of city and Temple.

[44]Thus Larry W. Hurtado, *Mark* (San Francisco etc.: Harper, 1983), 170.

[45]In addition to the oracles here adduced in the context of first-century citations, cf. also the survey of texts relating to temple "cleansing" in Evans, "Jesus' Action", 250–252.

[46]Compare Jeremiah 26.1–11.

[47]Cf. further Theissen, "Tempelweissagung", 157.

[48]Note the intriguingly compatible addition to Josephus, *War* 2.174f. in the Slavonic version (Loeb Classical Library edn., vol. 3, p. 650).

[49]Bruce Chilton, "Caiaphas", 805 suggests the Romans also accepted desecration of the Temple as grounds for capital punishment; evidence for this, however, seems to pertain primarily to Gentile trespassing past the wall of partition: Schürer/Vermes, *History*, see 1.378f.; 2.222 n. 85, 284–85.

[50]Jesus venerated the Temple as "the house of God" (Mark 11.17 par.; Matt. 23.21; also Luke 2.49). See William Horbury, "The Temple Tax", 284. What is more, both his participation in the Festivals and his teaching suggest that Jesus approved of sacrifice: thus especially Mark 1.44 par.; Matt. 5.23f.; 23.18–22; compare further Matt. 12.5 with Num. 28.9. It is worth noting especially that according to all four gospels Jesus *continues to teach in the Temple* after his "cleansing" demonstration. In Acts we find the early Christians participating in Temple worship (e.g. 2.46; 3.1ff.; 5.12; 22.17), and sacrifice (21.20–26; 24.17f.; cf. also Luke 2.22ff.). Note further Paul's continuing concern for the calendar of Jewish Temple festivals (Acts 20.16; 1 Cor. 16.8) and the early Christian tradition of James the Just, whose knees were calloused by continual prayer in the Temple (Hegesippus in Eusebius, *Ecclesiastical History* 2.23.6). Evidence of this kind would appear to cast doubt on "replacement" theories like that advanced e.g. by N. T. Wright, who asserts that Jesus claimed "to do and be what the temple was and did.... What he was claiming to do was to act as the replacement of the temple..." ("Jerusalem in the New Testament", in *Jerusalem Past and Present in the Purposes of God*, ed. P. W. L. Walker (Cambridge: Tyndale House, 1992), 58; cf. ibid., 62; compare also Crossan, *The Historical Jesus*, 355ff.). If so, the Synoptic evangelists and the early Palestinian church would appear to have profoundly misunderstood him.

[51]Thus e.g. Peter Stuhlmacher, "Existenzstellvertretung für die Vielen: Mk 10,45 (Mt 20,28)", in *Versöhnung, Gesetz und Gerechtigkeit: Aufsätze zur biblischen Theologie* (Göttingen: Vandenhoeck & Ruprecht, 1981), 38f. [E.T. *Reconciliation, Law, and Righteousness: Essays in Biblical Theology*, trans. E. R. Kalin (Philadelphia: Fortress, 1986)]; Joachim Jeremias, *New Testament Theology*, trans. John Bowden, vol. 1 (London: SCM, 1971), 292f. Both make reference to the (somewhat overrated?) verbal links with the Hebrew of Isaiah 53.10f., which describes the servant's suffering for the "many" as a sin offering.

Chapter Four: Did Jesus Fail?

[1]See Josephus, *War* 2.253, 3.321; and cf. Martin Hengel, *The Cross of the Son of God* (London: SCM, 1986), 138–142.

[2]E.g. Pliny, Tacitus, and others cited in Hengel, *Cross*, 93ff.

[3]The most recent example is perhaps Geza Vermes, *The Religion of Jesus the Jew* (London: SCM, 1993).

[4]A recently published text from the Dead Sea Scrolls speaks about the Spirit of the Lord "hovering" over his people in the age of redemption when he shall release the prisoners, give sight to the blind, resurrect the dead and proclaim joyful news to the poor. See Robert H. Eisenman, "A Messianic Vision", *Biblical Archaeology Review* 17 (November/December 1991) 65; Dale C. Allison, Jr., "The Baptism of Jesus and a New Dead Sea Scroll", *Biblical Archaeology Review* 18 (March/April 1992) 58–60.

[5]For the importance of this motif see William Horbury, "The Twelve and the Phylarchs", *New Testament Studies* 32 (1986) 503–527.

[6]The few exceptions pertain mostly to the hidden meaning of parables (Mark 4.10ff. par.), certain nature miracles (4.36–41 par.; 6.47–52 par.; possibly 6.35–44; 8.4, 14–21 par.) and God's purpose for the future (13.1–37 par.).

[7]See Geza Vermes, *Jesus the Jew*, 2nd edn. (London: SCM, 1983), 69–80 on the stories about Honi the Circle Drawer and Hanina ben Dosa.

[8]It is interesting to compare Josephus's note about the rebel leader John of Gischala, who "had unlawful food served at his table and abandoned the established rules of purity of our forefathers" (*War* 7.264).

[9]Relevant passages include Luke 8.2; 10.38–42; and especially the accounts of the crucifixion and resurrection. See the full discussion in Ben Witherington III, *Women in the Ministry of Jesus* (Cambridge etc.: Cambridge University Press, 1984).

[10]Cf. Mark 9.36f. par.; Matt. 21.15f. See J. D. M. Derrett, "Why Did Jesus Bless the Children?" *Novum Testamentum* 25 (1983) 1–18; E. LaVerdiere, "Children and the Kingdom of God", *Emmanuel* 98 (1992) 78–84, 130–135, 164; Joachim Jeremias, *New Testament Theology*, trans. J. Bowden (London: SCM, 1971), 227f.

[11]Compare Sanders, *Jesus and Judaism*, 206–208. However, Sanders is probably mistaken to deny Jesus' belief in the importance of repentance: see Mark 11.25 par. and passages like the conversion of Zacchaeus (Luke 19.1–10) or the parable of the unforgiving servant (Matt. 18.23–35); also John 5.14; 8.11.

[12]Compare also the delegation of three Pharisees and a priest dispatched to Galilee by the High Priest Ananus in order to infiltrate the political situation there: Josephus, *Life* 195ff.

[13]E.g. on the subject of divorce: see below, p. 109 and nn. 20f.

[14]Mark 3.4 par.; cf. Mishnah, *Yoma* 8.6.

[15]Mark 7.8–13 par.; cf. Mishnah, *Nedarim* 9.1; 11.4.

[16]In John cf. also the wine miracle at Cana: 2.9, 11.

[17]Cf. Hans F. Bayer, *Jesus' Predictions of Vindication and Resurrection* (Tübingen: Mohr (Siebeck), 1986), *passim*; also de Jonge, *Jesus the Servant Messiah*.

[18]The narrative context suggests a location near Caesarea Philippi in the Golan Heights for Mark 8.27–9.29 par. Since the 4th century (Cyril of Jerusalem, Jerome, Epiphanius), however, tradition has curiously opted for the top of Mt. Tabor – a suggestion made additionally improbable by the first-century village located there.

[19]The significance of this episode for the question at hand is also stressed most recently by Martin Hengel, "Jesus, der Messias Israels: Zum Streit über das 'messianische Sendungsbewußtsein' Jesu", in *Messiah and Christos: Studies in the Jewish Origins of Christianity Presented to David Flusser on the Occasion of His Seventy-Fifth Birthday*, ed. Ithamar Gruenwald et al. (Tübingen: Mohr (Siebeck), 1992), 174 and *passim*.

[20]Compare Heb. 11.35 with 2 Macc. 6–7.

[21]*Testament of Benjamin* 3.8 in the [uninterpolated] Armenian text says about Joseph, "In you will be fulfilled the heavenly prophecy which says that the spotless one will be defiled by lawless men and the sinless one will die for the sake of impious men." The third-century Rabbi Simlai quotes Isa. 53.12 in suggesting that Moses' request to be blotted out from the book of life (Exod. 32.32) means that he offered his life as an atonement for the people (B.T. *Sotah* 14a). Somewhat more fancifully, R. Ammi of the following generation explains why the notice of Miriam's death (Num. 20.1) follows immediately after the law about the Red Heifer: "As the red heifer brought atonement for sins, similarly does the death of the righteous bring atonement for sins" (B.T. *Mo'ed Qatan 28a; Pesiqta de-Rab Kahana* 26.11). Cf. further *Exodus Rabbah* 35.4; B.T. *Sanhedrin* 98b; *Pesiqta Rabbati* 36.2; 37.1 (on which see Arnold Goldberg, *Erlösung durch Leiden*, Frankfurter Judaistische Studien 4 (Frankfurt: Gesellschaft zur Förderung Judaistischer Studien, 1978), 47–64).

[22]Thus also e.g. J. C. O'Neill, "Why Did Jesus Go Up to Jerusalem?" in idem, *Messiah: Six Lectures on the Ministry of Jesus* (Cambridge: Cochrane, 1986), 50–54; and recently Martin Hengel, "Jesus, der Messias

Israels", 174. *Pace* C. F. D. Moule, *The Origin of Christology* (Cambridge etc.: Cambridge University Press, 1977), 109, for whom Jesus' last journey and death in Jerusalem were not a matter of deliberate purpose but the fatal and inevitable result of his inflexible devotion to the way of truth.

[23]This passage is also one of the stronger arguments against the position of those (like S. G. F. Brandon, e.g. *Jesus and the Zealots* (Manchester: Manchester University Press, 1967)) who have argued that Jesus himself was a zealot revolutionary. On this subject note also the telling comment of Sanders, *Jesus and Judaism*, 329: "From the fact that Jesus and not his disciples were put to death it follows that no one thought of Jesus as an insurgent." Note, too, the similarity of Mark 12.17 with Romans 13.7.

[24]Thus also the Jewish scholar David Flusser, "Caiaphas in the New Testament", *Atiqot* 21 (1992) 83, who continues: "History teaches that those who are accused of acting viciously do not commonly respond with repentance. On the contrary, they generally become even more obstinate and react to accusations by refusing to change their ways. This is what happened to Jesus' adversaries."

[25]Most prominently by Joachim Jeremias, *The Eucharistic Words of Jesus*, trans. N. Perrin (London: SCM, 1966), chapter 1; cf. his "This is My Body...", *Expository Times* 83 (1971–72) 201–202. See also, most recently, E. P. Sanders, *The Historical Figure of Jesus* (London: Allen Lane/Penguin, 1993), 250f.

[26]E.g. B.T. *Sanhedrin* 43a.

[27]See e.g. the discussion in Millar, "Reflections on the Trials [*sic*] of Jesus", 375–378.

[28]It should be noted that, despite Mark 14.12, 14 par., even the Synoptic Gospels never actually state that the paschal lamb was eaten at the Last Supper (*pace* Millar, "Reflections on the Trials [*sic*] of Jesus", 356).

[29]E.g. Annie Jaubert, *La date de la Cène*, Études Bibliques 15 (Paris: Gabalda, 1957), 116–133 and *passim*. The Essene solar calendar always made the 14th of Nisan a Tuesday.

[30]"I tell you I will not eat it [*sic*, Nestle-Aland[26]] until it is fulfilled in the Kingdom of God."

[31]See especially 1 Cor. 5.7; and cf. 1 Pet. 1.19; Rev. 5.6, 12; and a number of second-century church fathers including Justin Martyr (*Dialogue* 40) and Melito of Sardis.

[32]Even E. P. Sanders, *Jesus and Judaism*, 324 concedes, "The Christian interpretation of Jesus' death as atoning was so immediate and so thorough that one could argue that even here Jesus prepared his followers." For the idea of redemptive covenant blood see especially Exodus 24.8 and

Zechariah 9.11. The latter interestingly appears in the immediate context of the prophecy about the humble king riding into Zion on a donkey (9.9).

[33]*Gat shemanim* is Hebrew for an olive press. See Mark 14.32 par.; John 18.1.

[34]Cf. E. P. Sanders's analysis of Jesus' trial before the High Priest and his brief appearance before Pilate: *The Historical Figure of Jesus* (London: Allen Lane/Penguin, 1993), 271–74.

[35]I.e. Hebrew address and Aramaic question, as also in the *Targum* of Psalm 22.2. The originality of Matt. 27.46 is argued in Joachim Jeremias, *"Él(e)ias"*, *Theological Dictionary of the New Testament* 2 (1964) 935 and n.62.

[36]Cf. e.g. Sanders, *Judaism*, 332.

[37]Meyer, *The Aims of Jesus*, 252f. The paragraph quoted forms the end of Meyer's book.

[38]Ben F. Meyer, "Jesus's Scenario of the Future", *Downside Review* 109 (1991) 6.

[39]The classic exponent of this view is perhaps Albert Schweitzer in *The Quest of the Historical Jesus*. See also recently the rather more strident conclusions in P. M. Casey's *From Jewish Prophet to Gentile God: The Origins and Development of New Testament Christology* (Cambridge: Clarke; Louisville: Westminster/Knox, 1991), 170–174, though he prefers to speak of Jesus' "verifiable mistake" which in his view immediately "disproves a central tenet of orthodox christology", namely his infallibility (p.174). Casey discusses none of the three important mitigating considerations raised below.

[40]In this regard cf. also A. E. Harvey, *Jesus and the Constraints of History* (London: Duckworth, 1982), 93–95.

[41]This point is also well argued in David Wenham, "'This Generation Will not Pass...': A Study of Jesus' Future Expectation in Mark 13", in Harold H. Rowdon (ed.), *Christ the Lord: Studies in Christology presented to Donald Guthrie* (Leicester & Downers Grove: Inter-Varsity, 1982), 127–150. On the general question of Jesus' eschatology note further the circumspect remarks of C. E. B. Cranfield, "Thoughts on New Testament Eschatology", *Scottish Journal of Theology* 35 (1982) 507–509 and *passim*; also Meyer, "Jesus's Scenario", 1–14.

[42]Cf. Meyer, "Jesus's Scenario", 6. A full treatment of this question is August Strobel, *Untersuchungen zum eschatologischen Verzögerungs-problem auf Grund der spätjüdisch-urchristlichen Geschichte von Habakuk 2,2ff.*, Supplements to *Novum Testamentum* 2 (Leiden: Brill, 1961). See also the splendid discussion in A. E. Harvey, *Jesus and the Constraints of*

History, 72–76 and *passim*; Harvey's treatment shares in and conveys both the explanatory strengths and the dangers of reductionism inherent in the philosophy of Ernst Bloch, whom he cites repeatedly.

[43]Meyer, "Jesus's Scenario", 13 quite rightly concludes, "The question, 'Was Jesus mistaken about the future?', should accordingly first be reformulated as follows: Did Jesus have determinate knowledge of what God intended by the symbolic scheme of things that Jesus had been commissioned to announce? The answer to this questions seems quite clearly to be, No." See further the circumspect discussion in E. P. Sanders, *The Historical Figure of Jesus*, 169–188.

[44]In a criticism of the "failed eschatology" theory, A. E. Harvey rightly asks an even wider question: "Could a reputation such as Jesus has earned in history, and a world religion which has always given him such prominence, have been founded upon a scenario so naive that few of his followers have ever taken it literally?" (Review of G. Vermes, *The Religion of Jesus the Jew*, in *The Times Literary Supplement*, 9 April 1993, p. 4).

[45]See the discussion in J. N. D. Kelly, *Early Christian Doctrines*, 5th edn. (New York etc.: Harper & Row, 1978), 462–466, 479f.

Chapter Five: Was Jesus a Christian?

[1]Martin E. Marty, *Encyclopædia Britannica[15]* (1991), Macropædia, 16:251f.

[2]Among the most recent works is Geza Vermes, *The Religion of Jesus the Jew* (London: SCM, 1993), 11–45 and *passim*.

[3]See e.g. Martin Hengel, *Judaism and Hellenism: Studies in their Encounter in Palestine during the Early Hellenistic Period* (London: SCM, 1974); *The 'Hellenization' of Judaea in the First Century after Christ*, trans. J. Bowden (London: SCM; Philadelphia: TPI, 1989).

[4]*Pace* Fergus Millar, who oddly claims on the basis of John 6.1 (perhaps a peculiar interpretation of the Western text?) that Jesus went to Tiberias: "Reflections on the Trials [*sic*] of Jesus", 359. Note, however, John 6.23: some people came *from* Tiberias to hear Jesus.

[5]Thus E. P. Sanders, *Judaism*, 47; cf. James D. G. Dunn, *The Parting of the Ways Between Christianity and Judaism* (London: SCM, 1991), Ch. 2 and *passim*; and other recent authors. This is something of a contrast to the school of Jacob Neusner, which prefers to speak of different "Judaisms" before AD 70: e.g. Jacob Neusner et al. (eds.), *Judaisms and their Messiahs at the Turn of the Christian Era* (Cambridge etc.: Cambridge University Press, 1987).

[6]See e.g. Mark 7.1–13; 12.13–17, 18–27 and parallels. Cf. also Harold W. Hoehner, "Herodians", *The International Standard Bible Encyclopedia* 3 (1982) 684; Richard A. Horsley understands them more specifically as officials of Herod Antipas (e.g. *Sociology and the Jesus Movement* (New York: Crossroad, 1989), 78). Epiphanius (c. 315–403) claims in *Refutation of all Heresies* 20 that the Herodians were those who considered Herod (the Great) to be the Messiah; but this would seem anachronistic. (Incidentally, a similar belief about Herod is also supposed in the Slavonic version of Josephus' *War* 1.364–370 (pp. 636–638 in the Loeb edition). It is apparently based on a messianic reading of Gen. 49.10 according to which the Messiah would come when the government was taken away from Judah.)

[7]*Antiquities* 18.12–15, 16–17, 18–22, 23; 13.297f.; cf. *War* 2.120–161 (Essenes), 162f. (Pharisees), 164f. (Sadducees).

[8]The name arose in Hellenistic times, apparently in the second-century BC Hasmonean period. See further Anthony J. Saldarini, "Pharisees", *Anchor Bible Dictionary* 5 (1992) 300.

[9]For a discussion of recent scholarly debate about Pharisaism see e.g. Anthony J. Saldarini, "Pharisees", 289–291; D. R. de Lacey, "In Search of a Pharisee", *Tyndale Bulletin* 43.2 (1992) 353–72; N. T. Wright, *The New Testament and the People of God* (London: SPCK, 1992), 181–203. One of the key arguments concerns the degree of public influence which the Pharisees held. Jacob Neusner argues (e.g. in *From Politics to Piety* (Englewood Cliffs: Prentice-Hall, 1973); *Formative Judaism III: Torah, Pharisees, and Rabbis* (Chico: Scholars, 1983)) that by the first century the Pharisees had dropped out of the political arena and become a table fellowship primarily concerned with matters of purity. E. P. Sanders, by contrast, views the Pharisees as a large group enjoying considerable popular support but no formal power: e.g. in *Jewish Law from Jesus to the Mishnah* (London: SCM, 1990), 152–254; *Judaism: Practice and Belief* (London: SCM, 1992), 380–412.

[10]Sanders, *Judaism,* 388–404, follows Morton Smith, Martin Goodman and others in suggesting that while Josephus's summary statements can be misleading, his *case studies* show that the Pharisees enjoyed considerable popularity but no significant political or even religious control.

[11]From *halakh,* "to walk, to live" (Psa. 1, 15, Mic. 6:8 etc.). Halakhah attempts to answer the question, "How shall we live?"

[12]Josephus, especially *Antiquities* 13.297; cf. Mark 7.3ff.

[13]Tradition gives the correct interpretation of Scripture: Mishnah, *Abot* 3:15 (Rabbi Eleazar of Modiim, d. 135), "He who interprets the Torah not according to the halakhah, has no portion in the world to come." And yet:

all is contained in Torah; Scripture supports the halakhah. Rabbi Akiba, the great second-century scholar, stressed the need to find scriptural support for all halakhah. Cf. *Abot* 5.25: "Turn it and turn it, for all is in it."

[14]Mishnah, *Sanhedrin* 10.1: they will have no portion in the life to come; cf. 1 Cor. 15.

[15]Mishnah, *Abot* 3.19.

[16]Note the pensive remark of Rabbi Hanina, Prefect of the Priests: "Pray for the [Roman] Government, since but for the fear of it men would have swallowed each other alive" (Mishnah, *Abot* 3.2).

[17]It has frequently been pointed out that while Sadducees are prominent, the Pharisees play no part in the gospel accounts of Jesus' trial and execution. See recently Flusser, "Caiaphas", 85; and note William Horbury, "The 'Caiaphas' Ossuaries and Joseph Caiaphas", forthcoming in *Palestine Exploration Quarterly* 126 (1994).

[18]Mark 3.4: see CD 11.13f.; Mishnah, *Yoma* 8.6.

[19]Mishnah, *Nedarim* 9.1; 11.4.

[20]CD 4.19–21; cf. 11QTemple 57.17f.

[21]Mishnah, *Gittin* 9.10. See further Markus Bockmuehl, "Matthew 5.32; 19.9 in the Light of Pre-Rabbinic Halakhah", *New Testament Studies* 35 (1989) 291–95.

[22]Gary G. Porton, "Sadducees", *Anchor Bible Dictionary* 5 (1992) 892.

[23]Note, however, Martin Goodman's conclusion that the aristocracy in fact transferred their loyalties from the Romans to the nationalist rebels a few years before the revolt: *The Ruling Class of Judaea: The Origins of the Jewish Revolt against Rome AD 66–70* (Cambridge etc.: Cambridge University Press, 1987), 198–227 and *passim*.

[24]See also Sanders, *Judaism*, 332–336.

[25]Josephus, *Antiquities* 18.17; B.T. *Yoma* 19b; *Niddah* 33b. See also Porton, "Sadducees", 892f.

[26]Some have argued from exclusive reliance on the Pentateuch to explain the supposed Sadducean rejection of angels, which is attested only in Acts 23.8. Recently, however, Benedict T. Viviano and Justin Taylor have argued persuasively that this verse should be translated, "The Sadducees say that there is no resurrection either in the form of an angel or in the form of a spirit, but the Pharisees acknowledge them both" ("Sadducees, Angels, and Resurrection (Acts 23:8–9)", *Journal of Biblical Literature* 111 (1992) 496–498).

[27]See Porton, "Sadducees", 893.

[28]Pliny the Elder says specifically (*Natural History* 5.15 [73]) that the Essenes lived along the shores of the Dead Sea between Jericho and En

Gedi, which matches the location of Qumran.   In Josephus, see e.g. *Antiquities* 15.373ff.

[29]Note especially the work of Norman Golb, e.g. "Who Hid the Scrolls?", *Biblical Archaeologist* 48 (1985) 68–82.

[30]Geza Vermes, *The Dead Sea Scrolls in English*, 3rd edn. (London: Penguin, 1987), 30f.

[31]This text (4Q246=4QpsDan^d) was first published by Émile Puech, "Fragment d'une apocalypse en araméen (4Q246=pseudo-Dan^d) et le 'Royaume de Dieu'", *Revue Biblique* 99 (1992) 98–131; cf. also Robert H. Eisenman & Michael Wise, *The Dead Sea Scrolls Uncovered* (Shaftesbury etc.: Element, 1992), 68–71).   For its interpretation see further John J. Collins, "The 'Son of God' Text from Qumran", forthcoming in *From Jesus to John: Essays on Jesus and Christology in Honour of Marinus de Jonge*, ed. M. de Boer (Sheffield: Sheffield Academic Press, 1993).   A different interpretation, taking the "Son of God" as an evil usurper of the title, was proposed by David Flusser, "The Hubris of the Antichrist in a Fragment from Qumran", in *Judaism and the Origins of Christianity* (Jerusalem: Magnes, 1988), 207–13; compare further Geza Vermes, "Qumran Forum Miscellanea I", *Journal of Jewish Studies* 43 (1992) 301–303; and J. A. Fitzmyer, "The 'Son of God' Document from Qumran", *Biblica* 74 (1993) 153–174.   (Note, at any rate, that a messianic interpretation of the Son of Man of Daniel 7 is also present in other early sources: see below, p. 147 and n. 3.)

[32]This is despite the arguments of those (e.g. Robert H. Eisenman & Michael Wise, *The Dead Sea Scrolls Uncovered* (Rockport, MA: Element, 1992; Barbara Thiering, above, p. 11, n. 28) who have claimed unpersuasively that many of the Scrolls are in fact *about* early Christianity. This proposition, almost universally rejected among scholars, founders on the incompatible date and/or content of the documents.   A different argument, of greater scholarly integrity but probably lacking sufficient evidence, suggests that several tiny fragments of Greek papyrus from Cave 7 (7Q5) are in fact parts of New Testament manuscripts.   This case, first argued by José O'Callaghan in 1972 but never widely accepted, is most recently and most fully stated by Carsten Peter Thiede, *The Earliest Christian Gospel Manuscript?* (Exeter: Paternoster, 1992).

[33] David Flusser has argued that the term "children of light" in Luke 16.8 may be a deliberate reference to the self-designation of the Essenes and their rejection of money and material possessions: "Jesus' Opinion about the Essenes", in *Judaism and the Origins of Christianity*, 150–68; cf. also Chilton, *Temple of Jesus*, 142.

[34]For a seminal survey see Martin Hengel, *The Zealots*, trans. D. Smith (Edinburgh: T&T Clark, 1989); a contrasting and somewhat less persuasive position (Jewish resistance prior to AD 66 was non-violent and endorsed by Jesus) is represented by Richard A. Horsley, *Jesus and the Spiral of Violence: Popular Jewish Resistance in Roman Palestine* (San Francisco: Harper & Row, 1987). N. T. Wright assesses a variety of current scholarly positions in *The New Testament and the People of God*, 170–181.

[35]See further Hengel, *The Zealots*; Martin Goodman, *The Ruling Class of Judaea: The Origins of the Jewish Revolt against Rome AD 66–70* (Cambridge etc.: Cambridge University Press, 1987).

[36]Contrast the mysterious verse Luke 22.36. Commentators tend to agree that, in the overall context of both Luke-Acts and the ministry of Jesus, this passage is not likely to mean an endorsement of armed struggle but rather a metaphorical call to prepare for trouble. See the recent commentaries.

[37]See page 75 and n. 50, above.

[38]See e.g. Mark 1.44 par.; Luke 11.44; Matt. 7.6; 23.27; note also Mark 5.11–13 par. It is of course true, on the other hand, that Jesus was in dispute with the Pharisaic *interpretation* of the biblical purity laws, e.g. Mark 7.1ff. par.

[39]E.g. Friedrich Schleiermacher, F. C. Baur, Albrecht Ritschl, etc. See Colin Brown, *Jesus in European Protestant Thought 1778–1860* (Grand Rapids: Baker, c1985), 118f., 214f.; W. G. Kümmel, *The New Testament: The History of the Investigation of Its Problems* (London: SCM, c1972), 93f. and *passim*. Similar views continue to resurface periodically.

[40]Perhaps the two most recent examples at the time of writing are A. N. Wilson's *Jesus* (London: Sinclair-Stevenson, 1992), 239–256 and *passim*; and Geza Vermes's *The Religion of Jesus the Jew* (London: SCM, 1993), 208–215.

[41]See Acts 11.26. Josephus (*Ant.* 18.64), Pliny (*Letter* 10.96), Suetonius (*Nero* 16.2) and Tacitus (*Annals* 15.44) all discuss the "Christians" as an apparently new phenomenon.

[42]Note also recently Ben F. Meyer, who defends the legitimacy of the view that "Jesus... was indeed the founder of Christianity" ("Jesus Christ", *Anchor Bible Dictionary* 3 (1992) 795); cf. earlier C. H. Dodd, *The Founder of Christianity* (London: Collins, c1970).

[43]Thus also Sanders, *Jesus and Judaism*, 323.

[44]See James D. G. Dunn, *Jesus and the Spirit* (London: SCM, 1975), 92, 358f.; and cf. Marcus J. Borg, *Jesus: A New Vision* (San Francisco: Harper, 1987), 192–200.

Chapter Six: How Did Jesus Pray?

[1]The significance of Jesus' prayer life for an assessment of his (Jewish) faith is now also considered, albeit from a somewhat different angle, in Geza Vermes, *The Religion of Jesus the Jew* (London: SCM, 1993), 152–180.

[2]Cf. e.g. Sirach 6.34–36; Mishnah, *Abot* 1 4; 5.15, 18; 6.6; and see Strack/Stemberger, *Introduction to the Talmud and Midrash*, 14f. Imitation of one's teacher was also valued in Graeco-Roman thought at this time: see e.g. Lucretius, *De Rerum Natura* 3.1–30; Pliny, *Letter* 7.9; also Xenophon, *Memorabilia* 1.6.3ff., etc.

[3]These texts have been most fully treated by Ludger Feldkämper, *Der betende Jesus als Heilsmittler nach Lukas* (St. Augustin: Steyler Verlag, 1978), and more recently by David Crump, *Jesus the Intercessor: Prayer and Christology in Luke-Acts* (Tübingen: Mohr (Siebeck), 1992); Steven F. Plymale, *The Prayer Texts of Luke-Acts* (New York etc.: Peter Lang, 1991).

[4]The theological content of these prayers (but not, it seems, the form and setting) is reflected in the Lord's Prayer. See Asher Finkel, "The Prayer of Jesus in Matthew", in *Standing Before God: Studies on Prayer in Scriptures and in Tradition with Essays in Honor of John M. Oesterreicher*, ed. A. Finkel & L. Frizzell (New York: Ktav, 1981), 131–169; and e.g. Joseph Heinemann, "The Background of Jesus' Prayer in the Jewish Liturgical Tradition", in *The Lord's Prayer and Jewish Liturgy*, ed. J. J. Petuchowski (London: Burns & Oates, 1978), 81–89. See also Joachim Jeremias, *The Prayers of Jesus*, trans. J. Bowden et al. (London: SCM, 1967), 66–81.

[5]Cf. James D. G. Dunn, *Jesus and the Spirit* (London: SCM, 1975), 26–37.

[6]Probably only Mark 7.34; and see below on John 11.41f. Mark 6.41//Matt. 14.19//Luke 9.16 and Mark 8.6//Matt. 15.36 may have more to say about his (Jewish) custom of grace before meals: see further Mark 14.22 par.; Luke 24.30, etc. Note also the apparent (and unusual, perhaps elliptic?) blessing *of the loaves* in Luke 9.16.

[7]These qualities of prayer in the gospels are attractively summarized by the mainly devotional study of J. G. S. S. Thomson, *The Praying Christ: A Study of Jesus' Doctrine and Practice of Prayer* (Grand Rapids: Eerdmans, 1959), 12–22: importunity, tenacity, humility, charity, simplicity, intensity, unity, expectancy.

[8]Tertullian, *On Prayer*, 1. See also Heinz Schürmann, *Das Gebet des Herrn als Schlüssel zum Verstehen Jesu* (6th edn. Leipzig: St. Benno, 1981).

[9]Cf. e.g. Joachim Jeremias, *New Testament Theology*, trans. J. Bowden (London: SCM, 1971), 196; Finkel, "Prayer", 143 and *passim*.

[10]For this correction of the view of Joachim Jeremias (e.g. in *The Prayers of Jesus*, 11–65), see James Barr, "'Abba isn't 'Daddy'", *Journal of Theological Studies* N.S. 39 (1988) 28–47. Barr is also followed by Geza Vermes, *The Religion of Jesus the Jew* (London: SCM, 1993), 180–183.

[11]It may best reflect the complex evidence to say that Jesus' use of "Abba" was not a unique, but nevertheless an unusual and *distinctive* mark of his relationship with God. This is the line taken by James Dunn, who writes, "By 'distinctive' I mean both characteristic of Jesus and sufficiently unusual among his contemporaries, to mark him out, but not necessarily set him in a class apart" (*Jesus and the Spirit* (London: SCM, 1975), 366n.71). For other first-century examples of divine sonship, including Honi the Circle-Drawer and his grandson Hanan, see e.g. Mishnah, *Ta'anit* 3.8 and B.T. *Ta'anit* 23b (discussed e.g. in Geza Vermes, *Jesus the Jew*, 2nd edn. (London: SCM, 1983), 70, 211).

[12]"Lead us not into temptation" means "Do not let us succumb to the Trial": cf. 11QPs[a] 24.11. Note also B.T. *Berakhot* 60b, used in the morning service of the synagogue: "And do not bring us into the power [lit. hands] of sin, transgression, iniquity, temptation, or disgrace." Cf. *Authorised Daily Prayer Book*, ed. S. Singer (London: Eyre & Spottiswoode, 1962), 8. See further Jeremias, *The Prayers of Jesus*, 104–106.

[13]For a closer Old Testament parallel see perhaps Lam. 3.22, read in the context of 3.1–20.

[14]Although this prayer is absent from a significant part of the earliest manuscript evidence and perhaps not original in its present location, the clear trend in the majority of the tradition is towards its inclusion in the canonical text. As for its authenticity, the content makes a later invention seem unlikely, while an anti-Jewish motivation might well be thought to account for its omission from part of the tradition. (It is true that the theme of [pardonable] ignorance in the opponents of Jesus and Christianity is not uncommon in the New Testament (see Acts 3.17; 13.27; 1 Cor. 2.8), though it is difficult to prove which way the influence must have gone.) See further Bruce M. Metzger, *A Textual Commentary on the Greek New Testament* (rev. edn. London/New York: United Bible Societies, 1975), 180.

[15]This is argued in detail by Feldkämper, *Der betende Jesus*, 306–332.

[16]See e.g. Tertullian, *On Prayer*, 4; Cyprian, *On the Lord's Prayer*, 14. On the influence of this Prayer in early Christianity it is still worth consulting Frederic Henry Chase, *The Lord's Prayer in the Early Church*, Texts & Studies 1:3 (Cambridge: University Press, 1891).

[17]Acts 7.59f., there addressed to Jesus; cf. later e.g. Eusebius, *Ecclesiastical History* 5.2.5.

[18]Thus e.g. M. M. B. Turner, "Prayer in the Gospels and Acts", in *Teach Us to Pray: Prayer in the Bible and the World*, ed. D. A. Carson (Exeter: Paternoster; Grand Rapids: Baker/World Evangelical Fellowship, 1990), 77.

[19]Cf. further 15.7, 15: Jesus is sure to procure an answer to the prayers of his friends, those who abide in him.

[20]See further David Crump, "Jesus, the Victorious Scribal-Intercessor in Luke's Gospel", *New Testament Studies* 38 (1992) 51–65; and cf. note 3 above. More generally, compare also the interceding guardian angels of Matt. 18.10. This theme occurs previously in Tobit 12.12, 15, while 2 Maccabees 15.14–16 records a vision of Jeremiah's intercession for the people of God. Along with Matt. 18.10, these two texts from the Apocrypha were of pivotal importance in the patristic doctrine of the intercession of angels and saints (e.g. Origen, *On Prayer* 1.10.2–11.5; cf. 3.31.5).

[21]Also cf. possibly the language about Christ's ability to keep his people from falling etc.: Jude 24; cf. Heb. 2.18; Rom. 14.4; 2 Tim. 1.12.

[22]I am indebted to Dr. W. Horbury for this observation.

[23]Thus also Origen, *On Prayer*, 1.10.2: to pray aright is to share in the prayer of God's Logos who prays for and alongside those whose mediator, high priest and advocate he is; cf. similarly Cyprian, *On the Lord's Prayer*, 30. Origen considered that, since it is inappropriate to pray to someone who prays himself, one ought not to pray simply to Jesus; but that, on the other hand, prayer should not be addressed to God except *through* Jesus (*On Prayer*, 1.15.2 and *passim*; this point assumes additional poignancy in replying to the Jews: *Against Celsus* 3.34; 5.5; 8.13). See further Wilhelm Gessel, *Die Theologie des Gebetes nach 'De Oratione' von Origenes* (Munich, etc.: Schöningh, 1975), 204–206, 236–238.

Chapter Seven: Why Was Jesus Exalted to Heaven?

[1]Notable recent exceptions include M. de Jonge (*Jesus, the Servant Messiah*, passim) and to some extent E. P. Sanders (*Jesus and Judaism*, 18–22, 320, 323f., 334f.; *The Historical Figure of Jesus*, 2, 10–14, 276–281). Sanders thinks the relationship between smoke (the Church) and fire (the work *and intentions* of Jesus) has something to do with the apostolic resurrection experiences, but he comments on this only in passing (*Jesus and Judaism*, pp. 19, 22, 320; in this earlier work he does not mention the early tradition of the empty tomb). Significantly, he finds himself resorting to two older works by J. Klausner (1925) and H. J. Cadbury (1937) as conversation partners on the subject of continuity. Many others have of course recognized a diversity of *development* (e.g. recently Paula Fredriksen, *From Jesus to Christ: The Origins of the New Testament Images*

of Jesus (New Haven/London: Yale University Press, 1988), or even John Dominic Crossan, *The Historical Jesus* (see p. 4, note 10 above), but few have paid specific attention to the question of *continuity*. This is unfortunately the case, too, for Donald Goergen's thoughtful remarks on "The Jesus of Historiography and the Jesus of Faith", in *The Death and Resurrection of Jesus* (Wilmington: Glazier, 1986), 183–262.

[2]The numerous examples in Jewish texts include Philo's Logos doctrine, the Enoch literature, 11Q Melchizedek at Qumran, and the angel Yahoel in the *Apocalypse of Abraham*. See e.g. Larry W. Hurtado, *One God, One Lord* (London: SCM, 1988); Christopher Rowland, *The Open Heaven* (London: SPCK, 1982); Alan F. Segal, *Two Powers in Heaven* (Leiden: Brill, 1977).

[3]See e.g. John J. Collins, "The Son of Man in First-Century Judaism", *New Testament Studies* 38 (1992) 448–466; William Horbury, "The Messianic Associations of 'The Son of Man'", *Journal of Theological Studies* N.S. 36 (1985) 34–55; Seyoon Kim, *"The 'Son of Man'" as the Son of God* (Tübingen: Mohr (Siebeck), 1983).

[4]Thus perhaps most explicitly Ben Witherington III, *The Christology of Jesus* (Minneapolis: Fortress, 1990). See also Marinus de Jonge, *Christology in Context: The Earliest Christian Response to Jesus* (Philadelphia: Westminster, 1988) and *Jesus, the Servant-Messiah* (New Haven/London: Yale University Press, 1991).

[5]In his dispassionate account of the New Testament resurrection narratives, E. P. Sanders writes, "I do not regard deliberate fraud as a worthwhile explanation. Many of the people in these lists were to spend the rest of their lives proclaiming that they had seen the risen Lord, and several of them would die for their cause. Moreover, a calculated deception should have produced gretaer unanimity. Instead, there seem to have been *competitors*: 'I saw him first!' 'No! I did.' ... That Jesus' followers (and later Paul) had resurrection experiences is, in my judgement, a fact. What the reality was that gave rise to the experiences I do not know."

[6]This point also seems to be acknowledged by E. P. Sanders (*Jesus and Judaism*, p. 320), who is forever anxious to reassure his readers that he is "no theologian" (e.g. ibid., 331).

[7]For a recent summary of the arguments about the chronology of Jesus' passion and death, see e.g. Meier, *A Marginal Jew*, 1:386–402. The current state of discussion about AD 33 is summarized by Paul L. Maier, "The Date of the Nativity and the Chronology of Jesus' Life", in J. Vardaman & E. M. Yamauchi (eds.), *Chronos, Kairos, Christos: Nativity and Chronological Series. Presented to Jack Finegan* (Winona; Eisenbrauns, 1989), 113–130. Arguing that Jesus died in his late forties, Nikos Kokkinos in the same

volume presents "Crucifixion in AD 36: The Keystone for Dating the Birth of Jesus", ibid. pp. 131–163.

[8]Thus Ben F. Meyer, "Jesus Christ", *Anchor Bible Dictionary* 3 (1992) 793. See also e.g. William Lane Craig, "The Historicity of the Empty Tomb", *New Testament Studies* 31 (1984) 39–67.

[9]It is worth noting that if his followers had known the whereabouts of Jesus' body, the first-century Palestinian Jewish context would make it difficult to account for the absence of any kind of tomb veneration, such as was accorded to the tombs of other prophets and righteous men (Matt. 23.29 par.; *Lives of the Prophets*; cf. 2 Kings 13.21; Acts 2.29). As it is, the early Christians knew only the site of an *empty* tomb. This receives further confirmation in that early Christian apologetics, from Matt. 28.11–15 to Origen's *Against Celsus* 2.55–73; 5.56–58 (cf. also Chrysostom, *Homilies* 89.1; 90.1f. on Matthew), seems not to have faced challenges of the *facticity* of the empty tomb, but merely of the Christian *interpretation* of that fact.

[10]Note, however, C. F. D. Moule's suggestion that the Galilean disciples might well be expected to return to Galilee after Passover, and to travel to Jerusalem once again for Pentecost: idem (ed.), *The Significance of the Message of the Resurrection for Faith in Jesus Christ* (London: SCM, 1968), 4f.

[11]On this distinction see further Bockmuehl, *Revelation and Mystery*, chapter 9 *passim*. Note also that Luke describes the Damascus road incident as a "vision" (Acts 26.19) in the context of a bright light and audible voice (9.3ff.; 22.6ff.; 26.12ff.).

[12]This metaphorical sense is also how the ascension was most typically understood in the early church fathers. Compare E. G. Selwyn, *The Approach to Christianity* (London: Longmans, Green & Co., 1925), 195–197, who comments that resurrection and ascension are at once historical and symbolic events. Commenting on the frequent scholarly dismissal of Luke's account in this regard, H. E. W. Turner wisely cautions, "Let those who are guiltless of using spatial imagery in connexion with non-spatial subjects cast the first stone!" (*Jesus: Master and Lord* (London: Mowbray, 1953), 372).

[13]E. P. Sanders writes, "That Jesus' followers (and later Paul) had resurrection experiences is, in my judgement, a fact. What the reality was that gave rise to the experiences I do not know" (*The Historical Figure of Jesus*, 280).

[14]Although Paul does not mention the tradition of the empty tomb, it is significant that his account of the death and resurrection specifically stresses that Jesus' resurrection followed his *burial* (1 Cor. 15.4).

[15]These words derive from the hymn "Crown Him with Many Crowns", by Matthew Bridges (1800–94).

[16]It is highly likely that for most *Palestinian* Jews the idea of a resurrection would in some way have involved the actual bones – not least, perhaps, in view of the suggestive imagery of Old Testament texts like Isa. 26.19; Ezek. 37.1–14 and Dan. 12.1–4, 13. In this respect N. T. Wright makes a point worth pondering when he says that people with a resurrection hope like that of the Maccabean martyrs (2 Macc. 6–7) "would not be prepared to use the word 'resurrection' unless something emphatically physical had taken place" (*Who Was Jesus?*, 62). For the implications of this see further Moule, *Significance*, 8f.

[17]Sanders comments on the same dynamic (*Jesus and Judaism*, 320): "We have every reason to think that Jesus had led [his disciples] to expect a dramatic event which would establish the kingdom. The death and resurrection required them to adjust their expectation, but did not create a new one out of nothing. ... The disciples were prepared for *something*. *What* they received inspired them and empowered them."

[18]Dr. W. Horbury reminds me of possible exceptions including Mark 6.14–16 par. (John the Baptist revived) and *Testament of Benjamin* 10.6–8 (the sequence of resurrection); cf. Rev. 11.11 (the two witnesses). Note also the promised return of Elijah (Mal. 4.5; Mark 9.11–13 par.; John 1.21; etc.) and the occasional apocalyptic notion of Nero *redivivus*. Few of these examples, however, strictly anticipate the general resurrection.

[19]In regard to this passage, Rainer Riesner suggests that the exalted christology of the Fourth Gospel could be seen as spelling out in theological clarity what remained unspoken in Jesus' own pre-Easter claims: "Moderne Jesus-Bilder und der Christus der Evangelien", *Theologische Beiträge* 22 (1991) 331.

[20]*Pace* Lutheran authors like W. Michaelis, *"mimeomai ktl."*, *Theological Dictionary of the New Testament* 4 (1967) 672, who asserts that there is "no thought of an imitation... of the earthly life of Jesus in either individual features or total impress. The call for an *imitatio Christi* finds no support in the statements of Paul." For evidence to the contrary, see e.g. Chapter 6 above, *passim*, and note passages like 2 Cor. 8.9; Phil. 2.5ff., 3.10, etc.; cf. 1 Pet. 2.21.

[21]Even if one may not wish to follow the provocative theses of Margaret Barker, *The Great Angel: A Study of Israel's Second God* (London: SPCK, 1992), it is worth considering the evidence amassed by Alan F. Segal, *Two Powers in Heaven* (Leiden: Brill, 1977); Peter Hayman, "Monotheism – A Misused Word in Jewish Studies?" *Journal of Jewish Studies* 42 (1991) 1–

15; and Larry W. Hurtado (see below, n. 24). Hayman uses the term "monarchism" in this context.

[22]Cf. Larry W. Hurtado, "What Do We Mean by 'First-Century Jewish Monotheism'?", forthcoming in *Society of Biblical Literature Seminar Papers* 32 (Atlanta: Scholars, 1993).

[23]James D. G. Dunn, *The Partings of the Ways Between Christianity and Judaism and their Significance for the Character of Christianity* (London: SCM; Philadelphia: Trinity Press International, 1991), 230–239 and *passim*.

[24]See Larry W. Hurtado, *One God, One Lord: Early Christian Devotion and Ancient Jewish Monotheism* (Philadelphia: Fortress, 1988); also Dunn, *Partings*, 183–206.

[25]Richard Bauckham, "The Worship of Jesus", *Anchor Bible Dictionary* 3 (1992) 812–19 cites D. R. de Lacey and N. T. Wright in pointing out that 1 Cor. 8.6 indicates the monotheism of the *Shema* is reaffirmed, its "one God" being glossed with "the Father" and its "one Lord" with "Jesus Christ".

[26]Risky and sometimes heretical statements of christology have been one of the chief stumbling blocks in Christianity for both Jews and Muslims. No one should want to deny or downplay the scandal of the Cross, which is a necessary and integral part of what it means to be a follower of Jesus. But a grave responsibility lies with those who would question that God is One and thus create a stumbling block for entirely the wrong reasons. I am reminded of the founding inscription on the splendid Dome of the Rock in Jerusalem, which concludes its address to all People of the Book with this quotation from the Koran, 4.171: "Believe therefore in God and his apostles, and say not Three. It will be better for you. God is only one God. Far be it from his glory that he should have a son" (Cf. Jerome Murphy-O'Connor, *The Holy Land: An Archaeological Guide from Earliest Times to 1700*, 3rd edn. (Oxford/New York: Oxford University Press, 1992), 92). Might this be a good reaction to christology badly presented, e.g. by the largely Nestorian or Gnostic Christians of pre-Islamic Arabia?

[27]P. M. Casey, *From Jewish Prophet to Gentile God* (Cambridge: Clarke; Louisville: Westminster/Knox, 1991). Unfortunately Casey's provocative and challenging book, unlike that of James Dunn, shows no interaction with Hurtado and insufficient appreciation of the weight of Jewish background material on the origins of christology. (This is despite his claim that present-day Jewish views, *unlike* Christian ones, are "rooted in Jewish identity as it was at the time of Jesus", p. 175). His argument that there was a three-stage progression away from Jewish monotheism to a Gentile image of Christ's deity draws to a significant extent on a maximalist and remarkably ontological reading of Johannine christology, which he considers to be morally and historically false and deceptive (pp. 166, 178 and *passim*). He

prefers to ignore a number of passages containing the Gospel's explicit reaffirmation of monotheism (e.g. 5.44) and of a subordinationist christology (e.g. 14.28); 5.19–30 is cited (p. 37f.), but not satisfactorily accounted for. Despite John's daring christological statements I do *not* find here that reckless "final push for deity" of which Casey speaks (p. 157). Many things remain unsaid, and even in his explicit statements the Fourth Evangelist is rather more nuanced and subtle.

[28]2 Cor. 11.31; cf. Rom. 15.6; 2 Cor. 1.3; Eph. 1.3; 1 Pet. 1.3.

[29]Thus John Marriott in the familiar hymn "Thou Whose Almighty Word".

[30]Cf. also Dunn, *Partings*, 244–247 on the importance of reaffirming Christian monotheism in coming to terms with the Jewish origins of Christianity and its relationship to Judaism today. Some of the issues here raised have in the 20th century been given prominence in the work of Karl Rahner (e.g. *Grundkurs des Glaubens* (8th edn. Freiburg etc.: Herder, 1976), 139–142. See, however. the discussion and critique of Rahner in Jürgen Moltmann, *The Trinity and the Kingdom of God*, trans. M. Kohl (London: SCM, 1981), 144–148.

Conclusion: This Jesus

[1]See p. 21 above. It is perhaps worth noting that, in spite of Kähler's towering influence over 20th century theology, this point has continued to find a minority of senior scholarly advocates even in Germany. A key example must be the brilliant but widely ignored Adolf Schlatter (e.g. in *Die Geschichte des Christus* (3rd edn. Stuttgart: Calwer, 1977), 517–528); others include e.g. Otto Betz (*Was wissen wir von Jesus?* (Stuttgart: Kreuz, 1965; E.T. *What do we know about Jesus?*, trans. M. Kohl (London: SCM, 1968)); Leonhard Goppelt (*Theologie des Neuen Testaments*, ed. J. Roloff (3rd edn. Göttingen: Vandenhoeck & Ruprecht, 1976; E.T. *Theology of the New Testament*, trans. J. E. Alsup (Grand Rapids: Eerdmans, 1981–82)); Martin Hengel (e.g. the three studies contained in *The Cross of the Son of God*, trans. J. Bowden (London: SCM, 1986)); and Peter Stuhlmacher (*Jesus von Nazareth – Christus des Glaubens* (Stuttgart: Calwer, 1988). From a historical perspective it is also worth noting an interesting programmatic essay by a disaffected member of the Bultmann school: Hartwig Thyen, "Der irdische Jesus und die Kirche", in *Jesus Christus in Historie und Theologie: Neutestamentliche Festschrift für Hans Conzelmann zum 60. Geburtstag*, ed. G. Strecker (Tübingen: Mohr, 1975), 127–141.

[2]Thus e.g. A. N. Wilson, *Jesus*, 255. Recent writers who express a similar thesis somewhat more cautiously include Casey, *From Jewish Prophet to Gentile God*, and Vermes, *The Religion of Jesus the Jew*, 208–215.

[3]Wilson, *Jesus*, 241 (ital. mine).

Epilogue: Open Questions

[1]One might compare Matthew 23.13. I am also reminded of the behaviour of the watchman in a striking parable told by the Hasidic Rebbe Bunam of Pshiskhe (1762–1827): "A prince bought a pure-bred stallion, and to protect him from thieves, locked him into a stable built of stone. Its gate was bolted and guarded by an armed watchman. One night when he could not fall asleep, the prince went for a walk. He passed in front of the stable and thought that the watchman was looking perplexed. 'Hey,' he called to him, 'what's on your mind?' – 'There is this question that is bothering me: when you sink a nail into the wall, where does the mortar go?' – 'An important question,' said the prince. 'You do well to think about it.' And he went home and back to bed. An hour later he still could not fall asleep. So he went down again, out to the yard and the watchman, who sat there with his head propped in his hands meditating. 'What now,' said the prince, 'what are you thinking about now?' – 'Well, you see, it's like this: when you eat a bagel, what happens to the hole?' – 'A profound question,' said the prince. 'You do well to concern yourself with it.' And he went back to his quarters. He came down a third time, and for the third time the watchman seemed in a quandary. 'Another question?' asked the prince. 'Yes – and this is it: I tell myself that the stable is here, the walls are here and I am here – but the stallion, where in the world is he?'" (Elie Wiesel, *Souls on Fire* and *Somewhere a Master*, trans. Marion Wiesel (Harmondsworth: Penguin, 1984), 172).

[2]No. 12 of Maimonides' *Thirteen Principles of Faith*, part of the Jewish Morning Prayer service (see *Authorised Daily Prayer Book*, trans. S. Singer, 2nd edn. (London: Eyre & Spottiswoode, 1962), 90).

Index of Modern Authors

221

Index of Passages Cited

225

O. T. Pseudepigrapha

Dead Sea Scrolls

Philo of Alexandria

Josephus

Rabbinic Literature

Mishnah

Patristic Literature

Apostolic Fathers

Ignatius of Antioch

Justin Martyr

Greek and Roman Literature

Dio Cassius

Lucian of Samosata

Lucretius

Pliny the Younger

Pliny the Elder

Suetonius

Tacitus

Xenophon

The Koran